# GETTING RIGHT WITH GOD

# GETTING RIGHT WITH GOD
## JOSEPH C. WAY

Way throw a gasoline on the basic premises of the history of Christianity and lights a match with this provocative work. Writing for his fellow Christians, he takes as his central precept that God "is love and acts only from love," believing all other elements of religious faith can be derived from that concept, and that any claims contradicting it must necessarily be false. Among his other bold statements, he says that Jesus was a human, itinerant preacher who cared more about doing right while alive than about any notion of an afterlife; that the Bible isn't meant to be interpreted literally; and that a God who acts from love would never damn souls to eternal hellfire.

Way persuasively argues that a physical resurrection is impossible and unproven. He ask a series of challenging questions, including why Jesus was able to feed 5,000 people from "some-one's snack" a single time but not repeat the process to feed all the hungry people he encountered on a daily basis: "The argument that 'God can do anything,' 'It was only for Jesus,' or 'It was for that one special occasion' is totally, insufficient, and dodges the basic issue," he writes. He asserts that natural laws come directly from an unchanging God, so tales of miracles that contradict physics must only be stories. He also proposes that "Jesus made deliberate efforts to restore Jewish worship to its Hebrew core, not replace it" and didn't intend to start a new religion.

Many devout Christians will condemn the work as heretical, but open-minded readers may find Way's well-reasoned, passionate arguments compelling, and his refrain that God is love and there is no hell will ease the minds of those brought upon hellfire-and brimstone Christianity. This unusual view of Christianity raises far more questions than it answers and is likely to provoke deep thought and lively conversations.

*Open-minded Christians will be drawn in by Way's passionate arguments for a profoundly loving God and a pragmatic, fully human Jesus.*

— **BookLife Review**

# GETTING RIGHT WITH GOD

REVISED EDITION

JOSEPH C. WAY

B.A., B.D., MDiv.

| Library of Congress Control Number: | | 2020917016 |
|---|---|---|
| ISBN: | Hardcover | 978-1-6641-2950-4 |
| | Softcover | 978-1-6641-2952-8 |
| | eBook | 978-1-6641-2951-1 |

Scripture quotations are taken from the New Revised Standard Version of the Bible, Copyright © 1989, by the Division of Christian Education of the National Council of the Churches of Christ in the United States of America. Used by permission. All rights reserved.

All biblical references are from the *NRSV*. All references to the noncanonical Gospels are from *The Complete Gospels*, fourth edition, Robert J. Miller, editor.

Print information available on the last page.

Rev. date: 09/04/2020

**To order additional copies of this book, contact:**
Xlibris
844-714-8691
www.Xlibris.com
Orders@Xlibris.com
818790

This book is dedicated to the Pathfinders Sunday school class at First United Methodist Church, Georgetown, Texas, who encouraged me to search for truth and offered me the opportunity to share uncommon insights.

# CONTENTS

# PART III — FOLLOWERS OF JESUS

# PREFACE

"I will not stand for that!" shouted a young military officer as he rushed up the center aisle of an Air Force chapel. We had just completed an uneventful worship service with a hymn and a benediction. I was the chaplain in charge of the service but had no idea to what he referred. Rather bewildered by his unorthodox action and statement, I inquired into what he meant. "That last verse of that hymn," he said. "It reads, 'Help me to watch and pray, and on thyself rely, assured if I my trust betray, I shall forever die.'" He continued rather loudly, "I believe in 'once saved, always saved,' and that verse does not agree with me."

I politely replied, "Well, neither do I."

Another military man unexpectedly announced to me, "That was not a valid prayer you gave." At the request of the commanding officer, I gave a prayer during an official military gathering that included personnel from Christian, Jewish, and other faith groups. My prayer ended with, "We offer our prayer in the name of love" (or something similar). At the conclusion of the event, the man immediately confronted me with his statement. When I asked him why it was invalid, he replied, "Because you did not end it by saying 'in the name of Jesus.'"

In 1963, my life and career as a pastor were in serious jeopardy. Twenty-eight United Methodist ministers in Mississippi jointly and publicly declared our firm opposition to segregation. Because of my having signed the declaration, I was denied a pastoral appointment, even though church law mandated a pastoral appointment for me, and the declaration proclaimed the official position of the United Methodist Church. Severe hostility and firm opposition from local Methodist authorities, fellow pastors, parishioners, and the general public made it impossible for me to remain in the state as a Methodist minister.

These examples reflect three specific times someone confronted me because of different religious beliefs and behavior. Not one person differed with me because of me. They differed because they assumed they had the truth and I did not. We professing Christians seriously differ over the truth about God, Jesus, and us. All of us cannot be correct. Therefore, some of us may not be as Christian as we think.

"Always tell the truth" was an unwritten rule I inherited and accepted without awareness. My father's name was synonymous with truth, honesty, and integrity. As I was his child, he and others expected me to be like him. We lived on a small farm. I daily did whatever I could to accomplish the desired goal. I plowed with a mule, chopped cotton with a hoe, crawled on my knees or bent my back to transplant and later gather cabbage and tomatoes or picked cotton in the hot October sun. I soon learned disregard for truth would disrupt or destroy the desired outcome for each of those activities. I was unable to identify why I felt as I did, but I knew I was committed to the truth for required activities and me. Pursuing truth in all matters became more important than just protecting the family name, the crops, and my backside. I learned that even though the truths related to those matters are generally considered secular, "the truth of the matter" is those truths are definitely religious because they are connected to God and ultimate truth. Just as truth determines the proper time and depth to plant a cotton seed, transplant a tomato, etc., it also determines correct beliefs about the universe, God, Jesus, and us.

I learned the necessity to pursue truth and abide by it or suffer the consequences. I also learned the destructive results of mistaken beliefs and purposeful or accidental lies. Seeking and sharing truth has been a normal and necessary part of my life for more than eighty years. I will not give up now.

Truth was certainly important for Jesus. There is a powerful statement reportedly made by him: "You will know the truth, and the truth will make you free" (John 8:32). I fully agree. Truth offers freedom that is otherwise unavailable. However, I have added a phrase to Jesus's statement: "If anything can make you free." I added the phrase because there are two things Jesus's statement does not specifically say. First, if rightfully and properly applied, only truth can provide freedom from many things, but there are some things from which it may not quickly, if ever, free us (personal deformity, bodily pain, poverty, incurable disease, and being human). Even then, recognition, acceptance, and application of the truth can free us from some accompanying heavy burdens and excess baggage and thereby help us better manage the remainder. Our spirit and situation may be adjusted by truth, but we will neither be totally free from who we are nor free to do or be whatever we might imagine. Second, if we are committed to it, truth does not set us totally free from everything, because it binds us firmly to itself. It demands our conscious and constant commitment to it, or else we do not really believe in it. Truth also binds us because it is the inescapable law of God, the universe, and life. Truth contains laws we did not make and cannot break. No one can escape its control. It always has the last word. Ignorance of the truth does not free us from the consequences of our lies, denials, or false beliefs. Truth alone can set us as free as we can possibly be, even as it binds us to itself. Jesus understood our situation and called us to believe him and act like it.

If we are committed to truth, we do not get to select the situation or location to participate in or abide by it. Our commitment to it unavoidably leads to decisions and actions. If obedience to truth is a person's guide in life, it causes ordinary people to unexpectedly do extraordinary things such as supporting integration in Mississippi in 1963; breaking family ties and social customs in order to participate in a just cause (nonviolent demonstrations); pastors flirting with being defrocked by denominational authorities because they no longer believe certain doctrines (Protestant Reformation or modern clergy); or perhaps even dying on a cross rather than denying truth.

"Truth" is best understood and more likely accepted when supported by simplicity, practicality, rationality, continuity, and other widely accepted facts. However, those who contemplate and converse about God, Jesus, and religion have been too often scared away from relying on these. I am astonished at how many people have overlooked the simple truth about how we "get right and remain right with God," commonly called *salvation*. A sophisticated and complicated explanation of "truth" does not make it more truthful or more religious and may even diminish its application and appreciation. Simple and rational truth may be the most powerful of all. I have witnessed its power to reform seasoned alcoholics, provide religious insight for members of a small country church, compel the administrative body of a large city church to fight for integration and, in particular, "eliminate the squiggle in my own gizzard."

Discovering truth can diminish pain and produce joy. However, it hurts when we must surrender beliefs we have long considered valid, especially those related to and provided by our family and our religion. There are specific reasons I have challenged particular beliefs upon which much of Christianity was founded and why I question the beliefs of many who are presently professing Christians. I anticipate my comments will be pleasantly rewarding for some and very painful for others. Formulating this material took me to difficult places and led to conclusions far different from the norm. I am well aware that much of what I said will be adamantly opposed by many professing Christians, but that makes it neither correct nor incorrect. Much of what I have written is extremely radical, and I know it. I did not write this just to be different. I did it because I cannot do otherwise if I am truthful in what I believe and if I want to share truth as I understand it. I ask the reader to carefully ponder what I have said and why I said it before passing judgment. It will help if you identify your presuppositions as you ponder mine.

I do not claim perfection in what I believe. I admit I can be mistaken, but I have painstakingly tried to clearly state my beliefs and make them specific, anchored, systematic, logical, understandable, believable, and applicable to all people, places, and things. If there is no solid evidence for my conclusions, I have seriously tried to be logical, reasonable, consistent, and practical with my conjectures. I reserve the right to adjust my beliefs if new insight into truth comes. If anyone provides solid evidence of my mistake, I will gladly admit my error and abide by truth. I cannot absolutely prove every conclusion, but I am comfortable with my presuppositions and where they lead. If this material makes me or others seriously think and opens doors to new elements of truth, then great. If it only makes someone angry and they refuse to think about what they believe, their action will prove a point.

Some individuals who have heard me teach or are familiar with my two published books, *A Pain in the Gut* and *Could It Be, Biblical Gems from the Garbage Dump*, asked for additional thoughts and insights. Their encouragement, my desire to discover truth, and my wish to share what I believe are the reasons I wrote this book.

Numerous people have influenced me and affected my thoughts, but I cannot identify most of them. I have not quoted extensively from other authors. I tried to formulate my thoughts through specific words that came from and were purposely arranged by me. I trust the arrangement of the words is as original as possible, except for the noted material identified by quotations and credits. All biblical references are from the *NRSV.* All references to the noncanonical Gospels are from *The Complete Gospels*, fourth edition, Robert J. Miller, editor.

Years ago, I learned that a belief expressed in a song, a prayer, or a printed declaration may lead to appreciation or condemnation. Because of what I have said in this book, I anticipate both responses. Some of what I have written herein was based on my awareness of rules we did not make and cannot break, but it was based primarily on the fact that I believe Jesus.

# PART I
# GODS AND GOD

PART 1

GODS AND GOD

# CHAPTER 1

## THE INEVITABLE "GOD"

"They" led to our birth, will control our entire lives, and may determine how and when we die. Like sunshine and shadows, they surround us! They sneak up on us when we are unaware, and we also purposely pursue them. Between birth and death, we will each select one from among many to control us. *They* are presuppositions. They got their name because someone presumed something was true, that it worked a certain way, that it was a good guide for life and could be depended upon. Having been convinced that their idea was true, but without absolute proof, someone declared it a fundamental guide or directive for certain behaviors and beliefs. Based on its assumed validity, that person acted upon that presupposition and convinced others of its truth, who then acted upon it and convinced others of its truth, who acted upon it, and the process continued.

Presuppositions are problematic. Whether conceived or received, they are often subject to serious questions because they began at an unproven and unprovable point. They have no solid, provable foundation. Every presupposition begins at a point called *faith*. Someone presumed, or had faith, that the starting point was and is true and applicable. Having believed it was true, they acted like it, but they could not prove beyond doubt its validity. Every presupposition that controls anyone is based on faith and demonstrated by action. Every action is based on a presupposition.

Presuppositions that control us can be likened to many things. They are life's fundamental traffic signs that direct beliefs and behaviors. They are the invisible police officers who stand in the middle of the streets of our life. They tell us (sometimes yell at us) when to stop and when to go, when to turn left or right and when we must not enter. They are also the internal sergeant at arms we soon learn to consciously and subconsciously obey, even without a command given. They are the secret and unseen sentinels that authorize and justify beliefs and behaviors. They are the hidden gatekeepers that grant or deny authority to act or think certain ways. They arrived extremely early in our lives, often from unseen, unknown, and unexpected sources. Once they settle in, they are extremely difficult to deny or disregard.

Presuppositions are unavoidable. Daily life would be very difficult if prior to every individual act and specific decision we had to pause and ponder all the rules and possibilities for what to do, how and why. A decision could and would be made only after extended thought and time, if ever. Such necessary action would seriously delay every decision, reduce speech to a slow stutter, and confound clarity of purpose. Exuberant action would be extremely limited, if not totally lacking. Presuppositions come to the rescue and provide a shortcut. We subconsciously rely on obedience to the internal dictatorial gatekeepers, the ever-present police, and all others who provide instant instructions. They enable us to act with little or no thought.

What if there were no gatekeepers and no internal traffic cops? What if we had no instructions or connecting guidelines for acceptable thought, speech, or action and therefore used only spur-of-the-moment or off-the-wall instant decisions for each separate situation, action, or thought? Nothing would be subjected to anyone's judgment as right or wrong, good or bad, positive or negative. There could be no social order. If our lives proceeded at all, they would probably end sooner, be at a far faster pace but lose uniformity, consistency, and meaning. Without internal anchors and guiding principles, chaos would reign, and we would be without awareness of its cause or cure. Obedience to the gatekeepers is unavoidable for a meaningful life and social order. However, sometimes it is wise to fire the gatekeepers and get new ones!

At birth, everyone arrives with an empty internal "box" into which others inevitably try to implant specific gatekeepers, traffic cops, and rules by which to live. Others purposely provide specific directives for our beliefs and behaviors. Since each of us will be controlled by something (discussed later), the intent of others is to determine that which will eventually control us. People delight in trying to help us by forcefully stuffing the contents of their box into our box, with or without our awareness or permission. Some purposely seek to clone the contents of their box by implanting it into ours. That is not always bad, but it is always fraught with possible future danger. Throughout life, we also acquire some presuppositions through osmosis, observation, and thought. If we mature appropriately, we develop some control over what comes in or goes out of our individual box, but that comes with age, wisdom, and freedom to think independently, if it comes. However, the input into our box, the quality of the provided implants, our freedom and ability to think, the amount of increase of new contents, and the available sources from which to draw new presuppositions are determined by many things over which we may or may not have some control.

We never get a new box! Under certain conditions, we can get new contents and new cops. Under proper circumstances, we are able to purposely add to or subtract from what is in our box until its contents are basically new or radically refurbished with more purposefully chosen contents. However, that is too often the exception and not the rule. Too few people realize change is possible or permissible. They become locked in their box when they permit others to specify their gatekeepers and cops.

Some who thought they were helpful to those locked in their box offered the admonition to "think outside the box." That sounds good, but it is problematic. Our beliefs, behaviors, and thoughts are basically bound by the contents of our personal box. We are actually boxed in by its contents which contains, restrains, and largely defines us. However, no two boxes are identical. Thankfully, some boxes were initially implanted with the freedom and encouragement to think, question, reason, and choose, all of which are primary prerequisites for evaluating the contents of one's box and to consciously accept or change it. Sadly, others lack that freedom, and any forced change is extremely painful. The contents of our personal box, our presuppositions, are the key to who we are, what we believe, and what we do.

Regardless of how limited the contents of our box may be, from it we consciously or subconsciously choose a primary presupposition to control us, which makes it our "god." Because of our nature, the choice of a god is inevitable (discussed later). A chosen god may be later changed, given certain conditions and efforts. It is important for us to recognize the process by which we acquire the contents of our box and to understand how we choose our god so we may gain insight into our beliefs and behaviors. Since all behavior is in response to and controlled by our god, that makes all behaviors and beliefs unavoidably "religious" (discussed later).

Presuppositions from diverse sources, both known and unknown, come to us. Throughout life, many of us have repeatedly received and absorbed them from instructions, osmosis, accident, and design. From birth, authoritative figures quietly, accidentally, purposefully, and forcefully attempted to implant "proper" thoughts and actions into us (truth for them). During formative years, seldom were we encouraged to think for ourselves or make personal decisions. Without question or concern, we usually assumed our original authoritative informers were correct, if we were even capable of making such assumptions. We consciously and subconsciously accepted and absorbed their inputs, thoughtlessly making them our own (perhaps with some exception in our teenage years). From that point forward, even when the authority figures are not physically present, their previously implanted presuppositions loudly echo in our heads even when the persons are not present, when we are totally unaware of the process, and even after we have renounced specific presuppositions.

A perfect illustration of that continuing control comes from my family. During my childhood, no one was allowed to shoot a gun on Sunday unless a hawk was after the chickens or a crow was in the pecan tree. I am well aware there is nothing inherently evil about shooting a gun on Sunday. However, I left home two months before my eighteenth birthday, and my parents have been deceased for many years, but if I pick up a gun on Sunday, I hear and feel the prohibition I inherited more than eighty years ago. Old personal presuppositions seldom disappear or die. They either continue to direct us or they just hide for a while, periodically reappear, and make us miserable, even though we previously and consciously denied their validity.

Authority figures exist and operate within the family, community, church, country, and elsewhere, especially the family and church. They offer instructions to anyone who will listen, as well as those who will not. However, we eventually become responsible for our own beliefs and behaviors. Most often, we unconsciously copy or piggyback on what others provide without awareness or examination. If given an opportunity during the years of our personal development and experiences, we no doubt formulate a few personal beliefs from observation, insight, revelation, reason, imagination, and experimentation. If not, we are pathetic! If anyone assumes the authority to cobble together any presuppositions they might call their own, and if they consciously choose their god, it will most likely be after several birthdays, increased knowledge, expanded experience, freedom to think, and having wrestled with truth.

Presuppositions marched in an unending and authoritative line down through previous cultures, generations, family groups, and individuals. For thousands of years, that long, endless, powerful, and purposeful implantation process moved constantly forward from one generation to the next, often with little or no social and religious change, but with threats and punishments for any who differed. That long line now affects, involves, and includes us. Even now, people from that line are purposely trying to implant specific presupposition into us. Having joined the line, we are trying to return the favor for those around us. History often repeats itself through old, unchanged, or slightly changed personal presuppositions.

Even though all presuppositions are definitely religious, those commonly given that label are often considered more important and are the most difficult to change. That could be because of what we were taught, but I doubt that is the primary reason. From the dawn of civilization, most people have realized we do not control the universe and believe there is an "indescribable something" to which we are connected and by which we are affected. I believe the very core of our being subconsciously knows we must have a god, and we seek something that will give order and peace to life. St. Augustine, in his *Confessions,* addressed that issue when he said, "You have made us for yourself, O Lord, and our heart is restless until it rests in thee." As a professing Christian, I accept that concept, but I believe it is also correct in the broader non-Christian realm. All people, from all places and times, long for, and by nature must have, something beyond themselves which provides order for them, regardless of the name they give it or the process they use to worship it.

For that reason, individuals often grant greater authority to presuppositions they consider religious than to those they consider secular. Those assumed to be religious are also anchored more firmly and are usually more fervently defended. Many people adamantly refuse to surrender or adjust religious beliefs, even when confronted with strong contradictory evidence, threatened with severe personal punishment, or even threatened with death. That is not by accident.

Anyone who proposes a new or adjusted presupposition specifically identified as religious often receives a hostile response from other religious people. Some new presuppositions may deserve opposition but never just because they are new. Each new one needs to be carefully examined by a higher truth. Tightly held presuppositions empower nasty fights against any proposed change and perhaps against the one who proposed it. Religious wars have been waged when pastors used a different translation of scripture, announced a different "means of salvation," affirmed different requirements for social behavior toward those of a different race or sexual orientation, and so on. Having offered a different presupposition and possible truth, pastors and leaders have been severely chastised or abruptly dismissed by individual churches and denominations. Those who dismissed others were not receptive to new presuppositions because they thought they already had the truth.

The folly of such fights was demonstrated when a Mississippi Methodist pastor read his Sunday morning sermon text from the Revised Standard Version of the Bible. After the service, he was severely chastised by members of the congregation. They strongly insisted he read from the "original text," meaning the King James Version (perhaps the only one they knew), but they did not specify. Being a good pastor who listened to his parishioners, on the following Sunday the New Testament scripture for the sermon was read from the "original text," just as they requested—Greek! He did not last long as their pastor. They were so religious, they could not tolerate new truth. "Let everyone with ears, listen" (Matthew 11:15).

Acceptance of specific presuppositions creates a group. Likewise, a person who professes genuine adherence to a specific group is expected to give serious allegiance and homage to its affirmed presuppositions, whether a denominational, political, or family group. That is the meaning of *membership,* to be bound together and controlled by specific beliefs and actions based on prescribed presuppositions. Denial of the group's basic presuppositions actually severs one from the group, whether separation is declared or denied by the group or the individual. If one knowingly or unknowingly accepts and lives by the group's presuppositions, that person is a member of it, even if unintended or undeclared. The sad fact is that many of us have little knowledge about the basic presuppositions espoused by our chosen group, even if we really and freely chose the group. Because of the herd mentality and the likelihood we simply have little insight into what actually controls us or our chosen group, we can follow the leaders without awareness of what they profess, from where it came, or where it will lead. After all, the "authorities" assured us they were and are providing the gospel truth for our box, and to differ, doubt, or disbelieve them is an unforgivable sin. Furthermore, if we doubt or disobey, they promise we will be disowned by God, the Church, and both sides of our family, resulting in an eternity in hell, as well as no invitation to the family's next Thanksgiving dinner. Well, eating a peanut butter and jelly sandwich alone might not be all bad and sometimes advisable!

Presuppositions, like sunshine and shadows, surround us. Like the sun and shadows, we cannot truthfully deny their existence or live without them. We sometimes have a choice to be either in the sunshine or shadow. Likewise, we sometimes have a choice of the presuppositions that dictate our beliefs and behavior. Presuppositions are so important that we inevitably choose, either knowingly or unknowingly, one from among many that basically determines our beliefs and behaviors. Therefore, it is our god. The unavoidable necessity to choose a god illustrates a rule we did not make and cannot break.

# CHAPTER 2

# THE INDESCRIBABLE "GOD"

Since the dawn of civilization, personal experiences have convinced people they were not in complete control of their lives and the world around them. They sensed an "indescribable something," an unknown power, that exerted influence over them, even when uninvited and unwanted. Because of that presupposition, humanity has continually searched for what or who that unknown something is, how to describe it, and what it demands of us.

Throughout thousands of years, numerous delightful and frightening experiences have produced various presuppositions pertaining to an "indescribable something." From the earliest awareness of some outside control, people surely imparted and implanted presuppositions about this mysterious something, which became known as a god. Even though it remained indescribable, people provided firm ideas on what they thought it was and specific instructions on how to respond properly. People no doubt deferred to the judgment of those in authority. Professionals, parents, and others pondered with their kith and kin what it must be, the degree of its control, and the required response to their indescribable something. However, trouble arose when different segments of society declared diverse deities with very different demands and natures. Even though people knew *something* existed, they did not always know how best to describe it, how properly to respond, and they did not necessarily agree with others who thought they knew.

Down through the ages, humanity has unavoidably anthropomorphized the nature of their suspected and proclaimed deities. The reason is rather simple. Since we have no divine verbiage with which to discuss gods (or anything), we use human language in a feeble and unsuccessful attempt to partially describe and inadequately explain their assumed nature, character, behavior, and demands. Having no knowledge beyond the human (and no ability to use it if we had it), we envision and speak of any assumed deity in terms of what we believe is true about us, others, and our world. We attribute elevated human characteristics and nature to our identified deity, either by supersizing or downsizing specific aspects of our humanness. Actually, we inevitably create this god in our likeness! We speak about the indescribable something with words we also use to speak about ourselves and our world, but we remain unable to completely describe our god. In order to fully describe any god, we would have to be greater than it is. Any god we can fully describe is incapable of being a god! It is tremendously important to realize we cannot partially describe our god apart from ourselves; nor can we correctly describe ourselves apart from our god!

The multitude of named and claimed deities has been divided into gods and goddesses. The differences between the two are often more in name and gender than in action. The nature and purpose of both were or are to guide, control, and comfort their devotees. Since both terms refer to an indescribable something who controls, we will refer to all of them with the general term *gods* and disregard gender. Identifying all previously or presently proclaimed gods is impossible, and any effort to accurately speak about all of them is unreasonable. Regardless of when, where, or how the name *god* or a substitute is used, it always refers to an indescribable something that controls or directs someone.

We obviously have a serious problem when speaking about the indescribable something. How do we correctly speak about the unknown and the unknowable? How do we glean truth from the vastly different presuppositions and declarations proclaimed throughout centuries and cultures? Is there only one indescribable something, or are there many? Does the many eventually merge into the One? Does the One control me? Do different people have a different god? Numerous people, past and present, pursued and pursue truthful answers to these prolonged, profound, and personal questions. We now join them in the search for god.

Joseph Campbell spoke to this problem when he said, "God is a word referring us past anything that can be conceived of or named." That does not sound like Santa or Grandpa. Sir Lord Geering, from New Zealand, agrees when he states, "God remains as a symbolic term referring to all that transcends us, providing unity to the universe we live in." No super Santa, mansion in the sky, or streets of gold found here. Sam Keen reiterated the same idea when he said, "After we have said all we can say about God we are still surrounded by impenetrable silence."

All who search for better understanding of the indescribable something are bound together by three similar things, regardless of the period of history in which they search or the search method used. The first element is belief that the indescribable something may exist in some form. No one searches unless there is at least a serious question or strong suspicion *it* is out there. The second connection for all who search is a desire to discover what *it* is. The third connection, if found or assumed to be there, is the desire to find an appropriate response to it.

For all who believe *it* exists and intend to search for a better understanding of it, I propose a point at which to begin and a process by which to search. Both are contained in two fundamental definitions, which must always be pondered in the proper order. For our purpose, they are precise definitions of two specific words, *god* and *worship*. The two definitions apply to and encompass all people, all religions, all worship, and all declared or undeclared gods. These simple definitions may first appear inadequate to guide our quest, but simplicity is often an invaluable asset, and it sometimes wears a disguise. However, the ramifications of each definition are almost endless. If taken seriously, these two definitions may revolutionize, or at least seriously adjust, some of our presuppositions about God, gods, worship, and us.

## A. First Definition

The first definition declares the fundamental truth about "god." It states, *"Our god is that one thing which controls us, that to which we give ultimate allegiance."* This definition emphasizes the fact that one and only one thing rules a person, regardless of what that may be, by whatever name it is called or even if its name and control are unknown or undeclared. This definition gives us a solid foundation for pondering who or what "god" is for anyone. Different people have different gods that control them. The optimum word is *control.* There is nothing complicated in this straightforward definition. Complications come in discerning what actually controls us, but that discussion must be reserved until later. We now focus specifically on the definition. We must take it quite literally. It means exactly what it says. It applies to all, and it is true for all, whether a person's allegiance is given to something named or unnamed, known or unknown, God or idol. It is also applicable for any time and any person in human history and indicates the almost endless possibilities from which to choose a personal god.

Every normal person, regardless of color, creed, clan, or religion, is inevitably and always controlled by his or her one god, whether that fact is known, unknown, or denied. Modern insights into human behavior further emphasize the point that one thing from among many possibilities is most important for each of us. It is that one organizing element in our lives that controls us. A "normal person" cannot remain normal or survive for very long without a god. Attempted allegiance to more than one god is problematic and impossible, possibly illustrated by the New Testament stories of demon possession and by some present-day personality disorders. A person's god may be unknown to him or her or mistakenly identified. Since a person may be mistaken about it or may not want it known, this announced god may not necessarily be what actually controls them. Additionally, individuals live among us who do not recognize or will not declare they have a god.

Legions of available gods clamor for our primary allegiance. Given the number and nature of invitations, plus our various responses, it may first appear we have more than one god or that we alternate between them. However, in the final analysis, by definition and behavior, there is always only one god in control at any given time, or serious trouble ensues. Regardless of the verbiage used to speak about any god, language does not negate its control, its organizing force, or a response to it.

No one said we always make a healthy and wholesome choice of our god, but we always make a choice. Present-day disciplines of psychology, psychiatry, specialized counseling, recovery groups, and others daily deal with many who have had difficulty making a wise and productive choice about their organizing element (god). Search for clarity of commitment and truth consumes many hours and many dollars for many people. The recovery efforts made available by professionals are seldom considered to have any connection to today's normal concept of god. According to our definition, their efforts illustrate the very heart of the matter. The primary purpose of professionally trained helpers is to help clients discover their difficulty and effectively deal with the truth about unwanted control or the disruptive element(s) in their lives.

Religious leaders have always encouraged their constituents to have a single controlling element. Modern rabbis, priests, and pastors spend an inordinate amount of time providing parishioners an opportunity to identify their god. They repeatedly instruct and encourage their hearers to choose one particular organizing force in their life. From the pulpit and in print, many have identified and denounced idols that can—but should not—control. Judeo-Christian parishioners are admonished to forsake all else and serve one specific God or suffer the consequences. Believers are also reminded of their responsibility to assist others who may need to select the appropriate organizer for their life. One specific organizer is proclaimed, encouraged, and facilitated by clergy and the congregations they serve.

Old Testament passages provide the earliest biblical records that specifically address the subject of control by one god. It is the underlying issue in the biblical myth about Adam and Eve, when they were forced to decide what spirit would dominate their lives. The subject appears again and again in Hebrew history, often among its heroes and leaders. The Hebrews wrestled with the selection of one God and true obedience to him while living among those who worshipped pagan gods. During its history, biblical writers identified the cause of Israel's recurring problems as their failure to worship "the one God." Some prominent leader periodically came upon the scene, reminded the Hebrews the cause of their problem, and led them in a reaffirmation to consciously and personally serve their one God. Recovery usually came only after they renewed their covenant with the one God.

Moses and other ancient Hebrew leaders firmly admonished followers to become fully aware of the God that controlled them. Abraham may have been the first Hebrew person to emphasize there is only one God worthy of worship and then gave special instructions to facilitate the choice and worship of that one God and no other. The Bible indicates the Jewish "Shema" perhaps came from Moses. It has been daily quoted for centuries by devout Jews, reminding them, "Hear, O Israel: The Lord is our God, the Lord alone. You shall love the Lord your God with all your heart, and with all your soul, and with all your might" (Deuteronomy 6:4–5). At a later time, they were instructed to "Choose this day whom you will serve" (Joshua 24:15). Both statements reminded the Hebrews that they must choose and serve one God, or else additional trouble would ensue.

Many modern people assume those instructions to the early Hebrews were or are relevant only to the Hebrews, the present Jewish communities, and possibly all who presently take religion seriously. A careful examination of those instructions reveals they are as applicable to our modern day as they were to the ancient Hebrews. Abraham and Moses validated the above definition because they boldly affirmed that our God is always one. The overwhelming evidence, biblical and secular, declares the same.

By our nature, no person can escape the inevitable choice of one god. The ancient requirement remains: "Choose today the one god whom you will serve." We unavoidably do. Biblical records, modern medical personnel, Judeo-Christian leaders, and other enlightened people may use different verbiage but all affirm the necessity for one "controller." All encourage us to deliberately choose and to choose wisely. As insignificant as some people may consider the two above-mentioned Hebrew admonitions (choose one god and choose today), they contain profound and powerful truth that is more than just firm support for our first definition. They proclaim absolute truth, which we did not make and which we cannot break.

## B.  Second Definition

The second definition focuses on worship. It states, *"We unavoidably respond to whatever controls us (god) and our response to it is 'worship' of that god."* This definition, like the first, provides a specified point of departure for all searchers in all times and places. It automatically follows the first in lockstep and could be considered the continuation of it. Though closely connected, the two definitions are separate issues that require individual treatment for clearer understanding and greater impact.

Note the powerful verbiage in the definition. Human nature necessitates an unavoidable response to the god that controls us. Logically, there is no other option if we are to be mentally and emotionally healthy. Our god has ultimate worth to us and consequently dictates our behaviors. Ascribed worth engenders worship. Worship demonstrates worth. Worship identifies a person's god. Worship is a way of life in response to a god. Nothing about this second definition should confuse or mislead us. Our definition of god as "whatever controls a person" may surprise some, but perhaps more surprising is our definition of worship as response to that god, whatever that god may be. This second definition, like the first, is

15

logical, simple, straightforward, and clearly stated. It too is applicable to everyone, regardless of when they lived, who they are, or what their god may be. Whether one's god is named or unnamed, known or unknown, declared or undeclared changes nothing at this point. Worship is an unavoidable lifestyle in response to one's god. Our actions illustrate, if not guarantee, the worth of whatever we worship. According to this definition, there can be no atheists.

The control exerted by our god is truly affirmed and demonstrated when we consciously or unconsciously assume or duplicate its nature and spirit in our being and behavior (discussed later). The assumed spirit of the rock, bear, mountain, God, or whatever is a guiding force for those who worship them. Those who have no intent to imitate their god unavoidably do so by behavior and spirit. Anyone who does not imitate their proclaimed god in spirit and action has another god.

These two definitions do not provide complete information about an indescribable something. They do not say everyone has the same god or that there is only one possible choice or that everyone responds the same. They do explicitly declare everyone has only one god that they unavoidably worship. Furthermore, the definitions emphasize irrefutable facts that have too often been unknown, denied, or totally disregarded. Anyone's god falls within the parameters of these two simple definitions. The definitions' simplicity may be the reason they have eluded us far too long. These two definitions declare an equal and designated point of departure for all who now or ever did seek to learn more about the name and nature of their god and what it means to worship it. Given the truth contained in these two definitions, they define in broad terms what or who is "god" for anyone. They narrow our focus and provide undeniable clues to what god is for each of us. If taken seriously, these two definitions allow for further inquiry, possible discovery, and unexpected surprise. They are also rules we did not make and cannot break.

# CHAPTER 3

# UNKNOWN AND UNNAMED GODS

Everyone has a god, and the choices are far more extensive than perhaps initially assumed. If we mistakenly speak and think of a person's god only as an identified and named organizer, we totally disregard an extremely large and often overlooked group to whom god is also applicable and important. Some individuals are controlled by an unknown and unnamed god, a personal god of which they are unaware and, of course, to which they have given no thought or name. If we fail to recognize the existence of this large group of individuals, we not only disregard the two definitions, but we also overlook a vital avenue for understanding the behavior of many people.

Unknown and unnamed gods are worshipped by their devotees as faithfully as any who worship a named and claimed god. Those gods may or may not be made by human hands, but they were made gods by human choices. A list of possible choices would be almost limitless and would include anything imaginable that can control a person. If named deities are extremely diverse and distinctively different, unnamed and unknown gods are perhaps more diverse and different, but their controlling power is just as complete. One major difference between the two categories is that identified deities usually have particular designated characteristics, demands, and certain control over specified persons, places, and things. Unnamed and unrecognized gods naturally lack that stated specificity because they are not recognized as gods by those under their control. The one common characteristic for the named, unnamed, known, and unknown gods is the unavoidable control over the ones who worship them.

For practical purposes, I have divided gods into two general categories. The first category includes all identified deities purposely worshipped by someone. The second category includes the unnamed gods who are unknowingly worshipped by anyone. However, Jews and Christians also have two categories for deities, but the categories are very different from the two above. Their first category includes only their God, and the second category includes "all else." For Jews and Christians, there is only one God, and it is theirs. Worship of any other named, unnamed, or unknown god beyond their own is automatically dumped into the "all else" category and is called an "idol." Generally speaking, for Jews and Christians, everyone worships either their God or an idol, and there is no other category. This concept disregards the broader meaning of god, which we will later address. Even though these categories are not always acceptable, we will follow their terminology for now.

The term *idol* provides a useful and distinctive handle to grasp and use for further discussion. Its definition is elusive and often depends on who defines it. We must highlight the fact that what one person calls an idol may be a god for another person. Likewise, the professing Christian's God may be called an idol by a non-Christian and also by another professing Christian. Idols are identified and defined by the people who do not worship them.

Jews and Christians affirm that the object of worship is an idol if it is anything other than their personal god as they define it. Therefore, idols are abundant. Idols may range from persons to possessions, from jobs to joys, from something birthed to something bought, from something handmade to something heaven-sent, from anything actual to something only imagined, from something known to something unknown, from named to unnamed, etc. Idols rule behaviors and beliefs, due either to known, unknown, or unexamined choices. Just because professing Christians assume their beliefs are appropriate does not mean they are free from idol worship, nor does it mean they are correct when they declare the god of another is an idol (ouch). When examined by the highest standard, the long-held beliefs of professing Christians may unknowingly proclaim and promote idol worship. We may not be as Christian as we think.

Given the validity of the above two rules, it is safe to make some definite affirmations about the indescribable something. Regardless of the name or nature of a person's chosen god, it can be a singing bird, wild beast, stones, carved piece of wood, heavenly body, heavenly being, an addiction, etc. In the words of Sam Keen, "God (god) is the organizing principle of our life." There is a god, and everyone inevitably has one, whether we know it or not. It controls our lives, and we worship it. It is one but chosen from many. We tend to duplicate its spirit in our behavior. Jews and Christians call that which controls a person either "God" or "an idol." Whatever our god may be, it provides some order to our existence, has ultimate control over our beliefs and behavior, and we worship (value) it above all else. Expressed differently, our god is the primary presupposition from which we operate, and it is always the motivating spirit of our life, whether known or unknown.

# CHAPTER 4

# THE DISCOVERED GOD

All identified gods were discovered by someone who formulated an unprovable presupposition in reference to them. Gods never jumped from behind a bush and announced their name, nor did they write their name in the sky with clouds. Numerous situations and various circumstances in different times and distant places resulted in vastly different presuppositions and proclamations. Each proclaimed god has a history pertaining to its discovery. However, professing Christians are primarily concerned with their God, so we turn our attention to that subject.

Long ago, the Hebrews lived among people who proclaimed many different gods. Through an unknown process, a new presupposition arose among the Hebrews. Someone among them discovered and declared there was only one god worthy of their worship. It is important to notice they did not deny the existence of other gods. They had lived among people who worshipped various gods, and the Hebrews had previously joined with them in worship of those gods at certain times and at designated places. We do not know how the worship of pagan gods influenced the Hebrews' discovery of their prescribed deity. If the Hebrews seriously searched, we have little knowledge of how long they searched or how they reached their conclusions. The Hebrew concept and worship of their God probably developed out of pagan religion and in conjunction with it. We do not know if the early expressions of Hebrew faith and forms of worship were original with the Hebrews or if they were patterned after, borrowed from or in opposition to "outsiders" who existed both with and prior to them. The older Sumerian and Gilgamesh epics contain stories closely parallel to several biblical accounts. The two creation stories in the Bible have a strong resemblance to those creation stories in other ancient and pagan religions. Events in Genesis have Mesopotamian parallels. The idea of Satan or the Devil was probably borrowed from the Zoroastrians, who existed long before the Hebrews proclaimed their own God and proper worship. The degree to which the Hebrews simply borrowed, adjusted, sanctioned, or replaced pagan presuppositions and practices is beyond our knowledge and open to further research.

We can only surmise the confusion endured by the Hebrews and the time spent pondering former presuppositions and formulating new ones pertaining to their indescribable something. We lack information on who first proposed the new presupposition that declared only one particular God for them. In addition to understand God's nature, they also needed to know how to rightfully worship only him. Human nature and reason remind us that the formulation of their presupposition was not instantaneous and certainly not immediately or universally accepted. We get a brief glimpse of their struggle in the story of Abraham, who is credited as the first to conclude there was a different God for him and perhaps also the Hebrews. We have no record of how or why he reached that conclusion while many around him, including his own kin and clan, worshipped something else. From some unknown source or situation, he discovered a new god who had a new nature, new rules, and a new spirit. For the first time, it appears reason was purposely employed in choosing or discovering one's god. At some point, the Hebrews reasoned that God chose them only because he loved them and he only wanted a response of love from them. Perhaps this was the idea behind Abraham's conclusion. As the story goes, according to the dictates of his day and in response to worship of his pagan god, Abraham was preparing to slay and sacrifice his firstborn son when a new god was discovered or revealed. Through the use of logic, reason, and faith, he concluded the sacrifice of a firstborn son was totally unreasonable and absolutely unnecessary. We will never know what led to his conclusion or what part reason played in Abraham's new religion. (Some of us firmly believe reason and serious thought were the determining factors in his decision, and we are convinced that is the proper foundation for any valid Judeo-Christian proclamation.)

The Hebrews never tell us why they chose *he* as God's gender or why it was necessary to denote it. God has no gender. Apparently, that subject did not concern the early Hebrew people, but some modern folks believe God's gender is very important, and they are very sure they know it. We can probably guess why the male pronoun was used. Hebrew scriptures were formulated within a patriarchal society in which men definitely dominated. Therefore, the Hebrew writers assumed the gender of their anthropomorphized divine being who controlled them had to be male. However, the term *he* did not detract from their awareness that God was Spirit. The assumed male gender for God is presently problematic for some people. Since we think differently, or should, it is appropriate for us to use he or she or it because, like any name for God, each pronoun is only an incomplete symbol (and so is "God"). Some may find the use of one particular pronoun is less problematic and more meaningful than another. Other people prefer to use no pronoun, simply using the symbol *God,* which solves their gender problem.

We can only surmise what additional presuppositions grew and guided the Hebrews in their search for their God and his proper name, gender, character, and demands. At some period in their history, a prominent presupposition declared every personal name was extremely important and contained within itself a defining message about the named person's character and nature, when spoken or written. They believed if only they knew God's name, that would reflect his nature and character or vice versa. Herein lay their dilemma. If a name for God carried within it his nature and character, no person possessed the capabilities to declare a name for the indescribable something. Even though they needed and wanted a name that reflected God's nature, there was also a reasonable and agonizing question of whether their deity could or should be named by anyone (excellent question). Any attempt to do so would automatically be insufficient, presumptuous, and possibly dangerous.

Perhaps for that reason, in the story where Moses asked for God's name, all he got was "I am who I am" and nothing more. When Jacob had his wrestling match with God, he too asked for a name, but for the same reason, he did not get it. Those stories symbolize an ancient and basic truth about God. Based on their presupposition, God could not be named because he could not be fully understood, defined, or described (then or now). These no-name-for-God stories clearly portray the ingrained presupposition that God is beyond full human understanding and therefore must never have a restrictive and specifically defining name. He must always remain, to some degree, the indescribable something who deserves reverence.

The Hebrews' story gets somewhat convoluted (more than once). It was either later in the "no name for God" period or later than that period or from a different tradition and place or the opinion of a different writer when a different presupposition reared its head. We do not know if it was in opposition or in addition to the belief that "name reflects nature," but it does indicate change. Perhaps because of the passage of time, certain people discovered and affirmed God had a specific nature and name. Even though they thought they knew, they dared not speak or write them. They had a new and serious problem. How could they convey his presumed nature and name to others if they were forbidden to speak or write them? An answer apparently came to devout Hebrew worshippers who through experience, reason, revelation, observation, and faith thought they had discovered God's nature and therefore his name. Those devout believers resolved the dilemma with a new process that created "a name that was not a name" or a symbol. They began with a known word and removed the vowels, which resulted in no word but a symbol instead of a name. Since a collection of consonants without vowels spelled nothing, and even if that "no name" symbol referred specifically to God, they were not using his name. It was permissible to use a designed symbol for their chosen deity because the symbol was not an attempt to totally identify his character and nature. However, someone had to know the word and many others were smart enough to apply the vowels. This process appears useless to us because all words are symbols but it expressed their reverence for God, the indescribable something.

The story may be more parabolic than factual, but it reflects the Hebrews' struggle to develop the proper response to and worship of their God, even if they could not and would not name him. We have no idea how many Hebrews believed this. If the presupposition "name reflects character" was believed by most people in the secular world, the pagans also believed it. Pagan hecklers may have said "Your god is nothing and does not exist if he has no name." In response, the Hebrews may have forcefully declared that their God definitely had a specific nature and particular demands, even without a name. That did not stop the hecklers. Later, the Hebrews replied, perhaps from desperation, "He has a name, but we are not allowed to tell you. It is our secret." That response lacked force to win the argument, but what else could they say? Were the Hebrews forced to make a rational decision or renounce the faith? Regardless of the circumstances through which these stories arose and why they were later told, that new declaration may signify they had slowly discovered through experience a portion of their God's nature and demands. Therefore, out of awe, reverence, and limited knowledge, they offered a symbol, but not a totally defining name for the indescribable something.

The story about the origin of a symbolic name for their God may or may not be factual, but it contains undeniable truth. God is indescribable. He is beyond our ability to fully understand or describe. The story recognizes and emphasizes the significance of symbolic words, which always stand in the place of that to which they refer. A symbolic word points to something the word, in and of itself, is not. The word *God* was a symbol for them, and it is for us. At certain points in history, a different symbolic name may have been intended as a name for their deity, or it may have represented the view of a different writer with a different presupposition or tradition. We do know the ancient Hebrews chose other word symbols, which are later translated as "God," "the Lord God," "the Holy One," and others. At a time in history, or according to a different author, God was regularly called "Yahweh" and "Elohim." For their own religious reasons, different people at different times referred to God as "Jehovah," "Adonai," "El Shaddai," "Lord of Hosts," "the Lord," and others. Regardless of the symbol used, it respectfully referred to an awesome, wholly other, and indescribable something about whom they had certain presuppositions. Based on what they had seen and experienced, by faith they declared God does exist but has no physical features and is therefore Spirit. That very important point will be discussed later.

Over time, named and unnamed Hebrews developed additional discoveries or new presuppositions about God and humanity's proper response. Specific individuals received major credit for new presuppositions about God and appropriate human behavior, but they may not have deserved all of it. Some of those Hebrew directives are sprinkled throughout the Old Testament, especially among its first five books and the books of the prophets. The book of Leviticus provides specific examples of early directives for human behavior, perhaps reflecting what took many years to formulate. Likely written more than 3,500 years ago, and prior to the great prophets, it provides particular rules for worship and social activities. Called "a priest's manual" by some, it has six major divisions: laws dealing with sacrifices, the consecration of priests, what was clean and unclean, the ceremony for the annual Day of Atonement, guides to govern Israel's life as a holy people, and an appendix for religious vows. Among other things, people were instructed never to curse the deaf, never to put stumbling blocks in the path of the blind, never to falsify weights and measures, and never to glean the fields and orchards. These are rules by which to live in response to God.

Deuteronomy, the book following Leviticus, provides additional insight into the presumed nature and spirit of God and proper human behavior. The Shema and Ten Commandments are prime examples.

They indicate not only God's nature but also ours. They are the best-known rules within the present Judeo-Christian community. Even though we usually consider them rules for life, they are far more than that. The commandments contain specific presuppositions that state who God is, who the Hebrews were, and proper action for both. By slightly rephrasing some of the statements, the commandments become positive and describe the lifestyle and spirit of one who truly loves God. From this perspective, anyone who loves God above all else will not abuse God's name, make images of him, cheat, steal, etc. The commandments become statements of faithful behavior in response to God. In fact, people who faithfully follow them will act in the likeness of God and imitate his spirit. (Remember, we always imitate our god.)

The Hebrews proclaimed another radical presupposition. They were convinced God freely chose them because of his nature and not theirs and not because of anything they had done. (Perhaps God "chose" everyone, but only the Hebrews recognized it.) They believed God chose them because his nature is love. That was their first descriptive designation. In response to God's unmerited love for them, and because of what God did for them, they must choose him above all other gods and then love him above all else. Since God loved everyone, they must imitate God and love their neighbor. In addition to this directive and the commandments, the great prophets refined for their day God's character and requirements as one who loves mercy, justice, and obedience. The prophets forcefully condemned blood sacrifices and said meaningless, noisy assemblies were an abomination to God. From those prophets and Moses, Jesus got his primary message that God's spirit is love, and if we wish to get right and stay right with God, we must love God above all else, and we must love our neighbor as ourselves.

God never told the Hebrews his name, but they discovered his basic nature through the way he treated them. They discovered his nature from his actions, not his words. They discovered the indescribable something's spirit can be best described as self-giving love. Furthermore, they concluded God loved them, and all he asked of them in return was to love him above all else and then act like it with their neighbor, themselves, and the universe. Those Hebrew presuppositions were actually hammered out over time on the rocks of experience, revelation, reason, and faith. They became the basic foundation for Jesus's proclamations and practices, and they are the bedrock for Christianity.

# CHAPTER 5

## THE INHERITED GOD

Since Christianity was birthed within and grew out of the Hebrew religion, it unavoidably inherited many important presuppositions from its predecessor. For many professing Christians, the degree to which Christianity depends on those ancient beliefs is largely unknown, if not denied. Their concern too often begins and ends with Jesus. The early Christian development was directly influenced by two distinctly different people: Jesus and the apostle Paul. Both drew heavily from Hebrew and Jewish traditions, but each person emphasized presuppositions that resulted in very different doctrines. Jesus emphasized two longstanding Hebrew directives that stated if individuals want to get right and stay right with God, they must love God above all else and love their neighbor as themselves. Following Jesus's death and Paul's vision, Paul emphasized the necessity to believe in the crucified and resurrected Jesus as the means of salvation. Consequently, the new religious movement, later called Christianity, inherited its basic presuppositions about God and humanity from two people who were as different as night and day. Therefore, it is very important to examine what we inherited and what we now believe.

Our inherited beliefs require close examination, because they may not be as Christian as assumed. There are reasons. Our first introduction and instructions about God naturally came in early childhood and were limited to whatever religious authorities implanted in our box. The authority figures who taught us often knew very little about religious history and heritage, just like the authority figures who taught them knew very little, and so on. After our family tree grew for many years in its native and anemic soil, seldom supplemented by cross-pollination or fertilization from informed sources, we reaped from it whatever good or deformed fruit it produced. If someone offered "fertilizer" or an improved variety of fruit, our teachers too often did not like the looks of it, declared it defective, and punished the ones who offered or accepted it. Most of those who taught us did the best they could with what they had, and that was the basis from which our understanding of God grew, if it grew at all. Whatever our forefathers taught, it had a lasting effect on all generations that followed.

Since our god is the organizer of our lives and the object of our worship, ancient and present presuppositions about God are extremely significant and need careful scrutiny. Relatively recent insights may become an inheritance for any who find them meaningful. If professing Christians want to be what they profess they are, all inherited presuppositions about God must be carefully examined and evaluated by the highest available standard.

## A.  God of Creation

Jews and Christians inherited the affirmation that God created and controls the entire universe. It is his. Do not ask how he created it and the order of creation, because we really do not know. He had no assistant, regardless of what the Gospel of John states. He never asked for anyone's permission or instructions. He has no need for anyone to tell him how he should have done it, precisely how he did it, the order in which he did it, or how he should and will perform his next or final act. He allows us to have some awareness of his methodology, but we cannot completely duplicate everything he did. The biblical creation myth in Genesis makes a very, very significant point by stating creation was unfinished and God gave humanity some responsibility to care for and add to what God created. According to the creation myth, God deliberately depends on us to join him in caring for and continuing all dimensions of the creation process. Because of our nature, we either join in advancing creation or assist in its destruction, because there is no neutral ground. Fulfilling that responsibility to continue creation and properly care for the universe will depend on our ability to discern and abide by truth and love (discussed later). How well we have fulfilled our requirement to this point in time does not appear to have been our best. Based on available evidence, God seems to have done exceptionally well with his original design and intent, sometimes with and sometimes without our assistance.

We have only partially discerned knowledge of God's creation process. To know God's full secret would be too much knowledge. It is locked within some eternal truth beyond humanity's capability to discover or deduce. However, if our knowledge displeased God, why did he create us with the desire and ability to attain it? If anyone ever assumed God does not disclose how he gets things done, simple observation, modern scientific knowledge, and profound religious insight seriously challenge that assumption. Present knowledge provides greater insight into creation and humanity's intended participation in and preservation of it. We know enough to conclude we must purposely and willingly participate with God in creation, or we may inadvertently create something less than good, even something that will destroy us. It is essential we recognize the entire universe also functions on the "love principle," meaning when it is loved properly, it returns even greater gifts, but when mistreated, it will diminish in quality and quantity (plants, animals, soil, climate, people, etc.). Like God, its love is expressed through giving of itself and asks only for love in return.

Because of our nature, we always unavoidably participate in creation, but creation of what? Our deliberate effort to gain further insight into the intricate creation process and to consciously participate in it illustrate the awareness of our capabilities and responsibilities.

Scientific knowledge provides significant insight into how some of God's creation occurred and continues. Scientists with powerful telescopes, space stations, satellites, and such reveal vast wonders never before known or expected. Likewise, sophisticated microscopes uncover the once-hidden secrets of our innermost being. Truth discovered through research into space, human anatomy and behavior, the connectedness of all creation, climate change, and recently discovered biblical texts are among the many things that opened new and previously unimagined windows to God's action and truth. Given the amazing vastness of the universe, coupled with the many minuscule performing parts in it and us, how do we fit in or fulfill our proper part in continuing creation? We have no right to renounce God, even if recently discovered truth goes against strong and previously unexamined presuppositions. If God uses the slow evolutionary process to create things, even me, why should it bother me? If I am genetically related to monkeys and apes, it does not in any way deny God's action, change my skin color or my facial features. I am absolutely fascinated with the process, practicality, and ingenuity of God's creative action. If ontogeny recapitulates phylogeny (during its development, the human embryo retraces its entire evolutionary journey with tails, gill slits, etc.), my initial comment is "Wow! Look what God did! I am kin to all creation!" Furthermore, there is no reason to believe God is finished with creation or us.

Our nature, like God's, embodies the necessity to be creative. We have no choice. Our choice is to create what is good or its opposite. God offers us a partnership with him in maintaining and promoting that in which appropriate love and truth may be born and grow. We can function on the construction crew or refuse the offer and thereby automatically join the demolition crew. The nature of love and truth is creative, wherever and in whomever it is found. Any spirit other than appropriate love can only cause disruption, damage, and perhaps eventual destruction of that in which it dwells, along with others and the universe as we know it. God has decreed that humanity will largely determine the destiny of a portion of the universe, based on what and how we love. That does not indicate a weakness on God's part but indicates how important we are and the risk God willingly took with us. The admonition in Romans 12:21 may be far more significant than first thought: "Do not be overcome by evil, but overcome evil with good."

God is the primary creator of the universe. We are the secondary creators who, by nature, unavoidably create something. It is impossible for us to sit idle and let God do everything. We do have some choice of what to create. We can create not only something physical but also a spirit that promotes goodness or evil. Christians purposely participate with God in the creation of what is good, or else we deny the name.

## B. God Is Love

Christians inherited from the Hebrews the presupposition that God is love. He is revealed and demonstrated primarily through love for his entire creation. The Hebrews could affirm no other reason for God's expressed goodness or why he chose and cared for them. Likewise, because of God's nature, all humanity was chosen to receive that love, with a specific directive for all to imitate it. Since the directive to imitate God's love may boggle the mind, where and how do we begin? We begin where we are and with what truth we know. By nature, we must love something. If we love something, we value it. Love for something is a spirit within us that inevitably produces action. If we love God more than anything else, we will value him above all else, and we will seek to act like him where and when we can. That necessitates loving my neighbors as myself because God loves them just as he loves me. A possible definition of that kind of love states, "Love is wanting someone or something to have what they need for their health, happiness, and wholeness and wanting it to the extent I am willing to give up something I have in order for them to have what they need."

There is an interesting twist to this definition because it applies not only to us but also to God. It reflects the active process involved in loving by both God and us. Godlike love focuses not on getting all you can but on giving something you have to meet a need. To love is to give. "What is needed" may be debatable, but if in doubt, remember the rule that says we should treat others as we want them to treat us. (Love of self is also significant.)

The word *love* sometimes confuses us because it has two parts, both of which are encompassed in the above statement. Love is a noun that refers to a specific spirit residing in someone or something and usually directed toward or for something. Love is also a verb that requires action on behalf of someone or something. Action is the process by which the presence of a spirit is demonstrated. Action shows love of some kind. With little exception, we usually demonstrate the god we love by the spirit in us and by the action it produces. Love on behalf of another demands actions, whether from God or us!

The word "love" further confuses because for Jews and Christians, if not for everyone, it also refers to two opposite spirits, either appropriate love (Godlike) or inappropriate love (love of anything more than of God). Persons with appropriate love seek to value God above all else and then others as self. Those with inappropriate love have a different spirit, a different organizing element, and a different order for what is important. Inappropriate love is broadly defined as having primary allegiance to anything other than God (judged by Judeo-Christian principles). Love first affects *being* (what one is) and then *doing*. One must *be* before one can *do*. Our spirit, what and who we really are, is unavoidably followed by action. That is true whether we are speaking of God or us. Love on behalf of anyone demands actions, whether from God or us. That is a truth we did not make and cannot break.

In an effort to further describe God's love for us, I believe "God is love and acts only from love." This broad statement futilely attempts to encompasses the totality of God's being and behavior, but it is the best we can do. Any other truthful and appropriate statements about him must be commentary on and amplification of this one. That statement is the summation of all that is appropriate to believe, think, or say about God. It is the foundation upon which to base all other correct descriptive statements about him. It is the key by which we measure every action and word attributed to God. Even though we do not fully comprehend the parameters of the statement, it is the very best we can do with human words.

As professing Christians, the necessary and appropriate response to the above provocative presupposition is problematic. Given the encompassing nature of the statement, what more can we correctly say about God?

That provocative statement allows us to say much more but to say it with caution. With faith, reason, revelation, and experience, we can faithfully examine, ponder, and expand its relevance and meaning. There are three suggested guidelines to help us reasonably discern more about God. First, formulate no other presupposition outside the basic concept that God's nature is love and he always acts only from love when dealing with all humanity and all creation. In order to be correct, any explanation, belief, or expression pertaining to God's nature and action must agree with the basic affirmation that God is and acts only from love. It might help if we think of this guide as the template or the litmus test against which we measure every professed or proposed belief pertaining to God. This guideline emphasizes the specificity of the presupposition. It calls for meticulous evaluation of every proposed concept about God's being and behavior, and no concept will be acceptable if it does not coincide with the presupposition that God is love and acts only from love.

Second, all additions to the basic presupposition about God must be founded, formulated, guided, and concluded with deep dependence on faith, reason, factual data, revelation, research, and experience (with heavy emphasis on reasonable faith). This painstaking formulation process is not for the novice, highly emotional, or self-righteous. Cool heads, kind hearts, and keen minds are more likely to rely on and adhere to the basic guide for new insight. New presuppositions originate from individuals and may be absolutely correct, but given who we are, it is necessary to elicit further examination and affirmation from others who also seek to better understand God. An individual's shared insight or question may stimulate new and broader subjects for discussion and discovery. No person should widely publicize his or her individual belief about God until it is shared with and discussed among like-minded cohorts (the apostle Paul's problem). However, lack of support for an individual's presupposition does not necessarily mean it is erroneous; nor does community support guarantee its validity.

Third, formulate every presupposition with caution, clarity, and connectivity. Each new presupposition must clearly and logically comply with every other presupposition in the carefully selected belief system. No single idea or issue can stand alone, or disharmony will follow, because of lack of connectivity and uniformity. Logic and simplicity enable both connectivity and clarity. Each new addition and sub-presupposition must draw sustenance from the original, or it becomes invalid. The analogy of a vine and its branches is certainly applicable. Through this process of connecting one valid belief to another, we build beliefs with connecting steps that keep all secondary beliefs attached to the basic presupposition. In building our belief system and formulating our presuppositions, we must follow God's grand design, in which his nature and laws are interrelated, totally connected, and supportive of each other. Our accidental or deliberate disregard for disharmony, even when it sounds good or is called religious, will sooner or later disrupt, if not destroy, the belief assumed to be in harmony with the primary presupposition.

God is love and acts from love, and we are the recipients of it. That statement is the key by which we evaluate the truth of every attempt to speak about and for God with a presupposition, pronouncement, scripture passage, sermon, Sunday school lesson, or any expressed belief about God. From my perspective, any professing Christian who does not accept this one fundamental basis for proclaiming and evaluating all beliefs about God has misunderstood the ancient Hebrews' basic concept of him and disregarded the teachings of Jesus.

## C. God Is Spirit

To speak of God as "spirit" radically differs from what many of us were taught. We live in a world where physical things abound and spirit is seldom recognized. Therefore, if any thought is given to his nature, God is often thought to be physical rather than spirit. God is spirit, and there are other spirits that affect us daily. Spirits have no physical qualities and therefore cannot be weighed on a scale or measured with a ruler. A spirit is an invisible part of something in which it dwells and always affects the behavior of its host. An inner spirit is reflected by outside behavior.

*Spirit* is a human word. When used in reference to God, it firmly states he is not some physical being or person or object that occupies space. To say "God is spirit" removes all physical attributes from him. Therefore, it is essential that professing Christians learn he is not an extremely wise gray-haired and bearded old man on a golden throne who takes notes on our behavior both night and day while filling prayer requests and running the universe. (I am not sure exactly how a "she" would look or act, but she would probably be expected to spend her time in a similar way.) Even though this may radically differ from what we were taught, we must learn to think and speak of God as the spirit of positive, compassionate, self-giving, and active love.

Thinking of God as Spirit may be far less problematic than we first thought. Even if we have some difficulty associating the term *spirit* with God, we already use it in reference to other things. We actually know about certain types of spirits because we live among them. We already know how a prevailing spirit determines the attitude and actions of someone or something. We know that a dog or a donkey, a cat or a cow, a bull or a bee may have a docile or vicious spirit. Their behavior is always determined by an unseen but genuine inner spirit that dominates and dictates their behavior in a given situation. By their action, we know the spirit within. The same is true for God.

Speaking of spirit, here is the shocker: we are also spirit. The core of our being is spirit. The better we understand our spirit (who and what we are), the better we understand God's spirit. Our spirit makes us who we primarily are and determines how we act (and perhaps how we look). Our spirit is housed in physical flesh, but our spirit dominates. When we make reference to someone's behavior as good, bad, loving, caring, hateful, etc., we speak of their ruling spirit or its effect, not their physical body. We all have and are a spirit. When we recall someone no longer near us, either loved or disliked, we most often remember and speak about the spirit they possessed and shared. Their spirit touched our spirit. None of these spirits occupied space, but we knew they did and do exist. People are known and remembered primarily by the spirit that dominates them, not by their size, color of skin, hairstyle, or the house in which they lived.

We really do know something about spirits. We say someone possesses a dominant spirit, but the spirit basically possesses them and largely dictates their behavior. We are primarily possessed by a spirit. A person may become known by a secondary name (a nickname) that is synonymous with their particular behavior and prevailing spirit. We have heard stories about the town drunk, the wife beater, the helpful lady at the library, and the man you can always trust. In every case, each person was known by the indwelling, unseen, and definitely present spirit. Secondary names that correctly refer to the prominent spirit in us are very similar to the early Hebrew idea in which a name announced one's character. *Love* is God's second name, because it describes his nature, spirit, and action. He possesses, or is possessed by, the spirit of love and truth, which directs his actions toward us and the universe.

Wow! We really do know something about spirit. God is spirit, and so are we. Since we are basically spirit and God is spirit, how like God we are at the core of our being. At birth, we received a spirit that made us alive and, to some degree, like God. We were made in God's image, not only with and as a spirit but also a spirit that must love something in some way. That spirit given us at birth primarily develops according to the spirits that nurture it (very important point).

A statement reportedly made by Jesus becomes clearer: "But the hour is coming, and is now here, when the true worshipers will worship the Father in spirit and truth, for the Father seeks such as these to worship him. God is spirit and those who worship him must worship in spirit and truth" (John 4:23–24). When did you last hear a sermon on *that* text? In order to worship God, our spirit must be in tune with his spirit. The more closely our prevailing attitude and spirit imitate God's spirit, the more we participate in and help create his kingdom on earth by who we are and what we do. The apostle Paul correctly spoke of Godlike spirit and behavior when he wrote, "the fruit of the spirit is love, joy, peace, patience, kindness, generosity, faithfulness, gentleness and self-control" (Galatians 5:22–23a).

One further topic needs attention. Biblical writers refer to God, Jesus, and the Holy Spirit. At some point, the assumed significance of these three led to a presupposition for the Trinity. Father, Son, and Holy Spirit were identified as three different and separate entities or beings. Some believed the three eventually became one when Jesus and God merged and resulted in the formation of the Holy Spirit, said to have been birthed at Pentecost. I seriously differ with any who think this way, including the early church fathers and many modern believers.

Earlier we spoke of God as Spirit. God and Jesus were not and did not ever unite into one "being," because Jesus was and remained human (discussed later). He referred to God as "Father" in the same way we refer to God as "our Father." The human Jesus exemplified a Godlike spirit operating in a human life to the degree no one had ever seen or believed possible. Reference to Jesus as the "image of the invisible God" (Colossians 1:15) refers to the fact that the human Jesus was so saturated with a Godlike spirit that he enabled people to envision God, not that Jesus *was* God! Jesus was very much like God because he was saturated and motivated by love, which he demonstrated by behavior. That indwelling Godlike spirit in Jesus did not at any time make him God, just as that indwelling spirit in us does not make us God. In an effort to emphasize the abundance of Godlike spirit demonstrated by Jesus, he has been called "Son of God," "God among us," "the human image of God," etc. All of these refer to the likeness of Jesus's spirit to God's spirit and not to Jesus's physical lineage or transformation. Therefore, "Father" and "Son" do not refer to lineage and are not terms that unite them or make them equal. They emphasize the similarity of their spirit.

The Holy Spirit is not a third member of a unique group or a combination of the other two. It is not the spirit instituted by the human or resurrected Jesus. It is another name for the Godlike spirit, a name that distinguishes God's spirit from our human spirit and from unholy spirits that also exist. I prefer to call the Holy Spirit the spirit of holiness, because the term clarifies that it is Godlike spirit and guards against identifying it as another person or being. The spirit of holiness has been present throughout the ages because it is God's spirit. It was not a new addition from God or initiated by the death of Jesus. The spirit of holiness was not birthed at Pentecost (an already-established Jewish time of celebration and worship). The events that happened at Pentecost resulted in a conscious experience of some people becoming saturated with Godlike spirit, a recognition and reception of Godlike spirit that had always been available but basically unrecognized. Even though something dramatic occurred at Pentecost for some people, that event has been misunderstood or mislabeled, either by those who were there or those who reported it long after it happened, or perhaps purposely reshaped by writers.

There is a trinity of terms, each of which has an individual and specific meaning that must be maintained. They are closely connected by a similar spirit of love expressed by all three, but the three never became one. There is one God who is spirit and a human Jesus whose primary spirit was Godlike love, both of whom expressed and demonstrated the spirit of holiness, but the three never merged into one being. Emphasis on the doctrine of "the Trinity" can destroy the profound impact of each member within it.

## D. God Is Truth

Even though we refer to God as Spirit, we need other words to use in conjunction with it so that we may better comprehend and speak about his nature and action. *Spirit* acquires further meaning when attached to words like "the spirit of love, truth, forgiveness, and compassion." God is truth, and truth is an inseparable and indispensable part of God's being. Therefore, all truth is connected to God. "But the hour is coming, and is now here, when the true worship will worship the Father in spirit and truth" (John 4:24). (Here is another directive we did not make and cannot break.) Therefore, it appears that any worship not in keeping with truth is not worship of God. (That should alarm every professing Christian.) God's unending, unchanging, and self-giving spirit of love is always accompanied by truth that never wavers. He will always be true to his nature and spirit. He will always love. Truth encompasses and empowers each unchanging law that governs every action of God in the entire universe. Without God's adherence to truth, life would be unpredictable and meaningless, and the universe would probably cease. Love, spirit, and truth reflect the power of God. Love, spirit, and truth are the three primary supports under the table on which our understanding of God rests. There are other words used to speak about God, but these are basic, and if we disregard either of them, trouble ensues. Perhaps spirit, love, and truth are so connected that we cannot have one without the other. They are like identical triplets whose individual identity is often beyond our recognition.

Identifying truth is an imperfect process that stretches the mind. Even though we may not be able to fully discern it, its nature is continuity and connectivity. We may gain additional insight if, for clarity, we briefly distinguish between Truth (capital T) and truth (lowercase t). Let the first, Truth, refer to what we think of as the undeniable and unchangeable nature and laws of God that control and encompass the universe. Unbreakable and unchangeable laws in every form or place exemplify Truth in action. Let the second, truth, refer to the correctness of things that may or may not normally seem connected to God. This kind of truth is related to earthly things and activities associated with daily life. This truth deals primarily with the correctness of data or stated facts. Statements that are judged correct or accurate in reference to a person, place, or thing may on the surface seem to lack significant connection to the higher Truth.

However, truth cannot stand on its own and apart from the laws of God. It can survive only if it draws its validity and continuity from Truth that controls the universe. Therefore, Truth and truth are so interwoven they cannot be separated from each other. In the final analysis, there is only Truth expressed in many ways.

Perhaps an illustration will add clarity. I might say, "I see a white dog," and it would be correct, a fact or the truth. My announcement that I see a white dog seemingly has little connection to Truth. On further analysis, my ability to see and speak, or the dog's ability to move, etc. are interwoven with the unchanging laws of the universe and ultimate Truth. Under most circumstances, my statement would make little difference to anyone, but that did not disconnect it from Truth. I see a white dog. So what? However, under some circumstances, the importance of "so what" gets elevated. If all white dogs in the neighborhood are rabid and I truthfully say I see one, the "so what" becomes very significant and has wider implications. However, the larger the immediate significance of the "so what" for any true statement does not make it closer to Truth. Any correct expression of truth, even when it receives a casual "so what" or goes unnoticed, is ultimately connected to Truth, the ordered universe, and God. Meanwhile, any untrue statement, any denial of truth, even when connected to a casual "so what," can open a crack in the door to chaos and confusion. For instance, if people suspect all white dogs are dangerous and I forcefully but falsely say, "I see a white dog," chaos is likely to erupt. Likewise, any untrue declaration about God is also very dangerous and opens the door to chaos and confusion. (Professing Christians, beware.)

Perhaps another illustration will help us connect Truth and truth. The verbiage of a biblical passage will not be words written by God's hand, but if what it said is true (factual), then we may learn about Truth. God and Truth are one in nature, but everything we humans declare as truth, or true, may not be. Since truth, love, and spirit cannot be compartmentalized (except for emphasis), "truth" that includes earthly facts, honesty, and correctness is also a part of and accurately represents God's being and nature. Since God is love

41

and always loving, and since God is truth and always dependable, our participation in any truth in any manner is always connected to God's spirit.

The discovery of any new insight into truth is tantamount to receiving a communication from God (discussed elsewhere). We seldom, if ever, have recognized it as such, primarily because we were never informed. New insight into truth came to me when a farmer showed me his small turtle farm adjacent to his large field of cotton; when I discovered that, if possible, a cow will give birth to her next calf very near where she birthed the previous one; and that a disenfranchised piglet would run squealing to the back steps of our house to be bottle-fed while his siblings nursed their mother. God communicates truth in turtles, cows, cotton, piglets, and all manner of earthly things, but how often are we aware? Truth may also be discovered in a spoken word or a written text, from individual pursuit to group action, from scholars to uneducated peasants and all things great and small. Some nonfactual verbiage can also reflect truth (parables of Jesus). When we participate in revealing, proclaiming, and abiding by Truth and truth, we participate with God's spirit.

We should now understand the undeniable importance of knowing Truth and truth, in knowing true data and being totally truthful in every word we say or write. We need to know the truth in and about every personal presupposition believed and implanted, every doctrine believed and proclaimed, every biblical passage, every historical report in the Bible, every part of the universe, us, and others. Since truth is a part of God's being, any intended or accidental lie from us diminishes possibilities for greater love and truth in and among us. When we lie, purposefully or accidentally, we diminish the Godlike spirit in us and possibly others. Since God is truth, we can act like him only if we are truthful. We can correctly call ourselves Christian only when we deliberately and diligently seek and support truth in all we are, say, believe, and do.

## E.  God Is Unchangeable

God has been accused of changing his mind. Professing Christians sometimes stumble over this erroneous affirmation. The concept is invalid because it assumes God is physical and, like us, has a mind. It also disregards the fact that God can be only what he already is and has always been. If he did change, that would include changing his nature, which would also include his will and laws. Truth would vary and probably disappear. Some argue that God does change because the God portrayed in the Old Testament is far different from the one portrayed in the New Testament. Some say God acts differently under different situations and circumstances as well as during different times in history. If God rearranges his nature and rules to fit the occasion, devotees would never know his nature or requirements at any given time, would have to guess what he demands at the moment, and would likely live in fear instead of trust. It is absolutely impossible for God to change who he is, but people have obviously changed their understanding of him from the beginning of civilization to this day.

At different times in history, different people have perceived God differently, but that was because of them, not God. Some say Jesus radically changed humanity's understanding of God. If he did, it was not because God changed or because Jesus possessed a totally new insight about God. Jesus reiterated and explained in greater detail what should have been known for a long, long time. Jesus recognized the Judaism of his day had strayed from the core of ancient Hebrew religion, which was to love God above all else and your neighbor as yourself. He made an attempt to restore what had been overlooked, disregarded, and forgotten. People did not know, had forgotten, had been misled, or disregarded the truth proclaimed by Moses and the prophets. Jesus tried to restore proper spirit, beliefs, practices, and worship, but he did not proclaim anything new or start a new religion. He explained and exemplified the cornerstone of Hebrew religion. Any change promoted by him was because of his effort to correct the flaw in the current Judaism and not because of a new understanding of God.

Jesus never indicated or insinuated God had changed the requirement for salvation or that future salvation depended on what he was or did or what would be done to him. After Jesus's death, someone declared his death and resurrection became God's new source for salvation. However, that extended and convoluted presupposition was promoted by someone other than Jesus, and it is anchored in the Judaism Jesus denounced. Jesus's life and death did nothing to change God's mind, will, nature, or how people get right and stay right with God. Jesus's ancient Hebrew sources are closer to truth than some ideas proclaimed by present-day professing Christians who argue for a God who changed. Any biblical reports of God having changed his mind came from human misunderstanding, not from a divine decree.

The New Testament reports numerous suspensions, breaking, and outright defiance of natural laws, at least for a short period of time. That would mean God changed his nature. Many of those reports are associated with Jesus. If God adjusted his laws for a specific event, how do you explain a much larger problem of why the change did not adversely affect that same law elsewhere, as well as dependent, adjacent, and overlapping laws, plus adjacent people, places, and things? Additionally, the ever-widening and rippling effects of any change would be far-reaching, possibly encompassing those who were not knowingly involved but would be unexpectedly and adversely affected. At what point would it stop? For instance, how could you stop the water in a flowing stream without unavoidably changing its flow near and far, in both directions on the same stream and on other connected streams? If the water was firm enough for Jesus and Peter to walk on it, the fish could not swim in it, or was it firm only on the surface? Why would God change his rules and allow Jesus to change some water into wine for wealthy people but not allow him to do that for poor people with whom he regularly associated and who could not afford to buy it to supplement their meager food supply? Why allow Jesus to feed five thousand from someone's snack but not repeat the process in order to feed the hungry crowds he daily met and the poor with whom he closely associated? Proclamations of suspended laws are less than factual because a change in divine law, perhaps just one, would literally destroy the universe through a domino effect. The argument that "God can do anything," "It was only for Jesus," or "It was for that one special occasion" is totally illogical, insufficient, and dodges the basic issue.

God never suspended an old law or developed a new one in order to facilitate what he needed at any given moment. All universal and eternal laws with which we are familiar were always here, fixed, dependable, orderly, connected, and rational. It is both rational and religious to affirm that God never changes laws, but we may change our understanding of them and thereby change some beliefs and behavior. Under certain circumstances and conditions, situational ethics may be used by some of us as an excuse for bending or breaking laws, both divine and human, but situational ethics was not God's invention. There has been and will be no contradiction of himself or his laws, regardless of the situations, the people involved, how hard they pray to win the lottery, or how they may have interpreted his action. It is easier for some to argue God changed his mind than to change theirs.

However, we must admit we can never fully understand the total parameters of God's laws. Therefore, there may be dimensions and extensions beyond our present understanding of them. Someday, new discoveries of God's meticulous control over creation and creatures may far exceed what we presently know, but it will undoubtedly be in keeping with his demonstrated and unchangeable laws that we now know and on which we confidently rely. The ancient process to get right and stay right with God remains unchanged in our modern age. Space travels, deep probes among the planets, information on the life and death of stars and the discovery of mysteries never suspected have all resulted from using known, unchangeable, and eternal laws. Those laws are always operative out there, and they are certainly operative in and near us. Established laws undergirded recent discoveries about the origin of life, the nature of death, and everything between the two. My presupposition remains: God never changes his nature or laws. We did not make them, and we harm ourselves if we break them.

## F.   God Who Communicates

We have spoken extensively about God, but does he ever speak to us? Even though that phrase is frequently used, it is wiser to change the word to *communicate* instead of *speak*. The question sounds somewhat different when we ask, "Does God communicate with us?" *Speak* usually connotes talk and is more limited in scope than *communicate*. *Speak* normally indicates someone purposely uttered a verbal sound that was designed to convey recognizable information to another. A serious problem occurs when we misuse the two words by saying *talk* but really meaning *communicate*. The failure to recognize the difference between those two words has led to misunderstandings and arguments, even about God.

Some biblical stories indicate God spoke and certain people heard his voice. We must first ask were those reports examples of misusing the two words, either by the translator, author, or speaker? We must also ask if people thought they literally heard a voice attributed to God, or was that statement their way of affirming they believed God communicated to them a message of truth? Anyone who claims they actually heard audible words spoken by God causes serious question for those of us who have not experienced it. The fact that God is a spirit and therefore has no voice greatly reduces that probability. To assume he has a voice with which to speak reduces him to the human level and declares he has physical form (That's a big no-no.) Many who claimed they literally heard God speak were ecstatic, in an extremely stressful situation, had some emotional or mental problems, and often resided in an institution (or soon did). Even with these facts, many professing Christians believe God audibly communicated with certain people in the past and could now if he desired.

Biblical writers repeatedly record words like "God spoke" and "God said" or some variations of that verbiage. Precisely what they meant by those words is beyond our knowledge, but we have an idea. They did not hear the audible voice of God. It seems highly possible those are symbolic words used to convey their firm and honest conviction that God wanted them to communicate a message of truth to others. The manner and process through which the conviction came may have been usual, special, or spectacular, but their verbiage was designed to convey the importance of the message, not how they got it. "God said ... " may have reflected a speaker's new presupposition, as well as his attempt to get attention and to affirm the importance of the message. If that is how and why we have biblical statements of "God said ...," those passages tell us something about the speaker as well as something about their message. What they said may have contained unique elements of divine truth detected and reflected by them. On the other hand, just because they said their words were or contained a message directly from God does not make it true, even if they were sane and sincere. Believing someone received a communication from God or believing they received an audible message directly from him must never be confused. It seems safe to say God never offered audible comments to anyone but seeks to communicate with everyone.

There is a story about a man who could neither read nor write. He ran into a country store shouting, "The end of time has come! The end of time has come!" Someone quickly asked what made him think that. He answered, "God just wrote it in the sky!" A person who had entered the store just after him knew the truth and said, "No, no, no. That was just an airplane skywriting an advertisement for Pepsi-Cola." Discerning God's communication is not easy, instantaneous, or always correct. The biblical affirmations that "God said" must be carefully examined. It can be similar to the misunderstood writing in the sky because proper interpretation and explanation often came from those who are more enlightened.

God communicates in a particular way we seldom mention, at least by this name. Certain people communicate by using sign language, but only those with special training and awareness understand the message. The same is true for God, but only certain people seem able to understand the language. This does not insinuate only impaired or gifted people recognize God's sign language. The message is available to all who have proper training and awareness, but some may not recognize it or call it by that name. Psalms eight and nineteen are excellent examples of someone who recognized God's sign language is spoken by the stars, moon, etc. For some of us, the entire universe and all its parts tell of his greatness and reflect his dependable laws. God's "signing" is probably what first got the attention of the Hebrews and convinced them that he loved them. Many of us have seen signs because they are all around us, in the sky, on earth, in others, and in us. Few among us have seen anything that made us rush headlong into a crowd shouting a radically new and different message based solely on what God told us through a specific sign written in the sky. Specific signs from deep in space, from the action in a cancer cell or from the laughter of a child, may have caused us to identify truth not previously recognized and silently but surely, "Truth and God spoke."

God communicates by revelation of new truth through various ways. The term *revelation* has been used in ancient Judaism and modern Christianity. It does not necessarily mean God imposed something on us but usually refers to the sudden awareness of previously unknown truth (fact). It often implies the unexpected and unexplained arrival of any new insight, regardless of its source, when or how it came, or its subject. Sudden and new insights are more likely to be labeled revelation by those considered very religious, but others may use the term and connect it to some almost unbelievable learning experience. People with certain religious beliefs may attribute simpler occurrences to the same source.

All truth is from God and connected to God. Therefore, to speak of revelation is only a declaration of a new awareness, not the announcement of God's unusual act or ours. Since revelations also come to those who do not attribute their new awareness to God, one cannot correctly argue that it comes only to those with a special relationship with God or to the deeply religious, even though they are the ones who are more likely to use the word. Likewise, new insight often comes to those who have been seeking it but it may have been available long before it was discovered by those capable of discerning it. Human research and human effort enable revelation. Revelation is seldom used as a name for new truth communicated to us through common events and people, even though it is applicable. We must strongly emphasize that when a revelation of truth arrives, it is always aided by human perception, presupposition, and response. The word itself makes the very significant point that God uses fallible humanity to uncover new insight, which unlocks previously unknown dimensions of Truth and truth.

Even though God does not talk to us, he communicates with us through various ways. We sometimes recognize his communication through revelation, reason, meditation, scripture, conversation, experience, and love. Any process or place where truth is found reveals God's message, but he does not tap us on the shoulder, make a verbal announcement of its arrival, or write words in the sky.

## G. God Who Offers Only a Glimpse

Regardless of what some may proclaim, no one has ever seen God in his entirety or fully understood him. We have no monolith, no life-size statue that is an exact replica, no full description or definition chiseled in sacred stone tablets, nothing written in the cloudless sky or loudly announced from heaven. In spite of specific claims made by self-appointed preachers, pompous professors, prestigious pastors, or even those who speak in tongues, no professing Christian can speak with absolute authority about God (the indescribable something). However, we truly believe we know something about him (presuppositions). We feel sure we have had a glimpse of him, based on what we believe he has done. Since God is spirit and since every word we use to speak of God is symbolic, our words can provide only a glimpse of him. Given that fact, every attempt to make a true statement about God must be hesitantly made with reverence and reservation and only after serious thought and comparison with what we believe is truth. This statement applies to everyone who speaks about God, be they ancient or modern, biblical or secular, saint or sinner, prophet or preacher.

All we think we know about God originally began with someone's personal presupposition (ref. chapter 1). The original glimpse of God came to a person of faith and came primarily through revelation, reason, research, and experience. Some people presently believe they get a glimpse of God from scripture, prayer, dreams, and tradition. Others have suggested study, meditation, and conversation as sources for an additional glimpse.

Imagination has also been nominated as a valid process through which we glimpse God. Imagination is a wonderful human gift, but there are serious problems when depending on it for truth about anything, especially God. It has the strong potential for expressing what one wants and needs to be true instead of true discernment. Vivid imagination is most often unreasonable, illogical, and lacks connection to what we know as true or have experienced. It often arises from those who are either ecstatic or eccentric. It may come from those who are experiencing a miserable life and see little earthly hope but desperately want certain things to be true. It is often connected to something far beyond reality as we know it. Imagination coupled with debilitating pain and deep desire for change runs the risk of forsaking both human reason and divine rules that govern the universe.

Even though we do our best with what we have, we normally get a glimpse of God's nature and actions only from the back side. Biblical stories symbolically emphasize this point. Moses had to hide his face between the rocks when God "passes by" (Exodus 33:21–23), and Elijah waited inside a cave for God to act outside (1 Kings 19:11–13). They only saw the back side of God's actions. They did not witness it but affirmed he had acted in an unusual way, based on what they saw and believed. As it was with the Hebrews, it is with us. Using faith, revelation, reason, and experience, we surmise with some certainty that God was at work or he passed by, and we believe we got a glimpse of his action. These stories emphasize the fact that we do not fully understand God, but we often look back at some event and only then proclaim God was at work. We can also affirm we believe he is presently active everywhere and we can get a glimpse of his spirit acting among us. We are unable to boldly declare with similar certainty that God is going to act in an unusual way, at a designated place, or at a specific time. However, our insight into his nature and previous action enable us to affirm that wherever, however, and whenever he acts, he will continue to act in the same manner as he did in his previous passing, and a glimpse of his action is always available.

Some among us apparently believe they get a greater glimpse of God in miraculous, mysterious, magical, extraordinary, cataclysmic, and complex events. People of that persuasion have less emphasis and awareness of the little intricate and ordinary events in everyday life or the scripture. Spectacular action is proclaimed in selected scripture readings, proclamations, and conversations. Perhaps their purpose was or is to emphasize God's greatness and to elicit awe, wonder, and worship from some or to purposely engender deep fear in everyone. For certain individuals and denominations, that demonstrative verbiage reflects their present concept of God (more physical than spiritual). For others, that verbiage is less than helpful, even driving them away from organized worship. Those spectacular and mysterious actions of God may favorably or unfavorably affect some, but emphasis only on them seldom connects with our ordinary and daily lives. If God intervenes in our daily lives only through such extraordinary and spectacular events, we seldom hear from him, and he apparently has little time or concern for most of us. If God primarily acts only in distant places, for special people, and through supernatural ways, how concerned is he about average or disenfranchised people? If he reveals himself only in or by the spectacular and the extraordinary, does he know I exist, and does he have any serious concern for "little old me"? Is he ever active in my little world with only normal, everyday events? The use of magical, mysterious, and cataclysmic words in reference to God's nature and action inevitably add more confusion than clarity, more misinformation than truth, and disregard the presence of love and truth available to each of us right where we are.

In no way does this suggest God is not active in the cataclysmic occurrences, but is it a plea to recognize God's actions in all things great and small. Spectacular events lacking loud announcements are closer to us than we may realize. Ponder pregnancy and the birth of a baby, the blossom of a red rose on a green bush growing in black soil, a black cow who eats green grass and produces white milk with yellow butter, the intricate and diverse parts of our body that function simultaneously without our awareness or management and in so many other places. When God is understood as the spirit of love and truth that enfolds us, we also look at simple events where we are and marvel at such spectacular occurrences reflecting a glimpse of God. God's love and his concern always encompasses little old me and you right where we are. People who emphasize only the spectacular actions of God would do well to look for a glimpse of God in little things and quiet places, which also can be spectacular.

## H.  Conflicting Inheritance

Professing Christians have inherited radically different beliefs about God. It began for them with their first informers and continued thereafter, because of many existing things. It is important to recognize the different sources from which they drew their presuppositions and the sources from which they can presently draw them and affirmations about God. The present professing Christian community was affected by a major conflict that began long ago, because of a clear distinction between the beliefs of the original "Jesus movement" (Jesus and his followers) and later Christianity (the post-crucifixion movement) resulting primarily from the apostle Paul. These must be understood as basically two separate and extremely different movements or groups that are connected at far fewer places than we have been informed. It is significant to note that each group was formed by a different devout Jewish man. Each group was a "child of Judaism" but distinctively different from current Judaism and from each other. Each leader and group declared its own different beliefs about religious matters related to God, Jesus, and us. Each group seriously affected future beliefs within Christendom from its beginning to today.

The Jesus movement (sometimes called "the Way") was founded and led by a previously unknown Jewish man whose name was Jesus and about whom little other factual data is available. We do not know where or when he was born, his level of education, social status, occupation, and more. He may have once been a member of the peasant class, a temple child, a rabbi, or something in between. He inherited and fully accepted some original and basic Hebrew presuppositions, but disavowed certain parts of current Jewish beliefs, which thereby separated him from the Judaism of his day. His directives for life and salvation (for getting right and remaining right with God) were drawn (inherited) exclusively from early Hebrew beliefs and not current Judaism. His followers believed what he taught and joined with him in acting out of love for God, neighbor, and self. They seemingly renounced the necessity for blood sacrifices, ritualism, and legalism in worship.

The Jesus movement drew heavily from core Hebrew beliefs proclaimed in certain Old Testament passages. Jesus was not a Christian. He was born a Jew, loved, believed, and taught basic Hebrew concepts, and eventually died a Jew. Jesus purposely sought to restore the Judaism of his day to its original core of Hebrew worship as proclaimed by Moses and the great prophets, summarized as "Love God above all else and love our neighbor as yourself." Since God's nature is love, these requirements are the basis of all Jesus believed, taught, and did. Those were his directives on how to get right and stay right with God. That was the inheritance announced and offered by the Jesus movement.

The post-crucifixion group had little similarity to the Jesus movement. It was led by a dedicated Jew who was well educated, deeply committed to current Judaism, probably rich, held some authority within the Jewish community and possibly within the government. That leader, Paul, ignored the teachings from the human Jesus and radically changed the prescribed process by which a person could get right and remain right with God. Paul's dislike for the human Jesus and disapproval of Jesus's ministry were demonstrated by persecuting Jesus's followers prior to his vision and after it by renouncing and refusing to associate with Jesus's disciples.

Paul dearly loved the Judaism he inherited, but Jesus rejected much of it. Worship in Paul's original Judaism called for obedience to the law, specific sacrifices of shed blood, a high priest, a coming Messiah, etc. He originally accepted the Jewish doctrines pertaining to salvation and basically kept them after his vision, with some revisions. Following his vision, Paul said Jesus's sacrificial death and resurrection fulfilled those Jewish requirements for salvation because Jesus was the required ransom and a perfect sacrifice that negated any need for another. Paul affirmed Jesus was God's physical instrument for our salvation, which now comes not by keeping the Jewish laws but by faith in the crucified and resurrected Jesus, who fulfilled the law because he was God's anointed. Paul's prescribed process is convoluted, confusing, and questionable. The ramifications of his beliefs portray a much different God and a different requirement for salvation than proclaimed by the Hebrews, Moses, and Jesus.

The early Christian movement inherited very different beliefs about God from two different sources. It was, and remains, impossible for those two groups to purposely and peacefully merge. Throughout Christendom, a person's beliefs about God and the salvation process depended primarily on whether it was from Jesus and the Jesus movement or from Pauline influence. Even though the reference point for each group was and is Jesus, each began with a different Jesus, and therefore each had a different concept of God and a different salvation process. We cannot overemphasize the longstanding and different presuppositions held by and inherited from these two specific groups.

All of us inherited many beliefs about God. Most of them have existed for a long time. Most of us were never informed that our presuppositions about God are very important. Therefore, if we have not previously examined our beliefs about God, it is wise to closely examine what we inherited and consciously decide what we believe, because that basically determines how we live.

# CHAPTER 6

# BOTHERSOME BELIEFS

Given the two very different and significant sources from which professing Christians inherited and manufacture their presuppositions, different conclusions are unavoidable. Many professing Christians firmly believe they inherited all they need to know about God, what he expects of them, and how to get right with him. They want nothing else. If you seriously challenge their beliefs, some of them will do all manner of harm against you (in the name of Jesus, of course). When measured by the two commandments of Jesus and the affirmation "God is what he does and does what he is," some beliefs seriously bother me. It is impossible to name or offer alternatives to all proclaimed and bothersome beliefs about God's nature, action, and requirements, but I will select a few. I believe the Judeo-Christian God is first in all things, or he is not our God! (That's a rule we did not make and cannot break.)

The following comments on major beliefs may help those who have concerns and questions, those with disgust and distrust for some modern worship, those who are uninformed and misinformed, those who misbelieve and disbelieve, and those with little or great hope.

## A. Omnipotence

Some professing Christians believe God's primary nature is omnipotence, meaning he has unlimited physical power. The idea may have originated to properly emphasize the distinctive difference between God's power and ours. I affirm God cannot be destroyed. Any who attempt a hostile takeover will not succeed. If omnipotent means basically that God rules the universe, then fine. In no way is our power equal to the power of God. In that sense, God is omnipotent, but for some people, there is more to the belief than that.

God has always been in complete control. Therefore, the ancient story about "the fall of man" has no validity. There is only one God. There is no one, and never has been anyone, to whom a ransom had to be paid for humanity's release from evil deeds. Even though the idea of the fall is totally false, perhaps it can remind us of our imperfections and a future possibility where we could fail miserably and destroy ourselves. If humanity refuses to imitate God's nature and seriously disrupts love and God's laws, humanity as we know it will fall, not because God predetermined it, not because God ceased to love us, but only because we ceased to appropriately love him, each other, and his creation! That would not rob God of his control but rather confirm it. Perhaps it is safe to say love is God's first priority and omnipotence is his last resort, but even then, he will be guided by love.

Some argue that God is totally omnipotent and can do whatever he pleases whenever he chooses and without adherence to his established laws. In this belief, God's actions are not dictated by love but by what he needs or wants, according to the circumstances. If evil displeases him or persists among people, he can obliterate any or all without mercy. If people please him, he can reward them. In particular situations, he can make good things happen, regardless of what or who he has to harm or destroy on another's behalf. If that is true, there is no ordered universe upon which humanity can depend because God changes his mind and the rules, either as he pleases or as he thinks necessary. Under those conditions, humanity would live in danger of unexpected events, possible punishment for another's misdeeds, and in fear that they would unexpectedly displease God. Who can love a God like that?

The belief in omnipotence is problematic primarily because it misunderstands God's nature, which is limited by love. It erroneously assumes he is like us in behavior, shows partiality, can be swayed by people's behavior, or is directed by concern for himself instead of love for his creation. If this belief is taken at face value, people have once again created a super-powerful God who acts like them and of whom they are more likely afraid, because of his absolute power over them. This idea gets too close to anthropomorphizing God. There is no provable evidence where God interrupted and suspended any rule or acted against people to prove his power.

Emphasis on omnipotence is problematic because of what it may insinuate but does not actually say. It insinuates God controls everything and humanity controls nothing. Granted, we lack power to destroy God, but omnipotence neglects the fact that God has given us some freedom to choose, so that we may be cocreators and caretakers. Omnipotence overlooks the fact that God is limited by his own nature (acts only from love) and will even allow us to destroy certain parts of his creation, and eventually ourselves, if we insist. Any assumption that God absolutely controls humanity must be adjusted by the free will God purposely grants to us. Love never forces its will on another but always grants freedom to choose, within certain limits. We have limited freedom to briefly override and play loosely with some of God's rules, but we can never change, disregard, or entangle them to the degree they become inoperative and God loses control of the universe. God assumed the risk of allowing us the choice of participating with him in extending creation. He loves us and created us to be partners, not puppets.

One big problem with omnipotence is it usually emphasizes the physical power of God, but it neglects the power of his love. God has power to do whatever he chooses but he chooses to operate only from love. That statement may need some explanation. Since God's nature (spirit) is love, all God can do is love (action) and nothing else. God is what he does and does what he is. God has no further choice to make. He is not judge and jury, either now or later. We do not know exactly what he will do, but we know love will reign. That does not rob God of power but indicates how powerful God's love is. Sadly, few of us ever emphasize the tremendous power of God's love, which can change people and situations. It was an awareness of God's love, not judgment, that captured the attention of the Hebrews. Numerous conversions to Christianity have occurred when someone became convinced "God loves me, even me." I recall an elderly navy veteran in our recovery program for alcoholics who, with a tearstained face said, "It all changed when I realized God and the people at that little church really loved me." An awareness that God loves me, even me, in spite of who I am or what I have been, is powerful enough to change our lives and our world.

The belief in God's omnipotence may have developed to counteract experiences of humanity's ruthless power. In certain circles and circumstances, people have demonstrated almost unlimited power. Kings, warlords, religious authorities, landlords, merchants, and parents have severely dominated those who had few choices in life. Those who experienced ruthless power lorded over them may have promoted the idea of God's omnipotence because they believed God would eventually set right all the wrongs in the universe. They had no reasonable expectation for any change in their earthly lives. They longed for the day they and all their kind would be free from misery and would receive their rightful reward. That hope may be as old as humanity itself. It is the hope harbored in the marginalized, those under domination of mind and body, all under religious persecution and others. They are the multitudes who had or have nothing but hope, if even that. It is easy for those with religious beliefs to express their last hope in the mighty power of God. Biblical writers echo their point. Several New Testament writers obviously believed deliverance from domination was on its way and foretold a new beginning orchestrated by the mighty power of God. They expected God to eventually demonstrate his mighty power through a cataclysmic event and end this world as we know it and initiate something radically different for those entitled to it. People with no other hope may be driven to unusual conclusions and unhealthy presuppositions that satisfy them for the moment, but misery and misunderstanding do not guarantee correct conclusions, even about God.

Emphasis on God's power affirms he will orchestrate the closing of the curtain on the last act of human history, but that presupposes that there will be a last act. Appropriate love on our part could perhaps prevent a last act. If there is eventually a last act, it will be far different from that stipulated by the Bible and evangelical preachers. If there is a cataclysmic end, we will have triggered it, not God! If humanity chooses an overabundance of destructive behavior and inappropriate love, we will close the curtain on ourselves. The curtain may close on us but not on God and not necessarily on the entire universe.

My primary presupposition about God does not deny or doubt his power. It affirms God is and always will be in control by the power of laws and love. God's love for us means he gives of himself for our benefit, and he does not look for an opportunity to show us who is boss. Religious proclamations that focus on God's might, demands, and wrath may actually drive others away from him. If we affirm power is God's primary attribute, love becomes at least secondary. We are admonished to love God and act accordingly, not to fear his power.

## B. Omniscience

Some professing Christians affirm that God is omniscient or all-knowing. That is intended to emphasize the greatness of God but inadvertently does the opposite. Different explanations and meanings have been offered for this word, but they basically say God not only knows everything that has happened but also knows everything that is going to happen. The argument is sometimes tempered by saying we still have freedom to choose, but God knows in advance what our choices will be! That is a verbal dance that attempts to simultaneously protect both our free will and God's foreknowledge. That only compounds the problem and appears to be devoid of logic and love.

Omniscience emphasizes God's need for advance knowledge to protect his sovereignty, if not his dignity. It disregards the ultimate power of love. It presupposes God is weak and must have advance information or he could lose absolute control (again) or suddenly find himself confronting an unexpected and embarrassing emergency. The driving force behind this theory may be the erroneous belief in "the fall of man" during which God reportedly lost control of humanity. Does it say if God had known in advance, he would not have lost control? Does this indicate a change in God's nature after the fall, so that he is now equipped and determined to never again lose control? Even though designed to emphasize God's greatness, omniscience depicts God in an unfavorable manner, as if he is weak, does not trust us, is afraid of our free will, does not love us, etc. Furthermore, it seems illogical, impossible, and ridiculous to believe God has a corrected and complete report on everyone in the world at any given moment and is his own "advance scout" who sees the future for everyone.

If one accepts this belief, one must eventually raise ridiculous questions like, "How far in advance does God know?" "How much time do I have left to really change my mind?" "Do I really have a choice?" If God knows what I am going to do, that seems to be a form of predestination, because when he knows, I cannot change. The belief in omniscience is groundless because it goes against the major presuppositions about God's nature and ours. It indicates God needs protection from us, and that would mean he is less than God. It illustrates once again the strong tendency to liken God's nature and action to ours, by supersizing his abilities in comparison to our own.

## C. Predestination

Predestination is another belief somewhat similar to the beliefs that God is omnipotent and omniscient. Predestination actually encompasses portions of those two. It says God ordained everything in advance of its occurrence and there is no possibility for alteration, apparently even for God. For some people, this belief refers primarily to who will be "saved," but it encompasses far more. If predestination is applicable, there is no need for any of us to worry about anything, plan anything, or get disturbed about anything, because we cannot alter it or the outcome, and we are not really responsible for it. Therefore, there would be no sin for which we are responsible. Worry and anxiety about these matters were also predestined! Prayer would be a sham. Planning would be useless. Wars would be foreordained. Judas Iscariot did only what he had to do when he betrayed Jesus. Those who crucified Jesus did only what they had to do. Why blame them? We need not take safety precautions or be concerned about a proper diet. We could drink, drive, and text without fear because precautions change nothing. There would be no necessity for birth control, regardless of human knowledge, desire, or passion. There would be no rape or incest. Regardless of the circumstance under which a pregnancy occurred, it would be divinely planned. Why worry about our health and complain about or attempt to cure a disease if our time and exact method of death are predetermined? Concern for entering the kingdom of God or avoiding sin would be useless because the persons who will be saved are already decided, so eat, drink, and do whatever you please.

Predestination makes God a ruthless tyrant and humanity his helpless puppets. Not so. Not so. A thousand times, not so! That presupposition is repulsive! Where is God's love in it? Where are human choice, freedom, and responsibility? Where is there room for us to be helpers and cocreators with God, as indicated in the creation myth? Predestination denies and destroys personal choices at every level of our activities. It also provides any excuse we would ever need for disruptive and abusive behavior.

Predestination has a valid point if it is intended to affirm God's unchangeable nature and laws that operate in a precise manner. The rule, "God is love and acts only from love," is forever fixed. His nature and laws are predestined to remain as they are, set in stone forever. They establish the boundaries in which we and he operate. You can always count on them, even though scientists have learned to momentarily manipulate some of them. Laws may be purposely manipulated to some degree, but they can never be safely disregarded. The manipulation of one law depends on the absolute certainty of it and other laws.

Predestination must be carefully defined, or it is unbelievable, ridiculous, and definitely erroneous. It must never say or even insinuate God totally or partially preplanned everything and that we are only his puppets. Perhaps predestination can be likened to an enclosed pasture in which we find ourselves and from which we cannot escape. Between the distant boundaries is extensive space in which we have some freedom to decide where to settle or if and how far to roam. We have been advised how to make the most of our enclosure and have been told that some sections have more freedom to choose and move. Some sections are far more conducive to health and happiness than others. We must decide if we wish to abide by the rules or disregard them as long as possible. Our chosen behavior, while we roam and after we settle, is motivated either by appropriate or inappropriate love, and we are held accountable for our choices, wherever we are. Living by appropriate love increases the quality of life in the pasture and may extend the life of a person, other people, and the pasture. Inappropriate love diminishes, if not destroys, the person, other people, and the pasture. If we choose to disregard the rules and repeatedly run into the fence, it does no harm to the fence, but it can be very painful and possibly detrimental to ourselves and others. Regardless of our choices, we will always remain inside the fence. Both pasture and fence were created and are maintained by God's love.

God's laws are always operative, but he allows us some choice in response to them. Otherwise, predestination raises far more questions than can be rationally resolved.

## D.  Origin of Scripture

Particular presuppositions about the origin of scripture have inspired many, but erroneous presuppositions about the Bible have misled multitudes. Some believe the Bible is the absolute Word of God, while others say it is only the words of people. Opinions about the Bible's origin and content range from "God did it" to "The Bible is a unique, manmade selection and collection of diverse expressions of humanity's faith." The belief that "God did it" attributes its content primarily to God's dictation and effect. The other belief affirms humanity's extensive contributions to its content but does not deny God's help. Beliefs about its origin will inevitably affect its interpretation and application. A person's initial beliefs about the origin and interpretation of scripture are among those "first fruits gathered from the family tree." Professing Christians normally declare a deep love for scripture, but perhaps it is just awe and fear because they were told they must love it and are afraid to do otherwise. Some mistakenly worship it, not the God it proclaims, and thereby participate in idol worship.

The belief that "God did it" assumes all biblical statements are correct, regardless of the processes or person through which they came. This belief is known as "inerrancy of scripture." It believes there are no possible errors in it because God made no mistakes. Furthermore, since "God did it," it must be interpreted exactly as written. This belief is known as "literal interpretation" because the words mean exactly what they say, with no need to question them and no need for outside interpretation. Therefore, all prophecies and promises made or assumed in it must be fulfilled exactly as written. Inerrancy disregards the problem when direct contradictions occur, when impossibilities are reported, or when the same words are given different meanings in different places and by different people.

Through reason, research, and common sense, scholars have unquestionably concluded the belief in inerrancy and literal interpretation are erroneous. Extensive evidence and simple logic affirm humanity's contributions to the origin of scripture. Also, because of the obvious mistakes we know the Bible contains, we cannot claim inerrancy, that God wrote it; nor can we accept a literal interpretation. A multitude of scholars have validated these facts, and their findings are readily available. If presuppositions on inerrancy and literal interpretation intend to affirm the greatness of God, they only affirm the religious ignorance of some people.

If God did not control the writing of scripture, by what criteria do we properly measure the truth of its content, especially its comments about God? All statements about God's nature and actions in the Old and New Testament, along with any interpretation of them, must be measured by criteria beyond the words themselves. Words cannot be used to properly evaluate themselves. (For that reason alone, "inerrancy" is invalid.) For Jews and Christians, the basic criteria by which we evaluate any biblical statement about God's nature and actions is our primary affirmation about God. We affirmed "God is love and acts only from love." Therefore, every proclamation about God in the Bible must be measured by this criterion. Anything outside the boundaries of this statement about God's nature and action must be seriously questioned, whether in the Bible, doctrinal statements, sermons, or anywhere within Christendom. We must ask, "Does the particular scripture, comment, or belief under consideration support that affirmation?" If it does, wonderful, but if not, we must pause and ponder what was the purpose and presupposition from which the author(s) wrote or spoke. It is not a sin to be truthful about the origin and meaning of scripture, but to believe a lie is very dangerous, if not sinful.

Statements in the Bible considered historical must be examined by different standards, such as other indisputable truth and known facts, reason, logic, tradition, etc. Some stories were never intended as factual but as parables, allegories, metaphors, myths, etc., each designed to convey a broader truth and personal faith. Recognition and truthful interpretation of those stories are not always easy.

There are reasons for extensive, engrained, and erroneous presuppositions about the origin and interpretation of the Bible. For too many years and in too many places, local religious leaders lacked formal education but were considered the authorities on scripture. All statements, presuppositions about God, his requirements, and the words of Jesus (red letters, of course) were most often considered historical, factual, and beyond question (inerrancy). However, things are slowly changing. Some among us presently believe the primary purpose of biblical authors was to tell a story of faith, to proclaim truth, and to make and illustrate specific points that reflected their beliefs about God, Jesus, and humanity. We have learned to be less critical of why and how they wrote, but we also have no need to accept as true their stated beliefs and verbiage that do not meet the standard. It is not sinful to question biblical statements, but it may be sinful to proclaim those that are incorrect.

The Bible is a unique collection of human words that reflect humanity's presuppositions about the indescribable something. Many who wrote, originally read, or heard its words were smarter than we at a certain point because they could recognize facts, expressions of faith, symbolic words and expressions, metaphors, hyperboles, secondary messages, folk tales, etc. It is replete with irreplaceable data, firm expressions of faith, insights into God, statements of truth, and interpretative history. It offers keys for entering "the kingdom" and for living by appropriate love. Its major divisions provide important history, penetrating prophetic proclamations, unquestionable words of wisdom and worship, plus intriguing, strange, and questionable stories about a man named Jesus who changed the world. Expressions of faith reverberate through its pages, a faith that sometimes disregards facts. Discovering truth within its diverse pages demands rational research, and even then it may elude us. We must not judge the truth of something solely by what the Bible said about it, but we must determine if what the Bible said is true by using other dependable criteria. Even though the Bible contains great truths, if it is used to determine absolute truth in all matters, it becomes equal to God, the object of worship and an idol!

The words contained in the Bible are extremely important, but they were not dictated or written by God. Those words came to us over many years and from many different people. Even though a statement is in the Bible, that does not guarantee it is true. It is not sin to critically examine and correct scripture. However, it may be sinful if we refuse to apply research, reason, and known truth when identifying its origin and meaning. We must remember that every word in the Bible was written by someone very similar to you or me and most often written long after it reportedly happened.

## E.  Inerrancy of Scripture

"Inerrancy of scripture" is absolutely essential to some professing Christians, but it is extremely problematic for others. Even though that subject was mentioned above, further discussion seems wise, given the extent of its present emphasis. Let it be clearly understood that inerrancy of scripture is not the same as inspired scripture. *Inerrancy* means there is absolutely no error at any point in the scripture, even when direct opposites are stated. *Inspired* means the author had an inspiration, a sudden insight, or a life-changing concept. Even if it came through normal channels, the event inspired, enlightened, energized, and excited the receiver and was an expression of his or her faith at that time. An author may have felt inspired without having been absolutely or historically correct with his spoken or recorded words.

The belief in inerrancy of scripture must be denied. It will not stand under scholarly research and common sense. We can no longer defend it, because of the plethora of information discovered about the origin, formation, and duplication of biblical documents. Scholars have discovered and discussed the convoluted process through which many documents were composed and the circuitous journey through which they traveled to reach us in their present and sometimes various forms. Any who doubt the validity of this statement can find extensive support in readily available sources. In whatever form or by whatever route the biblical stories and records came to us, they all came through the assistance of those who were definitely human, often inspired, and sometimes inaccurate.

Scholars have found older and different translations for manuscripts plus purposeful alterations. Without question, biblical writers formulated their stories and documents from their own bias, presuppositions, faith, insights, oral tradition, and written records. Communal concerns and point of origin may have also governed certain portions or points from which they wrote. The authors believed their approach was necessary to proclaim their story of faith and history as they understood it or wanted it told. These facts are surely shocking, if not unbelievable, to any who believe God wrote scripture himself or personally dictated it in some mysterious way.

Some material in the Bible was deliberately designed by one author, later edited and altered by others in order to support a particular purpose or point. A scholarly study on the purpose of the four Gospels in the New Testament will fully authenticate the point. Matthew primarily sought to persuade the Jews that Jesus was the Messiah by quoting and misquoting the Old Testament as proof. By dividing his work into five distinct parts, it is as if he offered "five new books of the new Moses." From the first chapter, Mark portrays Jesus as a unique person, an active teacher, frequent healer, and in the opening line called him "the Son of God" (Mark 1:1). Mark apparently knew nothing about the Virgin Birth of Jesus. Luke's primary concern was to convince others that Jesus was the divine Savior who cared especially for the Gentiles. Luke apparently disliked the Jews and accused them of mistreating Jesus. He uses easily understood stories and parables to illustrate divine truth that Jesus offered. John's presupposition makes Jesus and God almost, if not completely, identical and seldom gets far from the implications of that belief. Obviously, each Gospel writer tells a rather different story about Jesus, all of which can hardly be true. Inerrancy denied.

Evidence also indicates biblical writers were not beyond manufacturing material when helpful for their purpose. Divergent records about Israel's history, selection, actions, specific leaders, and intended message illustrate how national pride, inadequate information, and personal desire probably shaped some stories. The political climate may have hampered honest or desirable verbiage in certain times. There were also writers whose imagination, perhaps hallucination, ran wild, and most of us have difficulty detecting God's message therein or believing God is the author.

Another powerful illustration against inerrancy is what we know about the formation of the Gospels of Matthew and Luke. Their authors were first-class plagiarists who borrowed without credit large amounts of material by basically following Mark's outline and copying verbatim large portions of Mark's material. They followed his format and made changes when desired, by deleting, correcting, or adding new material, pulling Mark's manuscript apart and inserting selected verbiage. They sometimes corrected Mark or added something of their own, even if it disagreed with Mark or each other. Matthew and Luke also had another unidentified source from which they both copied material into their own Gospel. Certain portions of their added material have almost exact verbiage, format, and ideas, which indicates it was undoubtedly copied from another source, known as "Q."

Most intelligent people find the foregoing evidence contradicts inerrancy of scripture and divine dictation. Any who continue to believe in inerrancy of scripture disregard extensive factual material, reason, and common sense. They may hold on to it because material in their "box" will allow for no other belief. The evidence against inerrancy does not argue against inspired scripture and leaves that subject open for further discussion.

In keeping with the above comments about the origin of our Bible and inerrancy of scripture, there is one small piece of information that may either shock or encourage further study, if not both. After years of extended debate by individuals, churches, and religious authorities, the first official listing of the twenty-seven New Testament books that was exactly as we now have them occurred in AD 367, in the thirty-ninth Festal Letter of Athanasius. After extensive debate over numerous possible choices, a list was eventually ratified as the official New Testament by both the Greek and Roman wings of Christendom. Some of the rejected books were later officially accepted as scripture by Catholics and others. The added books are individually named but are collectively called the Apocrypha and are included in some modern bibles.

## F.   Speaking "for" or "about" God

Did biblical writers assume they were speaking exact words from God, speaking specifically for God, or speaking about God as they understood him? There are no correct answers for these questions because we lack the ability to arbitrarily discern their thoughts and intended purpose. However, our belief in or rejection of inerrancy will help determine our answer. Given the information we have about the early Hebrew concept of God, it seems no one among them was bold enough to proclaim they were equal with God or could speak absolutely for God. Given the nature of God, they were correct. There may have been later presumptions that someone had that ability, but not originally. Even though someone affirmed "God said—" they had not heard the actual voice of God but sought to indicate the firmness of their conviction and their role as his special messengers. I suspect most of the "God said" reports were designed by people of faith to emphasize information and insight. However, since all were human, I also suspect there were some who erroneously spoke, even though they said, and perhaps thought, their message was from God.

The major designated divisions within the Bible (history, psalms, prophets, writings, and New Testament) may provide recognizable clues to the authors' opinions of what they were doing, but we must be careful when stating our assumption for any who spoke or wrote. In general, it seems Moses, many of the prophets, and Jesus thought of themselves as spokespersons on behalf of God. Several writers were concerned with divine action in history as they understood it or wanted it remembered. The Old and New Testament contain a mixture of possible assumptions by writers. In every case, it seems safe to say that biblical authors' primary purpose was to convey a message of faith as they understood it and in whatever way seemed appropriate. We must remain skeptical about the reports of God's verbal communication.

Some people may be very upset by the above statements pertaining to the Bible's source, verbal accuracy, overall content, and importance. Those comments are not meant to destroy or deny the Bible's importance for any Jew or Christian. Truthful insight into the Bible is liberating and leads us closer to God (who is truth). Since no other single collection of material has provided more guidance for so many Jews and Christians than this unique book, these statements are intended to enhance and facilitate understanding the Bible, God, and us. Sad as it may be, no other book has been more misinterpreted by so many people. Since all falsehood eventually diminishes or destroys, we need to know the truth. We need professionally trained teachers, truthful literature, honest discussions, and serious individual study if we are to better understand the truth in and about the Bible. However, let us remember every word in it, every revelation it reports, every admonition it offers, every profession of faith it makes, and every interpretation provided has the undeniable imprint of humanity stamped on each from start to finish. Therefore, it is essential to formulate all conclusions, especially about God and truth, with caution and wisdom.

## G. Let God or Jesus Do It

I am deeply disturbed by professing Christians who are apparently unaware of their responsibility and opportunity to join with God in creation, restoration, and preservation. It seems they expect God to do everything for them, and they have no responsibility to care for themselves other than "believe in Jesus" and ask Jesus (seldom God) to do whatever they want. They call that *prayer,* but it often reflects erroneous beliefs about God, Jesus, and us. Most prayers are expressions of wants. Having called Jesus's (seldom God's) attention to what they want, they wait expectantly for it to drop into their laps. Too many request and expect Jesus or God to get them out of the trouble they carelessly and foolishly created or failed to avoid, rearrange the laws of the universe for their selfish purposes, make sure they are comfy and cozy (even at the expense of others), and prepare them a cozy place in heaven, without expressing any willingness to do everything within their power to facilitate fulfillment of their request. They say, "The Bible says 'Ask for it and you will get it,' so let God or Jesus do it." Too many prayer requests say "give me, give me, give me" and never "help me, guide me, strengthen me, use me, thank you." The requests are usually selfish and indicate no awareness of our responsibility to ask "what can we do?" in order to participate with God and get what we and others need or want. Prayers that only make selfish requests from Jesus or God are neither prayers nor worship of God above all else, regardless of their sincerity and verbiage.

Belief in "let God or Jesus do it" leads to vociferous complaints that prayers are never answered. How would those who only ask know? They seldom offer a real one! God or Jesus is not the primary problem with unanswered prayers. We are! Many of us do not know what prayer really is. The difference between answered and unanswered prayer may depend on whether we do anything other than ask and wait for it to be provided. Prayers that only ask are similar to sending an order to a mail order firm. with specific direction to send what we designate but if not available, send the next-best thing and send it by overnight delivery. We may think all of our wishes and request are doable by "the divine," but that does not mean God will grant any request just because he loves us and we say we love him. God does not answer to us. If we put as much energy and thought into seeking guidance on how to prevent or solve our problems as we put into begging and waiting for Jesus or God to take care of it (and it is usually a problem that drives many to pray), we would have less need to beg Jesus or God for anything. Likewise, we would have far more time to praise God for what he has already done and is doing, and purposely give thanks for the opportunity to participate in his creation. That approach would result in a different kind of prayer and a different kind of person. God is able to do some things without us, but some things will get done only if we assist.

A refusal to do what we are equipped and expected to do turns our backs on the divine order of the universe and may illustrate worship of something other than God.

There is a story about a bashful country boy courting a lovely young lady. On a pleasant spring evening, they again sat in the front porch swing, he at one end and she at the other. He decided he really liked her and that it was time to demonstrate his interest. He turned his head toward her and said, "I wish I had a hundred eyes just to look at you." For a shy and inexperienced country boy, he thought that was a good move in the right direction. She simply sat there and said and did nothing. After a short delay, he decided to try again. He looked down the swing at her and said with great gusto, "I wish I had a hundred mouths just to tell you what I think of you." He knew that ought to impress her. She never moved a muscle or said a word. By this time, he knew something more was demanded. He slowly moved his hand toward her and was surprised to find her hand already resting halfway between them on the swing's seat. He softly held her hand in his. After a moment, he looked toward her and lovingly said, "I wish I had a hundred arms just to hold you close to me." That did It! She jumped up from the swing, slammed his hand down on the wooden seat, turned toward him, and with hands on her hips said, "Why don't you just shut your mouth if you are not going to use the two arms you have!"

That young lady's response is a packaged parable that contains far more truth than humor. It has a lesson for us, especially in reference to asking Jesus and God to do something. It tells us we must first be thankful for and then properly use what we have before we ask for more. It also tells us some extremely desirable things get done only if we get busy and participate. What was true for the boy in the swing is also true for us, because if certain things need to be done, God will participate, but he is not going to do it for us. The parable indicates that even though we may desperately desire something and even pray hard for it, when the time is right and the opportunity is available, we must either act or suffer the consequences. God loves us, but we are his helpers, not helpless.

## H.  Mr. Fix-It

Thinking of Jesus or God as "Mr. Fix-It" is only a slight variation on "let God or Jesus do it." The latter is more about personal needs or wants expressed in prayer, while "Mr. Fix-It" is expected to repair our personal frailties and the ills of our world. Too many of us expect God to be the magical Mr. Fix-It who always immediately comes to our rescue when called. Regardless of the unpleasant or threatening situation in which we find ourselves, many of us assume Jesus or God can and will fix it, most often with little or no cooperation from us. As proof of that point, pay attention to the prayers you hear, the ones you read in a devotional booklet or personally offer. If God were to do what some ask, it would be catastrophic, because they often ask God to fix something or someone that would renounce his rules.

There is a story told about a couple in desperate financial straits, primarily because of gross mismanagement and obvious waste. Calling themselves religious, they decided to pray for financial relief. Since the available lottery winnings would far exceed their need, they decided to pray to win the lottery. After several days and prayers, they did not win. They fervently begged, but still no win. One night, while on their knees beside their bed, loudly pleading with God to let them win, a booming voice from heaven declared, "For goodness sake, at least one of you go buy a ticket." Of course, the story is fictitious, but it has an inescapable meaning. The couple, like many others, saw God as Mr. Fix-It. However, his repair shop is not always open for service on our terms.

Make no mistake—God does fix things, with or without our awareness and with or without our help, or none of us would be here. That is the story of Judeo-Christian history. More than once, human survival was in serious jeopardy, and God is credited with saving the day. In most of those biblical events where God came to the rescue, he first intervened by way of a person who did what he or she could. God did not resort to some miraculous or cataclysmic repair job. Upon close examination, it appears biblical writers repeatedly reported how ordinary people, events, and things produced spectacular results. Some biblical writers were aware that God first needed a "fixed person" so that person could assist God in fixing other people and situations.

Perhaps God gets very tired of us asking him to fix what humanity willfully and continually disrupts and destroys. (What does that say about us?) Several biblical passages indicate God will eventually fix the entire universe through some cataclysmic intervention that will end time as we know it. That does not sound like a fix to me. That would cause a radical change but not a fix. That has not happened, even though some people presently think it is long overdue and near. God is not likely to fix today's evils through some catastrophic event, regardless of what some late-night television or radio evangelist tells us. Between you and me, I doubt that kind of fix will ever happen! God is not like that. Why would God decide to do more than he has already done and is presently doing? Why should he? Given his nature, he can do no more! He provided us with the ability and directions to fix (correct) the primary ills of humanity with appropriate love. He graciously gave us specific instructions on how to get right with him, especially through Moses, the great prophets, and Jesus. They all gave us directions for living by love and truth, the only fix for humanity there is! They all affirmed appropriate love equips us for proper living, but inappropriate love destroys us and the universe. Given his nature and ours, what more can God rightfully do without destroying his creation, himself, and us? The fixing of our destructive behavior is now up to us. We can only imagine how much fixing could be done if everyone in the world faithfully followed God's directives proclaimed by Moses and Jesus.

Jesus identified the key by which we can fix our relationship with God, our neighbor, and ourselves, but he did not, cannot, and will not fix it for us. Contrary to some proclamations by professing Christians, Jesus was not sent by God to fix humanity or the salvation process. There was no need to fix anything. God did his part long ago. By his grace and design, the final step is ours. Jesus told, showed, and reminded us what to do and be. We will always have our share of problems, but unless we do our best to love appropriately in what we are and do, many of our solvable problems will remain unfixed. Until we exhaust the available cure and corrective, it is rather ridiculous for us to depend on a Mr. Fix-It to lessen our responsibility. We must use the two arms we have. The good news is we already have a ticket to enter the arena of appropriate love.

There are more erroneous presuppositions about God than these identified few. All are, or border on, lies that unknowingly disrupt and destroy one's ability to love appropriately. Lies are the enemy of truth and God. That is why erroneous beliefs are so detrimental. I am concerned over the ease by which erroneous beliefs are acquired and the vehemence with which they are defended. Since our understanding of God determines what we are and what we do, we either get that right or nothing else can be. Truth sets us free.

# PART TWO

---

# JESUS

# CHAPTER 7

# SEARCHING FOR THE
# HISTORICAL JESUS

Professing Christians have an insatiable interest in Jesus, perhaps even more than in God. Jesus was and is the subject of countless pages of literature and unimaginable hours of verbal comments. There are probably more diverse beliefs held and more words written about him than any other person in human history. Presuppositions about him are possibly more prevalent and diverse than those about the Jews' and Christians' God. Words and beliefs about him range from the affirmation that he was only a unique man to the belief he was fully God. Our personal presuppositions about him place us somewhere on this continuum. Too frequently, professing Christians have no idea where they are on that continuum and do not know who Jesus really was. Many thoughtlessly accept their authorities' presuppositions and mimic the standard verbiage. That is the easy way out but dangerous!

Jesus was a Jew. His concepts about God's nature and requirements were primarily drawn from ancient Hebrews, not the Judaism of his time, a very important point. His lifestyle and teachings may have been new to his peers, but his message and ministry demonstrated the core belief of ancient Hebrews, which was basically disregarded in the Judaism of Jesus's day. In order to understand Jesus, we must understand the basic beliefs that directed his life and ministry. His presuppositions about God were his primary guide. Those of us who believe Jesus will agree with Jesus's basic beliefs about God. Likewise, our beliefs about Jesus must be based on and in agreement with what we first believe about God. This is an extremely crucial point about which there are major differences that seriously affect numerous beliefs across Christendom. Many begin with Jesus.

The majority of professing Christians express far more interest in Jesus than in God, if they know the difference. That point is easily confirmed by participating in a mainline or evangelical worship service, reading and listening to prayers, or engaging someone in a serious religious conversation. Jesus will be mentioned far more frequently than God, if God is mentioned. Beliefs that Jesus was more than human can easily make him the primary concern, and God becomes secondary. That can easily lead to no real distinction between Jesus and God, with erroneous beliefs about both. Those who make Jesus primary seriously misunderstand the nature of God and also the person and ministry of Jesus. They also disregard the teachings of Jesus and make him into something he never claimed for himself.

Our search for the human Jesus is thwarted by lack of valid information. The few source documents about him are convoluted collections of oral and written materials, much, if not all, of which defies validation, identity of authors, dates, and places of origin. The Gospel authors were primarily concerned with Jesus the Messiah and had almost no concern for Jesus the man. Therefore, most of the human elements and events in the life of Jesus were not particularly important to writers of the Gospels, except when they needed the events for other purposes. The majority of our written material about him was recorded long after the events to which they refer (forty to ninety years), by authors who were certainly not eyewitnesses and most likely did not even know any disciples or peers of Jesus. If Paul had firsthand information about the human Jesus, he refused to share it.

The Gospel writers did not personally know Jesus. (It is conceivable but highly doubtful that Mark did.) They depended on word of mouth, tradition, and written material that they adjusted according to their own faith, bias, and intent, with disregard for facts. Later translators and interpreters made their own adjustments. It seems safe to say we have no genuine original copy of any Gospel, if there was ever only one original copy. Scholars believe the oldest dated copy of a New Testament Gospel in existence, that is very similar to other copies we have of it, is from the late second or early third century. If our oldest copy of material surfaced about two hundred years after Jesus, some of us seriously question its accuracy when it speaks of Jesus. When was it actually written, composed, and edited, and by whom? What was changed from the original stories and events? How truthful can it be, given its basic presuppositions? Is it safe to base our interpretation of Jesus exclusively on convoluted documents that seemingly reached their revised form approximately two hundred years after his life? We continue to ask, "Who was Jesus?"

The existing Gospels often disagree with each other in reference to Jesus, sometimes at crucial points. Biblical scholars agree that authors wrote about Jesus for their particular purpose, shaped available sources to their point of view, expressed ideas beyond our belief and rationality, but they undoubtedly had some purpose for writing. Given this confusion and uncertainty about the Gospels, we tend to make up our own particulars about Jesus's birth and death, plus the significance of both and much that transpired between them. We who create our own God also create our own Jesus. If you doubt that, observe the next Christmas program or Good Friday service you attend. Visit different evangelical churches and pay close attention to the exuberant ministers who offer "the plan of salvation." Listen to sermons from different pastors on a similar subject, etc. Discuss the required method for baptism, its meaning, and necessity. At the conclusion of each, compare them with other comments. Check your own beliefs. Check the written record. Unless we are extremely cautious, we also tend to make up our stories.

As shocking as it may be, many Gospel writers and their sources may have done just what we often do. It appears they sometimes made up their stories about Jesus! Just like us, they had incomplete and conflicting materials. Just like us, they were somewhat unsure of all the details. Just like us, they had a hidden agenda. Long after Jesus's life, writers carefully cobbled together tidbits of information, oral reports, facts, historical data, traditions, customs, their personal religious beliefs, and personal biases, all of which they carefully selected and shaped by their overall theme and predetermined purpose for writing. Since the "Christ of faith" was the most important thing for Gospel writers, basic facts about the historical Jesus were not very important. Therefore, for that specific reason, their information about the historical Jesus likely had a secondary purpose and requires careful examination by us.

According to the canonical Gospels, Jesus's physical existence had a distinct, predefined, and predetermined end purpose, which he fulfilled. Their individual pronouncements about Jesus radically differ with what is probably true about him because they did not personally know him or know the truth about him. We have little information on the activities and messages of the Jesus Movement during Jesus's life. Much of the information we have is not about the historical Jesus but about a radically different movement, man, and message. The new man, the apostle Paul, proclaimed a new presupposition about Jesus and God, which focused primarily on the death and proclaimed resurrection of Jesus. Furthermore, he disregarded Jesus's earthly life, denied his original teachings, and developed a new basic presupposition regarding salvation. Paul's new presupposition was the prevailing presupposition proclaimed by the Gospels. It does nothing to help us discover the historical Jesus and may even prevent it.

The writers of the Gospels did not ask, "Who was Jesus?" They already knew—or assumed they did! From their beginning, each purposely set about to prove Jesus was the Messiah. The opening verse of Mark illustrates the point, saying, "The good news of Jesus Christ, the Son of God" (Mark 1:1). Gospel writers began with the conclusion and worked backward to prove their presupposition. In the midst of the religious chaos and confusion contained in the Gospels, there is no simple conclusion about the human Jesus. Most believable insights come through brief facts provided by statements reportedly made by Jesus, from snippets of information in the Gospels (sometimes unintentionally made), from noncanonical Gospels, from knowledge of human nature, from logic, and from common sense and reasonable conjecture. The search for the historical Jesus is indeed a search.

Our first necessary task is to identify the particular Jesus about whom we are speaking, because there were many. Do we mean the human Jesus or the post-crucifixion Jesus? Is it the Jesus of history or the Christ of faith? Are we primarily interested in the man or the proclaimed Messiah? Are we primarily interested in who Jesus was during his earthly ministry or in what some said he later became? The particular discussions for any one of these questions do not necessarily apply to the others. One person's response to any one of these question (and there are more questions) may be so radically different from another person's that an outsider would have difficulty believing both people are talking about the same Jesus. Who was Jesus?

Our uncertainty about Jesus is increased because the name "Jesus" and variations of it appear to have been common in the early first century. If Jesus had a last name, we do not know it, and that makes identity more difficult. Men were known and identified as the son of a specific man (Jesus, the son of Joseph the carpenter, not Joseph the butcher). If there were several men in the immediate community named Joseph, specific identity became problematic, and additional identifiers were necessary. They identified Jesus by his father's occupation and his brothers and sisters (Mark 6:3). There appears to have been other wandering preachers and miracle workers at or near the time of Jesus, some of whom may have been also called Jesus or a variation of the name. If one Jesus or more lived in or wandered into a location where another was or had been, that could easily confuse those who later attempted to tell the story of any one or all of them.

(Can you and a sibling agree on who said or did what, when and where last Thanksgiving?) We can only wonder what the specifics were for the wandering New Testament Jesus, the son of Joseph the carpenter, who may have crossed the paths of others with a similar name and behavior. Confusion created by various peasant preachers may or may not have had some influence on the information, or lack thereof, about the New Testament Jesus. We cannot be sure, but we must remain aware of that very real possibility.

Regardless of how desperately we long for facts about Jesus, we know few, if any, absolute certainties about him, other than he lived and was crucified. The more we learn about the compilation of the New Testament, the less we really know about the historical Jesus. Since we have conflicting personal beliefs, confusing biblical stories, and few solid sources, where does truth reside, and how do we answer "Who was Jesus?" In our everyday lives, we inadvertently and repeatedly bump into each other's beliefs. It is as if we unavoidably live in a bubbling pot of stew where different ingredients (ideas and issues) are often exposed by rolling to the surface, frequently determined by the heat under the pot. That stew of mixed beliefs is often flavored with identified and unidentified content, intellect, ignorance, and raw emotions. We each must contribute our own concoction to the big pot, some of which we may be unaware of its particular content and flavor. We tend to think, *my stew is better than your stew, and I will tell you why if I get a chance.* Anyone who vigorously stirs in another's stew or recommends something be added to or subtracted from their recipe is likely to get burned! We still ask, "Who was Jesus?"

It is impossible to find the historical Jesus. We cannot successfully separate and identify every ingredient in the stew. Therefore, we must be cautious in proclaiming what we believe to be true for Jesus. Bits of data, common sense, and reasonable conjecture suggest Jesus's parents birthed him in the normal way and with no abnormal pregnancy or publicity at his conception or birth. The social class of the family is unknown, but they were likely among the average poor, which means Jesus probably began life little different from many other ordinary and impoverished people around him. The emperor's humongous building project in the nearby city of Sepphoris may have provided his family an easy opportunity to earn a living wage and possibly an opportunity to improve their social and financial status. Based on reported behavior, Jesus appears to have been a very intelligent, uncompromising, eccentric religious revolutionary intent on reforming and restoring his beloved Judaism. None of this proves he was or was not poor, was always among the working class or from any specific class. His recognition of the need for and his effort to reform Judaism indicates above-average intelligence, especially for an ordinary layman or an uneducated peasant. His insistence that our salvation depends on love of God above all else and love of neighbor as ourselves was radically different from current Judaism. His religious knowledge and ability to minister to others may indicate special effort, interest, exceptional abilities, and unusual concern, if not more.

The Gospels of Mark, Matthew, Luke, and John, along with apostle Paul, largely disregard the physical life of Jesus. Either they simply did not know about the humanity of Jesus or they were afraid to reveal it because that might detract from their intended emphasis on his divinity. However, a careful study of their material tells very important things about the human Jesus.

Any search for Jesus begins with certain presuppositions that will determine where and how we look, as well as what we see. After many years of extensive research and reasoning, my basic presuppositions about Jesus are that he was and always remained human, never divine. There are numerous reasons for my conclusion. Furthermore, the declaration that he was or became divine, and the abundance of baggage that goes with that belief, has resulted in many questionable beliefs and behaviors that we now call *Christian*. I believe Jesus was a most unusual man in human history who purposely reiterated and demonstrated how to get right and stay right with God through appropriate love. He clearly stated that requirement when he said we must love God with all we have and are and we must also love our neighbor as ourselves. Jesus told and showed us how to do that by what he taught and how he lived. His teachings and lifestyle were so unique and meaningful that his hearers called him *Messiah,* meaning "one sent from God," and "Savior," meaning "one who saves us from Judaism's useless requirements and gives us hope," but all descriptive terms of that nature had no divine connotations. The argument, primarily from Paul, for a required and predetermined crucifixion, shed blood, a perfect sacrifice, a ransom, and a resurrection are unnecessary additions taken from Jewish influence that detract us from fulfilling Jesus's directives. Therefore, it is urgent for us to seek a fuller understand of the human Jesus so that we may be more like him in our God-given humanness.

# CHAPTER 8

# BIRTH STORIES

The story about Jesus's birth, or its absence, may help us discover more about him, the Gospels' authors, and Paul. The serious differences in the two birth stories we have and the absence of his birth story in the other two Gospels and Paul should sound an alarm. Their presence or absence are far more revealing than we first realized and have more significant ramifications than many will admit. Because of our present understanding of the birth process, we know more correct specifics about Jesus's birth than reported in the Gospels. His birth was likely more ordinary than many assume. In fact, it was probably very, very similar to our own.

From the beginning of human history, there has been an orderly birth process for everyone, because of God's fixed rules and predictability (no changing the rules). Personal experience, intelligent observations, and scientific research have uncovered the basic process of birth, life, and death. We are now able to verify and understand many precise rules and conditions related to each. If anyone declares the natural process has been altered for the birth of Jesus, questions quickly arise from many serious-minded people. Based on all we know about the fascinating but natural process of human conception and birth, why should God need to change the rules for the birth of Jesus? Every birth is close to a miracle, and if not a real miracle, then miraculous! Even then, it is governed by specific laws, and those same laws led to the birth of Jesus.

## A. No Birth Story from Paul

Paul, the earliest New Testament author, does not mention the birth of Jesus or awareness of an unusual conception. In Romans 1:3, Paul speaks of Jesus, "who was descended from David, according to the flesh." Likewise, in 9:5, he expresses the same idea by saying, "from them, according to the flesh, comes the Messiah." In 2 Corinthians 5:16, he states, "Even though we once knew Christ from a human point of view." In Galatians 4:4, he states, "God sent his son, born of a woman." From those statements, we surmise Paul apparently assumed Jesus's birth was by the natural process and his body was that of a normal human. Therefore, Paul's beliefs following his vision are far more extraordinary and revolutionary. Since he did not address a special birth process, it seems he recognized Jesus was human at some point and possibly his entire earthly life. However, he confuses us when, in Philippians 2:6, he states, "though he was in the form of God." Given Paul's pedigree and prominence, it is strange he indicated no knowledge of or interest in an unusual birth, if there was one. Given who Paul was, the time he lived, and the reported magnitude of events related to the birth of Jesus, how could Paul not hear about it and respond, if true? During his ardent persecutions of Christians, how did he not hear about it from them? It was probably because they had not heard the idea. Surely the disciples would have discussed it during Paul's brief association with them, immediately after his vision. Had he heard and believed the story, it would undoubtedly have been incorporated into his complex theology and extensive writings as proof of divinity. It seems logical to assume Paul did not know about a miraculous birth for Jesus because the story did not exist. I am convinced Paul considered Jesus totally human, at least until Paul had his vision.

## B. No Birth Story from Mark

Mark was the first of the four New Testament Gospels to be written. It contains no story about Jesus's birth, even though Mark calls him "the Son of God," which does not necessarily denote divinity. Jesus entered Mark's story as a grown man with no unusual qualifications or events prior to his baptism. Mark wrote near 70 CE, about forty years after the death of Jesus. Some scholars believe Mark was closely associated with the Jerusalem Christians and had extensive firsthand knowledge about Jesus, even if he came to Jerusalem long after Jesus's birth. If that is true, Mark would have heard all the stories about Jesus and, without doubt, the one about a special birth would have been foremost. Furthermore, if Mark was from Jerusalem, a story of this magnitude would have been repeatedly discussed, and Mark would have included it in what he wrote. If the early Christians knew an unusual birth story for Jesus, it is very strange that Mark did not hear it and tell it. Most likely, it did not exist.

## C. Matthew's Birth Story

Matthew's Gospel is dated approximately 80–85 CE, which was fifty or more years after Jesus's death. He is the first synoptic Gospel writer to tell about Jesus's mysterious and miraculous conception, followed by unusual events at and immediately after his birth. Since Matthew copied the majority of Mark's Gospel, did Matthew have sources Mark lacked, or did Matthew make up the birth story? Matthew and Luke also copied from the "Q" document that apparently had no birth story. If Matthew "made it up," what were his reasons? Matthew's Gospel provides strong hints that he created it and why.

Some people assume Matthew was a devout Jew. There is no doubt he was deeply concerned for them. Jesus's unique teachings and actions caused some observant people to ask (before and after his death) if this unusually compassionate person was the promised Messiah about whom the Old Testament spoke and for whom many

Jews waited. When Matthew began to write, there was no doubt in his mind that Jesus was the promised Messiah. That was his primary presupposition. We have no indication when or through what process Matthew reached that conclusion, but it was perhaps fifty years after the death of Jesus. Based on content and format of the Gospel, Matthew's intended audience was the Jews. Most Jews were very knowledgeable about the Old Testament and held a special fondness for it. If they were going to accept the premise that Jesus was the long-awaited and promised Messiah, Matthew's one hope was to firmly base his argument and evidence on and from the Old Testament.

Matthew's forceful attempts to prove his point with various biblical references and the format of his material may indicate the general lack of interest among the Jews. His problems with selected but incorrect proof may indicate he was not a Jew, possibly an uninformed Jew or desperate. Jewish authorities did not accept Jesus as the Messiah while Jesus lived, and they definitely had not accepted him as the Messiah by the time Matthew wrote. Matthew did not give up. Perhaps he was not a devout Jew but rather a very committed evangelist, with more desire than knowledge, who wanted to convert the Jews. Whatever he was, he knew just how to approach them. His one chance was to liken Jesus to Moses. Jesus was for Matthew the new Moses. Since Jesus was the new Moses, he must have more than an ordinary birth, just like the original Moses.

Dr. Dominic Crossan, a renowned Jesus Seminar scholar, believes Matthew patterned the birth stories of Jesus after the birth story of Moses (the most prominent man in Judaism and the Old Testament). Dr. Crossan believes both stories move in parallel scenes, steps, and stages in such a way that Matthew's story of Jesus's birth and early life are almost exact replicas of Moses. For Matthew, Jesus was the new Moses, who must also save God's people from bondage and lead them into the new "promised land" of correct beliefs. Matthew's insistence that Jesus was the new Moses is further emphasized when he divided his Gospel into five parts or books. His books are the five new books of the new Moses, which are like the five books of Moses in the Torah.

In an attempt to convince the Jews that Jesus was the Messiah, Matthew either purposely misquoted or seriously misunderstood the prominent prophet, Isaiah, who predicted the birth of a special baby (Isaiah 7:14–16). However, the baby's conception was not what made Isaiah's prediction special. That birth was to happen in Isaiah's lifetime, as a sign for the living king, to a woman of marriageable age, already old enough to have a baby, already married, and perhaps already pregnant. Her pregnancy would be, or had already occurred, by the natural process. Her sexual experience at the time of Isaiah's promise had nothing to do with her or the baby or the prediction of the Messiah. Isaiah's prediction had absolutely nothing to do with Jesus, but Matthew accidentally or purposefully assumed it did and misused it as leverage to prove his presupposition (a literal interpretation and its results.) We do not know if any members of the Jewish community accepted Matthew's serious misinterpretation of sacred scripture or if they laughed at him. We do know the Jewish authorities never believed Jesus was the Messiah for whom they waited. That should tell us something about Matthew. Many of us are seriously bothered by anyone who purposely misrepresents or seriously misunderstands scripture and who plagiarizes the major part of his material. Knowing someone did that, we question almost everything they said.

Matthew's grandiose story may have been influenced by readily available secular tales. Well-known secular stories of gods and great kings contained reports of unusual parentage, conceptions, births, and special abilities. People reportedly born under extraordinary conditions were automatically destined for great and unusual accomplishments. Conversely, people who had already accomplished unusual and great things were believed to have necessarily had special births, even if it was not recognized at their birth, until late in their life or if someone had to make it up after they died. Matthew's awareness of these beliefs may explain the reason he wrote as he did about Jesus. If Jesus was as important as Matthew believed, he had to have an unusual birth, actual or concocted. Matthew's Messiah must not only fulfill Old Testament prophecy (literal interpretation) but must also surpass all known messianic candidates, present or past, as well as all known earthly kings. It is as if Matthew said, figuratively or literally, "My Messiah is a bigger and better savior than all others, living or dead, real or imagined, and it all began with his birth." Using father Moses, sacred scripture, secular models of pagan rulers, wise men, kings, and gifts, Matthew composed a compelling story about the unsurpassable "New King" for a new age, for whom there was no equal in birth, life, or death.

## D. Luke's Birth Story

The second story of Jesus's uncommon birth is in Luke's Gospel, written about 90 CE. All who personally knew Jesus had surely passed from the scene after about sixty years, especially since life expectancy in those days was less than forty. Did Luke have another source for a totally different birth story, or did he compose it (which sounds better than "make it up") for his own purpose? He also wrote much later than Mark and also plagiarized the majority of Mark's Gospel and, like Matthew, made changes as he saw fit. Both Matthew and Luke add other very similar material, apparently copied from the "Q" source, but if that source contained a birth story, both of them either ignored it or one or both radically changed it. If there is a specific reason for Luke's birth story, it remains unknown. However, there are several possibilities.

As far as we know, Luke's birth story belongs totally to him. Scholars have not found anything that references a similar birth story in any other material. We do not know if Luke knew Matthew's birth story. Luke's long birth narrative connected numerous other people who became principal subjects in their own story. Perhaps Luke's unique birth story intended to purposely declare Jesus was more important than John the Baptist, an issue that seems to have been debated within the early Christian community and many years beyond. Otherwise, why did Luke go to great length to affirm Jesus's superiority over John?

For unknown reasons, Luke connects the birth story with unique, improbable, and impossible things, including unimaginable pregnancies, action by the Holy Spirit, angels singing to shepherds, a stationary star, and an absolutely dangerous (if not impossible) trip for a very pregnant woman. Among other things, it is significant that each of these items and events specifically emphasizes God's power. One very young female, a "virgin," was promised a special child at an unspecified future date. Her youth, possibly prior to puberty, and her virginity were emphasized in contrast with two much older married but once-barren women. Hanna (from the Old Testament) and Elizabeth (in the birth story) were both well beyond childbearing age but got pregnant anyway. For Luke, God's power can cause females to get pregnant before they are physically capable of having a child or long after their reproductive organs no longer function. The very young or the very old can get pregnant if God chooses. Luke's primary emphasis was divine power, and he used unimaginable pregnancies and heavenly events as proof of what God could do. However, we must ask just how different were all three pregnancies? The two older women got pregnant only through divine intervention, just like young Mary (if prior to puberty), but there were no miraculous birth stories connected to the older women. (We are not supposed to notice that!) For Luke, God can do whatever God chooses to do. Luke's birth story could be only a parable.

Even though Luke specified the young lady was a virgin at the time of the announcement to her, he does not state the age she will get pregnant or whether pregnancy will occur before or after the consummation of her marriage. Every promise or prediction made to or about her will be in the unspecified future. The common assumption has been that Mary's pregnancy came before puberty and definitely before her marriage. At no place is that affirmed in Luke's story. The argument that Jesus was a unique child from a unique conception has no factual basis if one reads Luke's story without preconceived notions or prior presuppositions. Was the announcement to her Luke's polite way of saying that was the time she learned of her betrothal and the time she first heard how women get pregnant? For a young, uninformed, and innocent girl, the startling news of a designated husband, a coming marriage, and possibility for an immediate pregnancy may have caused her to "see stars and hear voices." She surely pondered it in her heart, regardless if the news came from Mama, a playmate, or God. Social customs of that time decreed young girls were betrothed while very young but not necessarily immediately married, even though some were. Her betrothal, like all young girls, was made while she was young and well in advance of marriage in order to protect her social standing and from sexual abuse. Everyone knew she would probably get pregnant shortly after marriage, since there was little or no birth control. There is no evidence in this story, stated or implied, suggesting God changed the normal process for conception (Luke 1:26–38). Luke does nothing to refute the fact that God gives human life only through the normal process of human participation. (God does not change his rules.)

Luke's birth story may have been designed to give further credence to his later story about the astute twelve-year-old Jesus who slipped away from his parents and spent time in the temple conversing with learned men who were amazed with what he knew. When his parents finally found him and inquired why he was there, he answered, "Why were you searching for me? Did you not know I must be in my Father's house?" (Luke 2:49). This story agrees with the theory that people who have unusual abilities and events must have had a special birth. Jesus proved he was already special at age twelve. However, if there were a special birth, why were his parents surprised when they found him in the temple? It is important to remember that Jesus (in the temple) and Mary (at Jesus's birth) were not as young and immature as we often think, since for the Jews, a male was considered an adult at thirteen years of age and a female at twelve.

If Luke connected his birth story to the temple story about the twelve-year-old Jesus, it may have also been connection to or in support of another special story. Luke 4:18–19 has Jesus (no age given) in the synagogue reading from Isaiah. We do not know if Jesus actually read the passages in a regular synagogue gathering, if at some other point Jesus deliberately chose this passage as his road map for ministry or if Luke chose it for him. We are sure this passage basically describes what Luke believed Jesus actually did during his life and ministry. As Luke interpreted the life and ministry of Jesus, the Spirit of the Lord had to be upon Jesus in an unusual way in order for him to minister to the poor, blind, oppressed, etc., and to deal with the adverse conditions that confronted him during his ministry. It remains unclear if the temple and synagogue experiences were intended as proof of a special birth or were only indications of the uniqueness of Jesus. A special birth, a special twelve-year-old lad conversing with scholars in the temple, and a prophetic reading by him in the synagogue at an unknown age that foretold a special purpose for his ministry all agree.

There may be an additional issue related to Luke's birth story. During his writing, there seems to have been an argument over who was greater, Jesus or John. The question was possibly created because, following Jesus's baptism, he apparently was a follower of John. Scholars believe for some unknown reason they later went separate ways and simultaneously traveled, preached, and baptized. An argument later arose among their followers over who was greater and, most likely, which was the Messiah (or perhaps just *a* messiah). Writing long after the event, Luke sought to resolve the argument at the beginning of his Gospel by ascribing to Jesus an unusual birth, but not for John, which automatically made Jesus greater than John the Baptist. Luke has John admit the superiority of Jesus. Hidden in the shadows of this argument is the firm indication the expected Messiah was to be only human (a very significant point).

There is a haunting question that hangs over the birth story in Luke. If the birth was as spectacular as proclaimed, if it was far beyond the ordinary process of conception and birth, if heaven and earth proclaimed it, then why do we have no specific secular verification or date for the events? Such events would have disrupted surrounding society, if not a large portion of the world. Surely, no spectacular event with such magnitude could have actually happened without public recognition and records. Apparently, Luke composed the story for his purposes.

## E. No Birth Story from John

The Gospel of John has no birth story for Jesus. The Gospel was probably written after AD 100. The date is questioned by some scholars, but the distance in time between Jesus's life and the writing of this Gospel demands careful attention. John remained absolutely silent about Jesus's physical birth, as if he were never born. John had no need for a birth story because he said Jesus existed before the foundations of the world. John does not tell us how Jesus came to live among us in human form. Since John wrote long after the other Gospel writers and may have known their birth stories, perhaps this is John's way of saying, "Ha! I can top your Virgin Birth story. He always existed!" With this proclamation, how could Jesus be born in human form? Even though John indicates Jesus had a physical existence, Jesus's unique nature was very different from ours. Given John's claims for Jesus, no ordinary birth would suffice for his predetermined mission. John may have also assumed, perhaps like Matthew and Luke, that a special beginning (actual or imagined) was absolutely necessary to equip or empower Jesus for his special ministry. If John's followers were going to believe him, he needed to tell them something unique about Jesus. Is this another illustration of beginning with a conclusion and making up the story in an attempt to justify it?

John vacillates between the affirmation that Jesus and God were sometimes, if not always, one and the same, but he also identifies Jesus as God's son. There is some strange logic here, or is he speaking of oneness in spirit, which may be closer to truth than we have realized? Jesus also refers to God as "Father" and prays to him, which adds further confusion to exactly what John thought or was saying. A large part of his Gospel consists of long discourses on themes not found in the other three and for which there is no known parallel material. There is no indication he knew the other Gospels existed or anything about the two birth stories. (Some scholars now question that.) He made extensive use of common words, simple stories, and known human experiences in order to convey the unusual significance of Jesus for everyone. For John, Jesus needed no special birth, because he was what God is: "the bread of life," "the Good Shepherd," "the light of the world," and more. Jesus performs many miracles, but John calls them "signs" because they are signs of how special Jesus is and what God can do. The arrival of John's Jesus is radically different from the other three Gospels and further confuses the question, "Who was Jesus?"

## F.   Summary

The presence or absence of a birth story provides further confusion about the historical Jesus. The inclusion or exclusion of a birth story provides more information about the author's presuppositions and purpose than it does about Jesus. The two birth stories were composed for the purposes of the authors. It is highly possible the verbiage contained within the stories about Jesus's unique arrival on earth was symbolic and parabolic. Eventually, the symbolism was lost and mistakenly interpreted as factual, even by the majority of professing Christians today.

Scholars are convinced that significant insight into Jesus comes from a few practical and pithy statements attributed to him in noncanonical Gospels. They reflect some of his beliefs about God, humanity, and himself. Scholars believe they are among the first recorded statements of Jesus and stories about him. Some of the noncanonical Gospels are very helpful, partially because of what they do not say. It is very significant this material contains no special birth story, no indications Jesus considered himself special, no announcement of his predetermined death, and no indication he would become special after his death. They agree with the conviction that a careful study of the birth stories in the Gospels provides no evidence for an unusual pregnancy and birth. Given extensive evidence and common logic, God did not break his regular rules in the birth of Jesus. Jesus was, and remained, as human as we are.

# CHAPTER 9

# FROM MAN TO MESSIAH

Most professing Christians firmly believe in the "incarnation theory" which means "God took on human form and lived among us." They affirm Jesus became divine, either by birth or otherwise. Many proclaim Jesus the man became Jesus the divine Messiah because God designed it that way; end of story and end of discussion, without any questions or concern for how, why, or when. They accept the fruit from their family tree and believe the authorities who assure them, "It's true because it's in the Bible." Few will accept the fact that even though Jesus was called *Messiah* and *Son of God,* those terms did not necessarily mean he was assumed divine by those who first used them.

I previously declared Jesus was born human and he remained human. Furthermore, I am convinced that proclamation of the incarnation theory seriously damaged and disrupted the religious movement begun by Jesus. Therefore, since most professing Christians firmly believe in the incarnation, my firm rejection of that major presupposition requires a lengthy and rational response.

Few professing Christians ever asked the origin of the idea that the human Jesus became the divine Messiah. Jesus never indicated he was, or was to become, more than human, even if some writers say he did. It seems that the early followers of Jesus expected their Messiah to be only a human who would be an ideal leader, possibly a king, and do great things for them, including deliverance, national renewal, and lasting peace. (A different but true meaning for "messiah.") There are several strong hints his followers wanted Jesus to be a Messiah-King who would be a person in the likeness of David (triumphant entry event). Charges against Jesus at his trial suggest the authorities were afraid of that possibility instead of his religious beliefs. That is why they killed him and not because anyone among them thought he was or would ever be divine. From the little believable information provided by the Gospels, Jesus's closest and personally trained disciples never considered him more than a magnificent and unusual man. Believable noncanonical Gospels firmly emphasize a human Jesus who was not assumed divine by anyone at any time. During Paul's persecution of Christians, he never considered their leader was more than human.

Professing Christians need to be aware of some most disturbing, interesting, and enlightening facts. Pagan gods (Attis, Mithra, Osiris, and others) were worshipped during Paul's lifetime and during the formation of the Gospels. Stories about some of those gods provide an almost exact parallel to the Gospel stories about Jesus. As an example, Attis reportedly had a virgin birth and was born on December 25. He was called a shepherd, the only begotten son, and the Logos. He was slain for the salvation of mankind. He was crucified on a tree, and holy blood ran down to redeem the earth. He descended into the underworld and rose after three days to become the most-high god. After his death, his followers had sacrificial meals where bread was eaten as his body by his worshippers. (Does this sound familiar?)

The Gospels, written long after Jesus's death and Paul's vision, obviously began with a belief in incarnation. Apparently, all of them promoted the presupposition that Jesus was divine and God became man. However, they obviously disagree when and how it happened. They do not tell us why they begin with that presupposition or from where the theory came. Whatever the source, they set out to promote and prove that Jesus was the divine Messiah and not a human messiah. We do not know if that was the only belief they knew, the most prominent of their time or their personal choice. The Gospel writers repeatedly offer support for their presupposition, but in the process of trying to prove their point, they tell things about Jesus and the disciples that apparently were incorrect and sometimes beyond belief. None of their support for their belief in incarnation tells from where came the belief that Jesus transitioned from human to divine or how God became a man. They attempt to justify it with the virgin birth, a baptism, miracles, the Logos, and stories attributed to Jesus, some of which may have been borrowed from folklore and pagan religions.

I think it is necessary to point out the possibility there were two separate messiahs addressed in the Gospels and elsewhere. The problem occurred because of different meanings of the word *messiah*. It is important to separate the messiah who remained human from the Messiah who reportedly was divine. The first refers to a godly man filled with a loving spirit who rescued numerous people from various things and was given the special title of messiah or savior without divine connotation. The second refers to one who was considered divine, God among us in human form. It is impossible to date the beginning of either theory or when they became prevalent. However, the development of the human messiah is more obvious because of Jesus's ministry. The idea that Jesus was or became divine certainly was not present in his teachings or in the Jesus Movement immediately after his death. It seems Jesus never mentioned the matter. Emphasis on the divinity of Jesus became prominent only after his crucifixion and probably after Paul's vision. Belief in Jesus's divinity apparently arose in that unknown time span between the crucifixion of Jesus and the formation of Mark's Gospel, with further development thereafter. Paul's contribution to the incarnation theory is unknown but probably very extensive.

The belief that Jesus was a human messiah has many roots. Reasonable conjecture, drawn from tidbits of information, indicates the idea may have been understandably aided by many well-meaning people who knew or knew about Jesus. His unusual spirit and ministry, witnessed by so many, caused them to affirm he was a most unusual man who rescued them and taught them how to live; therefore, a true messiah. Because of their religious concepts, they could have believed he was sent from God without believing he was divine. However, because of outside help, what they believed and said may later have been misunderstood and misstated as support for a divine Jesus.

The uniqueness of Jesus was inadvertently supported by those who did not personally know him, especially the marginalized and desperate. They heard about a unique man who reportedly possessed unusual abilities and demonstrated personal care for the needy in very unexpected and unorthodox ways. They kept alive the unusual stories about Jesus and may have embellished them. Unusual stories connected to religious matters were probably more frequently and fervently told and believed. People on the fringes of his influence spoke highly of him and considered him a very special person.

The idea of a human messiah could have been encouraged by the many uneducated peasants who gladly listened to Jesus speak, who closely observed his behavior or had been personally helped by him. If Jesus traveled extensively, many different peasants would have had firsthand experiences with the man who demonstrated compassion and unusual care for their kind. However, we may have been misled by reports on the extent of Jesus's travel. If he was gainfully employed, he may have confronted some of the marginalized more than once. If he spent extended time in a certain place, side trips from a base of operation appear more rational, practical, and effective. Because of the tendency for Gospel writers to adjust their data as desired, some of those trips may have been in the mind of the author and not on Jesus's travelogue. Assuredly, Jesus was concerned for the poor and either went where they were or gladly welcomed them when they came where he was. He freely associated with the poor and ate with the unclean, sick, tax collectors, zealots, and women. That inclusive behavior was beyond anything they had ever seen or expected and was the subject of many serious conversations. Those disenfranchised people had no known category into which Jesus fit. His compassion, care, and religious insight were considered, for the lack of a more appropriate terms, "miracles" to them (just highly unusual and unexpected actions). Jesus must have a fitting title, so he became their messiah (one who came to their rescue them and set them free). Because of the beliefs of that day, they may have also considered he was sent from God, without thinking he was divine. Reports on the importance of an unusual man most likely grew in number, meaning, and size with the passage of time and much retelling. Those who had experienced the ministry of Jesus felt compelled to give him a significant and descriptive title. As in ancient times, his name depicted character and actions.

Those who traveled with Jesus, including the disciples, knew him exceptionally well and may have purposely contributed to his special title of a human messiah. If Jesus gave "so much to so many," his traveling companions probably spoke highly of him wherever they went. They knowingly employed superlatives in an effort to convey accolades that ordinary words could not. Those who originally spoke the words knew what they were doing when they applied those high accolades to a man who was truly a human messiah. They spoke very highly of Jesus until the outsiders, and especially the next generation who only heard about him, assumed the superlatives were literal descriptions and mistakenly elevated Jesus above the human level. Those simple, grateful, descriptive, metaphorical, and symbolic words about the human Jesus were later misunderstood and used to mistakenly transform and elevate the human messiah.

Jesus's behavior was obviously instrumental in receiving a special title. Was he so intent on helping the marginalized that he did not recognize his effect on them? I think he knew his effect and purposely sought to guard against false assumptions, which is the reason for the "Messianic secret" (do not tell who he is) in Mark's Gospel. We cannot escape the probability that some of the things he did were interpreted as exceptional because his words and actions were beyond anything many had ever heard, seen, experienced, or expected. When he purposely did for them what another person could have done but did not, that made him very special. His general knowledge about healing and wholeness may have been little different from others who also knew how to help, but they simply refused, for numerous reasons, to associate with the marginalized. The place, nature, and amount of Jesus's assistance was never intended to facilitate the incarnation theory, but we can understand how special Jesus was to so many. Their exuberance could not be contained and may have been misinterpreted and misnamed, both then and later.

Jesus's renunciation of some Jewish beliefs and worship practices may have added to the belief that he was a messiah. We have no indication when Jesus became deeply dissatisfied with Jewish worship or beliefs. It seems the poor were not warmly welcomed in regular temple worship, but the synagogue requirements may have been different. If the poor and sick were forbidden to attend one or both, did Jesus refuse to participate because they could not (a boycott)? We have firm indications that anyone who participated in Jewish worship was expected, if not required, to offer sacrifices, at least on specific occasions. That would be expensive and perhaps impossible for the poor and seriously ill. Is that why we have no record of Jesus ever personally offering an animal sacrifice of any kind? Did he believe it was useless? Jesus's strong opposition to the beliefs and practices of local Jewish worship, along with his instigation of a radically different form of worship, may have earned him recognition and a special title as a human messiah, which was later misunderstood. If Jesus revolutionized worship for some who were struggling with Judaism, they likely used descriptive titles when they spoke of him. In different situations and times, people applied such titles as *Savior* (one who saves us from Judaism's useless requirements and gives us hope), *Messiah* (one sent from God to teach us), and others, but none of which declared or was intended to say Jesus was divine. It was extremely easy for people to later misuse those terms and mistakenly elevate the nature of Jesus.

Jewish converts may have unknowingly supported the idea of a human messiah. The Gospels provide no information on Jesus stealing Jewish worshippers, but it is rational to assume some gladly joined with him in his attempt to reform, not refute, Jewish worship. Previously, they had regularly or occasionally participated in organized Jewish worship and had accepted, or were well aware of, certain Jewish beliefs pertaining to sacrifices. If they seriously listened to what Jesus said and carefully observed what he did, they recognized how different he was. During their personal association with Jesus, they experienced and observed what it meant to love God and serve your neighbor without offering animal sacrifices. Jesus's followers, who were steeped in Judaism, knew about the meaning of a sacrifice, and it was not unusual in their day for a person to be sacrificed for a cause. If they believed and proclaimed Jesus was a sacrifice for their cause or his, that means he gave himself totally to a specific cause, but it does not in any way suggest they believed he was divine. It simply states Jesus gave his life in support of a cause or belief. That interpretation could have been eventually misunderstood and enlarged. If anyone believed Jesus was sacrificed for his cause, that may have grown into "a sacrifice for the sins of the world." That added interpretation inadvertently could move Jesus the human messiah to Jesus the divine Messiah, even though originally it was only a descriptive statement about the human Jesus.

We were led to believe Jesus spent a large portion of his ministry in and around Capernaum. If he lived there for an extended time, those people would have specific opinions about him, his ministry, and its effects. If those followers knew about a divine Jesus, we have no indication of it. They gave no indication he was more than uniquely human. The silence from Jesus's followers in Capernaum seriously robs us of valid information on what he did and how he was perceived. Likewise, the same is true for Jerusalem. If he lived there for an extended time, those people would have known about him, his ministry, and its effects. The effort in Jerusalem to make him a messiah-king indicates they did not consider him divine (triumphant entry). It is difficult to believe those core groups remained silent if they believed Jesus was divine. Absence of any information may not mean there was no information from them. If any support for the divinity of Jesus had come from these two significant places, the Gospel writers would have certainly used it to the fullest extent by quoting them as evidence and proof for their point.

I cannot be sure, but I am convinced that members of the above-mentioned groups believed Jesus was human but considered him an exceptional man with a Godlike spirit for whom the term *messiah* fully applied without any divine connotations. Because of their religious concepts, all of them could affirm he was "sent from God" without believing he was divine. They had longed for a leader-king, like David, who would be filled with a righteous spirit and who could and would save them from their troubles (a genuine messiah). They saw or heard about a man who demonstrated such a unique spirit, who had such genuine care and concern for everyone, that they believed Jesus was the one to lead them. Their experiences with Jesus were so different and unusual that they knew he was special and must have a special title. Therefore, they gave him the title *Messiah,* which meant "the human one who came to save us and lead us," but they never thought he was the divine messiah expected by the Jews.

The cruel crucifixion of Jesus left these groups terribly confused and vulnerable. Apparently, they lacked a strong leader, had no idea of how to interpret his death, and were unsure of their next move. Suddenly, Paul came upon the scene and offered a package containing all three, centered around a divine Messiah.

## A. Paul's Influence and Domination

I previously spoke of two messiahs proclaimed in the New Testament. The above-mentioned human messiah was totally unacceptable to Paul, and he proclaimed the second type, a "divine Messiah" sent purposely from God. I have limited knowledge about Paul, and I am confused about his beliefs. Present-day scholars are also confused because they do not agree on what he believed. Of one thing I am sure, he obviously influenced Christendom from his day to this. He most likely did not know the human Jesus and, for some unknown reason, exerted great effort to destroy Jesus's followers (certainly before his vision and perhaps, in some manner, also after it). According to his own words (Galatians 1:11–17), Paul received no information from any of Jesus's closest disciples or from any other person who helped shape his beliefs and proclamations about Jesus. It came to him from God through a vision (revelation) that focused on the "anointed Jesus," who was sent from God as the promised divine Messiah. However, Paul seemed to tell a different story when he affirmed his message about Christ's resurrection and appearance was based on what he had received (1 Corinthians 15:3–9) but does not identify the source.

The presupposition with which Jesus and his followers began was vastly different from the one from which Paul began, specifically about Jesus and the kind of messiah he was. These two basic presuppositions are so radically different that it is impossible to dovetail them into one. From existing records, it appears the Pauline concept became predominant within a few years after Jesus's death. If it actually did, it was because a skilled, highly educated, and determined spokesperson purposely transplanted a new "rootstock" that he fervently fertilized, trained, and pruned until, like kudzu on a Mississippi hillside, it jeopardized all else nearby. It dominated Christendom from that day to this. However, we know the Jesus Movement did not die, even though we have very little information about it during the time of Paul and later.

We must hasten to point out that Paul's dominance of the new religious movement may not have been as instant and complete as indicated. We must seriously ask just how strong the Jesus movement was if it was easily commandeered soon after Jesus's death by someone with such radical ideas. There are three possible answers. First, members of the Jesus movement were completely devastated and lacked the ability to respond appropriately. Second, a forceful and powerful person burst upon the scene at an opportune time and skillfully took full advantage of the devastated people. Third, Paul did not commandeer the Jesus movement, and it quietly continued much like it had during Jesus's life while Paul went his separate way. The third option is most probable, based on the modicum of information available. If Paul's writings about himself and his ministry had not been preserved, we probably would have little or no information about him. Also, Paul's influence may have been less than we first thought.

According to Paul, he had been entrusted with the gospel of the resurrected Jesus for the uncircumcised (Gentiles), while Peter, James, and John were the "acknowledged pillars" of the gospel to the "circumcised" (Galatians 2:7–9). We have no indication by whom, how, when, or if that was decided. Paul also said he never wanted to proclaim the good news where Christ had already been proclaimed because he did not want to build on another's foundation (Romans 15:20). Since Paul refused to learn anything about Jesus from the disciples, since he was determined where and to whom he would preach, and since he wanted no predecessor who had proclaimed Christ, he must have been fully aware that he and the disciples proclaimed a different message about Jesus and God. Given the environment in which Jesus and Paul lived and the diverse people they reportedly affected, it is very difficult to believe the Jesus movement was directed only to the Jews or that Paul preached only to Gentiles. I believe the reports we have indicate otherwise.

I am fully convinced Paul was the primary source through which "the Jesus of history" was elevated to "the Christ of faith" or the "divine Messiah." The emphasis of a peasant preacher who had demonstrated and advocated God's requirements for appropriate love and compassion was replaced with Paul's primary emphasis on the results of the anointed, crucified, and resurrected Jesus. That new proclamation came from a man who probably did not personally know Jesus, who may have never seen Jesus or heard him speak, who had no interest in the historical Jesus, and who did not want to associate with Jesus's disciples. (That would be an excellent announcement in the Sunday worship guide.)

Paul became the leader of what can only be called a new religious movement. He disregarded the Jesus of history, denied the beliefs and practices of the early Jesus Movement (sometimes called "The Way"), changed Jesus's salvation statements, and reconstructed current Judaism. As a devout Jew, Paul concluded Jesus was the divine Messiah expected in Judaism. Even after Paul's vision, many of his beliefs depended far more on Judaism than on Jesus. Paul used Jesus to augment his basic Jewish doctrines through add-ons by which he inserted Jesus into Judaism's empty spaces and interpreted Jesus on the basis of his Judaism. Even though Paul's vision radically changed his concept of God, Judaism remained primary, and Jesus was secondary. The Jewish authorities firmly rejected Paul's idea that Jesus was the expected Messiah. Paul's new religious movement was based specifically on what the Jewish authorities rejected. The Jewish authorities believed they had correctly interpreted the Old Testament passages about the promised Messiah and were firmly convinced Jesus did not fulfill the requirements. The response, or lack thereof, from the powerful Jewish authorities clearly indicates they concluded Jesus was only human.

Following his vision, Paul was technically no longer a valid member of the Jewish faith, even though he otherwise believed much like them. He was not, and had never been, a follower of Jesus. He stood totally alone in his primary religious presuppositions. Paul started what must be correctly called a new religion because it agreed with neither Judaism nor "The Way." Any attempt to infuse his belief system into either one of the other two is futile. As preposterous as it may seem, just one man's vision, knowledge, hubris, and effort changed the emphasis *of Jesus* to the emphasis *on Jesus,* and it largely remains there today.

Paul's new presuppositions instigated a gigantic divide, which is often unknown, primarily overlooked, and deliberately denied. That divide cannot be called any other name. He denied the basic teachings of Jesus and disregarded the method of Jesus's ministry. He deliberately separated himself from Jesus's disciples. His basic proclamations about Jesus were foreign to anything Jesus believed or said about himself. Given those obvious facts, how can anyone logically deny Paul started a new religion and proclaimed a divine Messiah?

Because of Paul's influence and domination, there are presently two basic presuppositions undergirding the current Christian community, even if one has largely overshadowed the other. Each affirms a different presupposition about Jesus and the kind of messiah he was. One basic presupposition states, "Believe the directions from the human Jesus." It affirms our salvation comes through following the requirements announced and lived by him. He was a spokesperson for God, who lived by and echoed the core beliefs of ancient Judaism, emphasized by other major spokesmen for God. Members in this group believe the process for getting right with God and remaining right with him is to "love God above all else and love your neighbor as yourself," which has remained the same from the time of the ancient Hebrews. It was not changed by Jesus or by what happened to him.

The second basic presupposition for professing Christians came primarily from Paul. Members of this group believe Jesus was at some point divine and his preordained cruel death and resurrection were necessary for our salvation. They assume Jesus was purposely sent from God as a special agent who was the patch for human depravity and was designed to set us free from the wrath of God we deserve by virtue of sin, original sin, and "the fall." They also believe Jesus was the required blood sacrifice that somehow washed away our sin, and his death paid God, or someone, a ransom so that we may have salvation.

Those in the first group believe salvation comes through following the *words* of Jesus. If we believe God freely offers salvation, then we must act like it with appropriate love. Those in the second group believe salvation comes through claiming the *works* of Jesus, that Jesus physically did something that enables individual salvation. The foundation of the first group's beliefs is in the core of ancient Hebrew religion. The foundation of the second group is one man's personal vision and his adherence to his current Jewish beliefs. Those who believe in the works of Jesus base their belief on the words of someone other than Jesus.

Even though these two presuppositions may overlap at certain points, they are radically different and cannot be dovetailed into one. Their irreconcilable difference is illustrated when the first presupposition declares Jesus only sought to change errant Judaism back to its original core, but the second presupposition changed Jesus into what Judaism lacked.

## B. Transition in the Synoptic Gospels

The Gospel writers began with the presupposition that affirmed who the earthly Jesus became, not who he initially was. They began with the intended purpose of proving Jesus was the divine Messiah, the Son of God. Historical data is almost accidental or adjusted to prove their point, not to correctly report on the human Jesus. For them, there is little distance for him to go from human to divine, if he is not considered divine from the beginning. They all began with that conclusion and worked backward to the beginning, seeking and creating data to justify what they already believed. Mark begins his Gospel by saying, "The beginning of the good news of Jesus Christ, the Son of God" (Mark 1:1). Matthew and Luke begin with a virgin birth affirmation. The author of John's Gospel joins with the Synoptic Gospels and states what was probably true for all Gospel writers when very early he said, "We have found him about whom Moses in the Law and also the prophets wrote, Jesus, son of Joseph from Nazareth," (John 1:45b). Since all Gospel writers apparently began with the primary purpose of proving and promoting their presupposition, there is little chance to get truthful data about the actions or teachings of the human Jesus.

Many of us had originally assumed, and many still do, the Gospels provided accurate reports about the historical Jesus and the early Christian community. All of the Gospels portray major events in the life of Jesus as if they were totally spontaneous and without precedence. We now know some significant events and stories were borrowed, misquoted, and embellished. Some were apparently Old Testament stories, renovated and reported as if they were historical events in the life of Jesus. As examples, consider Isaiah 7:14 for Jesus's birth, Zechariah 9:9 for the triumphant entry, and Isaiah 53:4–12 for the major ideas, events, and actions that parallel the events of Holy Week. The extreme similarities of those Old

Testament passages to stories describing Jesus are too repetitious for us to believe they first occurred in the life of Jesus. Certain passages are not fulfillment of prophecy, as some people profess. (Recall inerrancy and literal interpretation.) The Gospel writers would have us believe their reported comments attributed to Jesus were verbatim, about a certain situation, at specific locations and times, including the lengthy discourses in John. It is very unwise to believe that. Given what we know about Gospel writers' purpose and approach, it is very possible that no event in the life of Jesus occurred exactly as recorded by them. Also, did they incorporate pagan concepts into their stories, and if so, to what degree? Apparently, Gospel writers' sole purpose was to prove the historical Jesus had been transformed into the Christ of faith with little regard for truth.

Two Gospel writers may have recognized the difficulty of convincing others that the human Jesus moved from human to divine. It is possible that Mark's Gospel was not widely accepted because of its claims about Jesus. Matthew and Luke indicated their general acceptance of Mark's premise by each wrapping his Gospel around Mark's and adjusting Mark's stories as they felt necessary. One adjustment in each was a unique birth story. Did Matthew and Luke make a deliberate effort to facilitate acceptance of man to divine Messiah by declaring Jesus had a special birth or being because of divine intervention?

Gospel writers led us to believe they were either present at the events with Jesus or consulted eyewitnesses. Given the dates when they wrote, that cannot be correct. There is evidence they enhanced, embellished, and rearranged their source material to fit their own purpose, but we have no way of knowing exactly what, when, or to what extent. Did the Gospel writers really care or know what the initial followers of Jesus knew or believed? Did they care about the earthly life of Jesus, other than the points within it that they use to prove and promote their presuppositions? With the possible but doubtful exception of Mark, the writers had no association with eyewitnesses or early followers of Jesus, and Mark has no birth story. In reference to the transition theory, it seems the Gospel writers began with what they heard or read or believed and created much of the remainder. However, Paul's prevalent theology was very helpful to them.

Another possible practice raises further question on the accuracy of the Gospels' transition stories. It affirms that some writers sought to prove the magnificence of someone by attributing to them borrowed hero stories from known classical Greek literature (very similar to borrowed stories about pagan gods or Matthew's new Moses). Authors may have used known stories and characters from famous literature and substituted the name of Jesus in the place of the main character or hero in those stories. If the Gospel writers did this, who would challenge them? Whatever truth there is in this possibility, it really tells us nothing about Jesus or his early followers, but it may say something about Gospel writers' determination to promote their purpose through any possible means. (Keep in mind, these are human words by human writers who were driven by a specific and personal presupposition.) A fundamental question remains unanswered. Did the Synoptic Gospel writers create the idea that Jesus was divine, or did they accept, adjust, and promote the belief that had already been formulated? The latter is more likely.

## C.  No Distinction in John

The Gospel of John is distinctively different from the other three canonical Gospels. He wrote long after the others, perhaps about 100 CE. John has a different and strange "transition theory," if it can be correctly called that. Each of the Synoptic Gospels presents a somewhat similar process through which Jesus gradually moved from human to divine. John accepts no part of that. For him, Jesus was "divine upon arrival," but he does not explain. Compare that with Paul's assumption that Jesus became divine through his death and resurrection. Obviously, early New Testament writers did not agree on the transition theory.

Technically, John does not move Jesus from human to divine, because there was no natural man. Even though John recognizes

Jesus had an earthly beginning, he does not describe or date it. From the beginning of time, Jesus was coequal with God and participated with God in creation. (The virgin birth in Matthew and Luke is not too far removed from being always with God.) Perhaps for that specific reason, John's Jesus purposely possesses fewer human characteristics than in the other three Gospels. Jesus took on human form to live among us and show and tell us how we should live. John does not explain just how Jesus can do that if Jesus is not completely one of us. More importantly, Jesus is primarily God's special agent through which signs of God's power and love are demonstrated. He was also predestined from before creation to die for humanity's sin as proof of God's love for us. That is strange logic and radical theology, if all of this was ordained and predestined prior to the creation of the universe.

For John, it seems Jesus was predestined to rotate from one level to the other because John has difficulty keeping God and Jesus separated. At some points, Jesus and God are one, but at other times Jesus refers to God as Father. Jesus prays to God on several occasions. Jesus's acts of healing are not from a compassionate peasant who seeks to help others, because of love, but are usually the occasions to illustrate God's power and to emphasize the importance of Jesus as God's agent. John's "I Am" statements are frequently supported by a sign or story on the same subject, but those statements would have far more relevance if they were attributed to God rather than Jesus. However, for John, Jesus is what God is: love, light, bread, living water, and more.

John provides comments that are noticeably different and clearly contradict several statements recorded in the earlier Gospels. We can only question who is correct, if either! The earlier Gospels indicate Jesus made only one trip to Jerusalem during his earthly ministry, but John indicated he made more trips and spent more time there. John repositions a crucial story. The other three Gospels locate the cleansing of the temple near the end of Jesus's ministry, and it creates serious discord, which contributed to Jesus's arrest. John moves that event near the beginning of Jesus's ministry. Repositioning that story reduces its importance and eliminates one major reason for Jesus's troubles during his last week in Jerusalem. For John, there was no need for further provocation because Jesus was going to die then and there as predetermined by God. That was Jesus's purpose for coming to earth and for going to Jerusalem at that time. Apparently, John believed Jesus had absolutely no choice in this entire process and had dutifully moved through necessary steps toward a predetermined end in order to prove he was divine and the promised Messiah.

Compared with other Gospels, John reports different activities during the last week of Jesus's life. John gives a different time for Jesus's arrest in relationship to Passover activities. He closely aligns the time of Jesus death with the Passover sacrifice. There is foot washing only in John, and Jesus gave no instructions to continue the Last Supper in remembrance of him. The Synoptic Gospels indicate Jesus's ministry lasted one year or less, but John clearly thinks it lasted at least two years or more. (Verification of how little the Gospel writers knew about Jesus.) John delivers extensive discourses supposedly from the mouth of Jesus, the likes of which do not appear in the other three Gospels or in any other known complete or partial manuscripts related to Jesus. Many of those long speeches are John's compositions for his intended purposes. Those extended discourses are far removed from the pithy and pointed statements in the Sermon on the Mount or those proclaimed by a compassionate person who simply said love God and your neighbor appropriately.

John also began with the conclusion that Jesus was the divine Messiah and proceeded with his attempt to prove it, but he took a different approach. He clearly stated his purpose in what was probably the closing verse of his original Gospel, before someone added another chapter. In the closing verse of the next-to-last chapter, he makes a specific point and also provides the reason he wrote. He states, "But these are written so that you may come to believe that Jesus is the Messiah, the son of God, and that through believing you may have life in his name" (John 20:31). Even though John's was the last New Testament Gospel written, his convoluted presuppositions permeate much of modern Christianity, and his Gospel is dearly loved, believed, read, and quoted more than the others. John 3:16 is probably the best-known and most frequently quoted Bible verse for professing Christians (maybe the only one some of them know). There is no significant transition in John because, for him, Jesus was divine from the beginning.

The Gospel of John adds yet another interesting, unexpected, inexplicable, and significant twist to the transformation theory by interjecting John the Baptist into his reports. We can only speculate why John's Gospel commented far more about John the Baptist than the other Gospels. It seems to include conflicting conclusions. Surely, it was not just a human-interest story. Did someone later supplement John's Gospel for some specific reason? The most probable reason was because of a lingering debate, either within the community where John lived or on a larger scale, if not both. Apparently, people were seriously debating who had been more important, Jesus or John the Baptist. John the Baptist had been extremely popular during his lifetime and also after his death. Luke went to great lengths to specifically declare John the Baptist had a natural birth. The Gospel of John simply says he was a man sent from God (John 1:6). The baptizer had a large following, some of whom apparently assumed he was the or a messiah. Scholars firmly believe Jesus was originally a student/follower of John the Baptizer but separated from him for unknown reasons and at an unknown time. Scholars now believe John and Jesus were itinerant preachers simultaneously conducting a similar ministry by preaching repentance of sin and baptizing but in separate locations. It seems at some unknown time, the followers of John and the followers of Jesus had a disagreement, probably over which one was the true messiah. (John and Luke hint at this but do not tell us that complete story.) From within the shadows of recorded stories, it seems John the Baptist may have been more important in some circles than Jesus and was therefore considered the messiah by them. That unsettled matter lingered long after Jesus and John died, perhaps for at least eighty years. The author of John's Gospel sought to settle the argument. From the very beginning of John's Gospel, he deliberately and decisively determined to resolve that issue by the way he tells the story and affirms John the Baptizer was in every way human and subordinate to Jesus. That argument had obviously lingered within some portion of the Christian community, or why was it necessary for the writer of John's Gospel to settle it after all those years? If the writer of John's Gospel was attempting to settle that issue, it indicates at least two very, very significant points. First, they were concerned with which man was most important and not concerned if one of them was divine. Second, the lingering argument among the followers of Jesus and John affirms the expected messiah was only human. Truth occasionally slipped through. This lingering concern over who was greater, Jesus or John the Baptist, raises serious questions, such as what was the origin of the idea of a divine Jesus, and who believed it?

## D. The Council of Nicaea

Jesus's nature, whether human or divine, remained unresolved during early Christianity. Available literature reflects conflicting beliefs among the early church fathers, and serious debate continued for years. Emperor Constantine was converted to Christianity on October 28, 312 CE, and later became disgusted with the conflicting arguments related to Jesus's nature. He directed a council to convene and resolve the issue. In 325, participants at the Council of Nicaea wrestled to decide Jesus's nature. Eventually, they concluded he was fully human and simultaneously fully divine. The early Christian authorities simply kicked the can down the road by declaring the impossible. Obviously, that really did not settle the matter, even though some thought it did, then and now. Proclamation of the New Testament writers, the early church fathers, the Council of Nicaea, and the Council of Chalcedon did not resolve the issue or provide logical reasons for their conclusions. Most modern creedal statements, priests, pastors, and parishioners presently declare, without question or reservation, that Jesus transitioned from human to divine, but based on what?

## E. Conclusions about the Transition Theory

There are many reasons I do not believe in the divinity of Jesus. First, it simply does not fit. Everything I believe about the actions of God fits into a systematic and orderly process. The universe depends on absolute continuity and connectivity. The rules that govern the universe never change. God's design for humanity has been absolutely consistent throughout recorded history. It does not seem God would suddenly change his rules and provide one divine individual but never before or after that one time.

Second, this idea is predicated on the theory that the depth of human depravity demanded something more than human to redeem us. The argument continues by affirming Jesus had to be divine in order to be a savior or a messiah for fallen humanity. That belief comes from misinterpretation of several Old Testament passages. The proper understanding of God's nature and ours affirms he never lost control of humanity, and humanity was never totally depraved. The basis for the theory is untrue.

Third, the Gospel writers do not justify their conclusions. They begin with the assurance of his divinity and proceed to prove it. Each tells a different story, some parts of which are radically different and cannot be reconciled. They offer no hard proof. Because of their belief in the inerrancy of scripture and literal interpretation of Old Testament prophecies, they offer as proof of his divinity the fulfilled biblical predictions, the virgin birth stories, Jesus's miracles, Jesus's ministry to the marginalized, and John's assumption, all of which are questionable. They conclude with an inexplicable predesigned crucifixion and a resurrection. We are asked to believe this because "they said it." However, there are no outside records of these unusual and contradictory events. When records and events are carefully analyzed without prior conclusions, there is no proof or logical reason for Jesus's basic nature to have been any different from ours (to be discussed later). People could believe he was sent from God without declaring he was divine. There is no logical justification in the Gospels for the divinity of Jesus.

Fourth, I reject the transition theory because it declares a change in God's original process for humanity to get right and remain right with him. There was no need or possibility for change. Under no condition did Jesus, by word or deed, initiate the process or a new process to get right and remain right with God. Like those ancient spokespersons whom he quoted, Jesus was committed to loving God above all else and his neighbor as himself. God's free offer of salvation has been the same from the beginning of time. Therefore, our appropriate love of God, neighbor, and self is the key to our salvation, not a belief that God had to send someone to correct the salvation process through a cruel crucifixion, ransom, and resurrection.

Fifth, the human-to-divine theory promotes not only a false salvation process but also an inappropriate lifestyle resulting from it. According to the theory, just believing the right things pertaining to the life, death, and resurrection of the divine Jesus is basically all one needs in order to get right and stay right with God, both here and hereafter. In this theory, beliefs get primary emphasis, and if appropriate love is required, it is given a secondary role. The belief emphasizes love for Jesus but not for God or neighbor or self, and the responsibility to appropriately love everyone is put on the back burner because we just need to believe in Jesus, and he takes care of everything! It affirms, "Just believing" in a divine Jesus automatically and miraculously rescues us if and when we fail. The thrust here is to believe in Jesus and depend on him to correct all our errors, cover all our inappropriate love, and eventually transport us into the kingdom. There are obvious difficulties with this concept because it tends to dodge personal responsibility for what we are, what we do, and how we do it. Correct beliefs are important, but more is demanded. We must love appropriately and act accordingly.

Sixth, I deny the divinity of Jesus because the theory attempts to make Jesus into what he was not so that we may be set free from being what we unavoidably are. The theory denies the basic nature of Jesus and us. Neither needed or could be changed. If Jesus was divine, that would not automatically change our nature, even if it

119

needed to be changed. A divine Jesus would not inject us with a saving substance and make us different than we are. A unique life or a cruel death does not automatically change everyone else. A Jesus whose nature was like ours has far more possibilities for helping us be what we were created to be than a Jesus who was declared to be what he was not so that we may become what we are not. We were, are, and always will be human. Jesus's death did not and cannot free us from our humanity, nor did it free us from the hard work of holy living. Jesus was as human as we are and did nothing to automatically change basic human nature, but he did show us our full human potential and responsibility, both of which may deeply disturb us.

Seventh, I renounce the divinity of Jesus because it provides us an escape from being like Jesus or taking his teachings seriously. If Jesus was divine, we cannot be expected to live as he lived. This belief provides us with the perfect and only excuse we will ever need for our misdeeds: "Well, I'm only human." However, if Jesus was human and one of us, that places demands for holy living on us if we want to follow him.

Eighth, I disbelieve the divinity of Jesus because of its probable author and origin. Even though others may have adjusted Paul's presuppositions, I am convinced he was the primary originator and promoter of a new salvation process that radically differs from what Jesus and Moses taught. During the time of Jesus, Judaism had drifted far from what its founding fathers taught and practiced. Paul was deeply immersed in the religion of his day. Even though he was a very devout Jew, his association with and persecution of the followers of Jesus must have caused him to question his Jewish beliefs. Paul was a severely conflicted man who was about to lose his mind. In that chaotic condition, he had a vision that resulted in beliefs that were neither Jewish nor patterned after Jesus. Following his vision, Paul could not renounce his Jewish doctrines or separate himself from some ideas about Jesus. Instead of separating from either, he declared Jesus was actually secondary to his current Jewish doctrines and plugged the crucified Jesus into its holes to make his Judaism complete. That combination resulted in Paul's declaration that God's original design for salvation was null and void. I prefer to believe Jesus and Moses instead of Paul.

Ninth, if we can believe the reports, perhaps the most compelling reason to disbelieve Jesus was divine is that no member of his family ever gave any indication they believed it, even his mother. If they had believed, their response on several occasions would have been very different, especially the parents' response to the twelve-year-old in the temple, the family thinking Jesus was unstable, the neighbors not knowing Jesus was different, and Mary being totally unprepared for the reported crucifixion and resurrection. Based on these events, it seems rather obvious that the family did not consider Jesus divine, and their responses seriously undermine that belief.

In summary, the transition theory is totally erroneous and unnecessary. It has too many obvious flaws. Obedience to the two directives prescribed by Jesus fulfills God's ancient and modern requirements for salvation and thereby negates any need for Jesus to be more than a unique human. His two directives need nothing added. Jesus, Moses, and the great prophets believed we were fully capable of meeting those two primary directives, or they would not have accepted their sufficiency and directed us to abide by them. Since neither the original Hebrew directives nor Jesus ever predicated our salvation on the coming of a divine Messiah, why should we express a need for one or declare Jesus was it? The transition theory appears to have originated primarily from one man's attempt to keep his entrenched Jewish beliefs after he recognized Jesus was important. However, his new ideas did not follow ancient truth, reason, or common sense. Based on what appears to be the authentic words of Jesus, Moses, and others, plus sound theology, logic, reason, believable reports, and common sense, we need no transformation of Jesus from man to Messiah, no divine Jesus, no living blood sacrifice, no high priest, and no resurrected Jesus in order to get right and stay right with God. Jesus was as human as we are, but wow, what a remarkable human!

# CHAPTER 10

# THE HUMAN JESUS

Since Jesus was always and in every way just as human as we are, a major portion of the belief system and doctrinal foundation of denominations, congregations, and individuals is null and void. That unexpected awareness of his humanness may wash over someone like a giant tsunami from the sea, inundating everything, destroying some "sacred cows" while rearranging other beliefs and leaving in place only those things that are securely anchored by the two great commandments identified by Jesus. Since the essence of genuine Christianity consists primarily of living by those two specific commandments and not by believing only in a divine, crucified, and resurrected Jesus, the foundation under the religious house in which many have lived for roughly two thousand years is seriously damaged, if not destroyed.

That means much of what is said and done by professing Christians has not been and is not "Christian" by any stretch of generosity. In certain instances, organized church groups have been the most unchristian groups in town, and certain church members have been mistakenly called Christian. Some who heard Jesus probably did not believe his answer to the inquirer's question about salvation. Multitudes of professing Christians do not believe it today. We are presently in a situation similar to Jesus when he confronted the religious people where he lived and taught. Before they listened to him explain what he said, because of their presuppositions, they concluded he was mistaken. Need I say more?

Jesus was a most unusual man and a dedicated spokesperson for God. He possessed and was possessed by the spirit of appropriate love, which led to unusual labels being placed on him. He invited and encouraged others to love God appropriately and sought to show them what that meant. He freely gave of himself to express God's indwelling love for the benefit of others, often at his expense (which is what love means). I want it clearly understood that I believe the human Jesus is certainly our Savior. In the basic sense of the word, he is one who showed us how to worship and serve God because: (1) he told us and showed us how to get right and stay right with God through appropriate love; (2) he told us to believe him and act like him in order to be saved from the sin of inappropriate love, from getting lost in the pursuit of an erroneous salvation process that leads to a totally irrational and misdirected lifestyle; (3) he demonstrated how to negotiate life's maze and how to successfully overcome the numerous and ever-present temptations to love inappropriately; and (4) he demonstrated that Godlike love is the only key to a meaningful life, but if you get killed because you have loved appropriately, you have participated in the kingdom and should have no regrets. All of this is fully possible without having a divine Jesus and a physical resurrection.

## A. Paul's Opinion

It is difficult to know what Paul believed. Scholars cannot agree, even if Paul knew. If Paul ever believed Jesus was human at any point, he carefully avoided discussing it. After Paul's vision, Jesus became far more than human for him. As best we can tell, no other single person in New Testament times exerted as much effort as Paul to spread the Gospel (more correctly stated, to spread "his gospel") about Jesus. Following his conversion, there is no indication Paul deliberately sought to destroy the followers of Jesus, but there is obvious evidence he radically differed with them and wanted no association with them.

We do not know when Paul first attempted to destroy the followers of Jesus or when he supposedly became one of them (in name only). At some unknown time, he had full authorization and an avid determination to destroy, or at least make miserable, all available followers of the human Jesus. While on the road to Damascus, we assume for that specific purpose, a totally unexpected and dramatic vision of or about Jesus came to Paul. It would be very informative if we knew exactly what transpired just before and during that vision. Had Paul recently caused serious bodily harm, even death, to some followers of Jesus whose behavior and witness deeply affected him? Did he have their blood on his tunic? Apparently, because of that one vision, and with no help from Ananias or other disciples, Paul considered himself immediately equal, if not superior, to the original disciples of Jesus. That should be a clear warning sign about the nature and beliefs of this man and his brand of Christianity. He claimed full knowledge of the mission and purpose of Jesus, even though he "learned nothing from any human" (Galatians 1:12) and had no prior interaction with Jesus or his disciples, other than what he learned while persecuting the disciples and a brief stay with Ananias. Paul firmly believed his vision of a resurrected Jesus superseded what Jesus taught and what the Jesus movement believed. (Apparently, he thought he knew more than Jesus!) He did not need any information from the followers of Jesus because none of what they believed was important to him. (How did he know what Jesus believed and taught?) Paul obviously believed that Jesus and his followers believed incorrectly. The power of that one vision transformed and informed Paul, but it actually had as much, if not more, to do with adjusting his Judaism as with Jesus. His vision changed his concept of God, Jesus, Jewish law, and faith. Paul's radical assumption and presumption reveal volumes about his nature and theology, as well as his lack of knowledge about the human Jesus. Paul's response to his vision provides a clear clue to Paul's personality and indicates how forceful he was in denying the significance of the human Jesus and the teachings of those who knew Jesus best.

The lives of Paul and Jesus likely overlapped, and Paul could have personally known Jesus. No one, to my knowledge, has suggested Paul had met or heard Jesus speak. Do not eliminate those possibilities. Paul reportedly said, "Even though we once knew Christ from a human point of view" (2 Corinthians 5:16), but was that a personal we or a general we? Logically, there had to be some particular reason Paul adamantly disliked the followers of Jesus, if not Jesus himself. Paul was seriously upset with the human Jesus and wanted to forget about him but told no one why.

Had Paul been personally offended or adversely affected by something Jesus said or did, either to him or other devout Jews? Did Paul hear or hear about something Jesus or his followers proclaimed that was in serious conflict with Paul's strict religious beliefs? Given Paul's fondness for the Jewish law, perhaps Jesus's proclaiming the ancient sufficiency for salvation was too much for the legalistic Paul to tolerate. Did the practical and doable teachings of Jesus, compared to Paul's legalism, infuriate Paul? If so, did the hot-tempered, know-it-all, perfectly religious, and pompous Paul carry a deep grudge against Jesus and his followers that caused him to retaliate by persecuting if not Jesus, then Jesus's followers? Paul's deep-seated dislike for Jesus may be the reason he refused to mention Jesus's earthly existence. How did Paul, a devout Jew, interpret Judaism in a way that allowed him to maim and murder those who differed with him? Did Paul begin his persecution of Jesus's followers before or after Jesus's death? Did Paul have a personal altercation with Jesus? Where was Paul, the prominent and powerful Jew, during Jesus's trial and crucifixion? Because of his power and prominence, perhaps Paul was involved in causing or encouraging them, and maybe present at them. He was just the kind of man who would have been in attendance and in support of the trial and crucifixion. Personal participation in those events could have later caused such inner turmoil that he "went blind" and "lost his way." We usually call that a mental breakdown.

Jesus and his followers were undoubtedly interfering with Judaism. Whatever that interference was, it must have been more extensive than ever told and more detrimental to the Jewish community than ever indicated. That interference was either extremely serious or very personal because Paul was determined to demolish it through imprisonment and death for those who followed Jesus.

The mystery continues. Paul was a sophisticated Jewish scholar, which automatically placed him at the level of daily life far from the environment in which Jesus was probably born and in which Jesus reportedly spent a large portion of his time. Paul's pedigree and social position meant he knew little or nothing about life for the poor. The insignificant social class into which Jesus was probably born and the extended recognition Jesus gained may have been more than a jealous Paul could tolerate. Was Paul's negative response his personal initiative, or did Jesus irritate the religious authorities to the degree they directed Paul to destroy Jesus and his followers? Without doubt, there are many unknown parts to the puzzle of why Paul responded as he did. However, at no point during his persecution period did Paul indicate Jesus was more than human.

Paul expressed no interest in the birth of Jesus and apparently considered his birth as normal as any other person's. In Galatians 4:4, he said, "God sent his son, born of a woman." In Romans 1:3, he said Jesus "was descended from David according to the flesh." Apparently, Paul believed Jesus was originally human but became divine only through his death and resurrection. Paul challenged his followers to be Christlike, but precisely what that meant is unclear. It likely had nothing to do with the activities of the earthly Jesus in whom Paul had no interest. If Jesus's earthly life was unimportant, why imitate him in our lives? Paul never quoted words from Jesus or praised him for his unique earthly ministry. He never suggests why he thought God chose this unimportant human Jesus to became the unique and crucial part of a new salvation process.

Paul's ethical teachings and directives for Christian action and nature eventually came close to Jesus's emphasis on love. Romans 13:8–10 contains verbiage similar to words of Jesus but not the spirit of Jesus when Paul speaks about the necessity to love your neighbor as yourself because that "fulfills the law." Elsewhere, especially in 1 Corinthians 13:13, when he said, "the greatest of these is love," he moves closer to the love Jesus preached and practiced. Paul admonishes, "Let love be genuine; hate what is evil, hold fast to what is good; love one another with mutual affection" (Romans 12:9–21). Paul's seven "fruits of the Spirit" (Galatians 5:22–23) are exemplary action that agrees with the spirit of love promoted and prompted by Jesus. These and other comments basically agree with Jesus's two directives for appropriate love, but Paul never admits any connection with Jesus or gives any credit to him.

For Paul, we love in order to fulfill the law, but the righteous will live by faith. That is a significant change in his understanding of God. We are able to love when we have been transformed through a process that includes belief in the death and resurrection of Jesus, baptism, and the infusion of the Holy Spirit. It seems proper ethical behavior and the ability to love come from something infused in us, seemingly by belief and baptism (injection process not fully disclosed). Since the capability to love appropriately is not in our original human nature, it must be infused in us from elsewhere. Furthermore, we love God because of what he did with and in Jesus and not because of who God is apart from Jesus. We must love God because God rearranged the salvation process for us by sending Jesus.

Contrary to Paul, followers of Jesus believe we love because love is a part of our nature. We love because we are loved and our nature is to love. Nothing from outside us changes our nature, but it may inform, encourage, and accompany us.

Paul, an erudite, pompous, and educated Jew, shunned the disciples and original followers of Jesus, most of whom were likely unlearned laymen. They and Paul probably had difficulty conversing with each other, let alone agreeing. The disciples probably wanted to talk about the life and teachings of the earthly Jesus they knew, but Paul wanted to talk only about the theological ramifications of the resurrected Jesus. If he did not already think they were uninformed, his brief time with a few disciples soon after his vision convinced him the disciples were radically different, totally incorrect in belief and behavior, that he had nothing in common with them and he wanted or needed absolutely nothing from them. The disciples' simple beliefs were insufficient for the sophisticated newcomer. It appears Paul's religion came primarily from his head, but the religion of Jesus and the disciples came first from their hearts. Three years after his vision, Paul reported a visit with Cephas and remained fifteen days but only saw Cephas and James, the Lord's brother (Galatians 1:18–19). Fourteen years later, he went to Jerusalem and visited James, Cephas, and John who were "acknowledged pillars" (Galatians 2:1–10). He and they agreed to go peacefully their separate ways, he to the Gentiles and they to the Jews. If correct, that information is extremely important because it affirms the Jesus movement was still very much alive and still very different from Paul long after Jesus's death.

Given his limited background and lack of knowledge or experience, how could the pompous Paul properly understand and then loudly proclaim the correct message of Jesus? He could not and did not. That type of self-selection and self-appointment is certainly unacceptable in our day. If someone was convicted of murder but declared he had a conversion experience the next day while in jail, we would not immediately appoint him pastor of a big church. Even if a janitor lived in a specifically named motel and daily cleaned a hospital operating room, we would not appoint him within a week as the chief surgeon in that hospital. Why should Paul be an exception to sound judgment? Why should he instantly become chief advocate and judge for all followers of Jesus? Why should he be allowed to redefine the nature of Jesus and what it means to be Christian? Why should his definition basically dominate Christianity to this day? The rational answer to all these questions is he should not. He appointed himself and got by with it. His selection was not democratic, not by committee, not by the disciples, and perhaps not by God.

We do not know the degree of conflict that existed between Paul and members of the Jesus movement, but reasonable conjecture indicates there had to be some. The followers of Jesus did not surrender. In fact, they may not have known of Paul's activities until long after his vision and perhaps paid little attention to him when they did know. They were accustomed to various religious proclamations. There may have been little public conflict between the two groups because their beliefs and behavior were so dissimilar that each group went their separate way. Apparently, the disciples disregarded or denied Paul's presuppositions and continued in their own way. That might provide a clue to why the Gospels say little about them, since the Gospels support the Pauline doctrine.

Ephesians 4:1 indicates Paul possibly called himself "a prisoner of the Lord," but he may be best described as "a prisoner of himself," or more correctly "a prisoner of Judaism." His prior Jewish beliefs that bound him so tightly were augmented by the person of Jesus and not by the professions of Jesus (a very important distinction). If one wanted to get right and stay right with God, Paul originally believed a person must periodically offer a living sacrifice for their sin because people and sacrifices were imperfect. By some process, the human Jesus became a perfect living sacrifice whose shed blood (his death) was powerful enough to negate the need for anything to shed its blood as a sacrifice. Jesus was important because he was "the Anointed" who was crucified and resurrected, and that qualified him to permanently fill Judaism's empty spaces into which Paul stuffed him. Paul's Jewish beliefs included a Messiah, a living sacrifice, shed blood, a ransom, and a high priest. These five fundamental elements were prominent in Paul's preaching. They were taken directly from the current Judaism he knew so well. Jesus's teachings and ministry had no importance for Paul.

We must ask, why was the unimportant human Jesus (according to Paul) selected for the all-important final, unblemished blood sacrifice? Why him and not an unknown homeless peasant or a famous rabbi? We get no answer from Paul, but there must be some connection to what Paul personally knew about Jesus or what he learned from persecuting the followers of Jesus. The human Jesus must have been more important to Paul than he revealed.

Paul became a most unusual person. He was a Jew who no longer believed like other Jews, and he was also a professing Christian who did not really believe the messages of Jesus. He did not fit in either group. In spite of all he reportedly did, he is not mentioned in any nonbiblical literature of his day. The great and famous historian Josephus made no mention of him. That may tell how unimportant Paul really was in the secular world, if not also in religious circles. Was Paul the primary and biggest supporter of Paul? From what we know, that would not be surprising. Was Paul less famous than we were led to believe, or was he known primarily within certain religious communities established under his direction? Would he have been important if he had not written his many letters that survived? Was Christendom very unwise when it closely followed Paul and not the human Jesus?

Was Paul successful because his gospel provided exact and sometimes easy answers to people who were confused over the death of Jesus? The timing, conditions, and his answers may have contributed greatly to his success. Within that particular environment, Paul's success was due primarily to his own tireless effort in large and small communities in different and distant places where Jesus's disciples had not visited. Did his brand of Christianity largely truncate the Jesus movement, or did the disciples just need a publicist?

## B. The Gospels Downplay Jesus's Humanity

Each Gospel declared Jesus was, at some point, more than an ordinary man, and each one sought to prove that point in their own purposeful way. Beginning with Mark and moving through Matthew, Luke, and John, we discover, for lack of a better term, somewhat of an upward movement for the nature of Jesus. There is some truth in saying, "The later the Gospel, the less human Jesus was." Generally speaking, Jesus was a preacher, teacher, and healer in Mark; a new Moses in Matthew; God's messenger to the Gentiles in Luke; and equal to God in John. It is significant to note that John's Gospel is perhaps the best loved, most quoted, and the longest, but also the last written. The elevation of Jesus's nature reflected in the Gospels likely began shortly after his death and continued over approximately eighty years between his crucifixion and the writing of John's Gospel. The attempts by the Gospel writers to justify their presupposition took various routes, but no Gospel strayed far from its basic presupposition that Jesus was more than human. If they gave tidbits of information about the life and ministry of the human Jesus (sometimes by accident), that never detracted from eventually declaring he was more than human. Because of the lapse of time between the life of Jesus and the writing of the Gospels, the authors obviously inherited the prevailing presupposition pertaining to Jesus's nature, the majority of which was probably from Paul's influence. They quickly move to the requirement that one must believe Jesus became divine and was resurrected. If Jesus was ever considered only human by the New Testament Gospels, that belief was soon left behind and ignored.

## C.  The Human Jesus and Us

Many professing Christians firmly believe they desperately need Jesus to have been something we are not. Many have been convinced they are less than good, in serious trouble, and can do nothing about it if left to their own strength. They have been repeatedly told, and they believe, they need an outside "savior" who will do for them what they cannot do for themselves. (Let Jesus do it.) They believe a divine Jesus fills that need and he can magically do something special for them that no human Jesus could do. They think if they "believe in him" (whatever that means) and believe he was divine, they are no longer responsible for what happens to them because they "gave everything to Jesus." Like the lizard whose color is determined by what it touches, their entrance into the kingdom is determined by whether or not they "hold on to Jesus." He (notice it is Jesus, not God) will give them "salvation," if only they believe in him. He swaps belief in him for their personal salvation, but he can do that only because he was divine and only if they believe in him.

Therefore, if one "grabs hold of Jesus" or believes in him, nothing else matters. In their minds, it is just that simple. In this hectic world, they want someone who will quickly free them from responsibilities for themselves and who quickly sets right all that is possibly wrong within them and their world, with little or no help from them. They hold on to their belief in a divine Jesus and proudly say, "He walks with me and talks with me. He chucks me on my chin. He pats me on my back and says how good I've been. All I need is my Jesus."

There are at least three huge flaws with this belief. The first is its false assumption about our human nature. The belief radically differs from how Jesus saw us and himself. He began with the affirmation that we are perfectly capable of obeying his two commandments without any divine infusion or intrusion. Our salvation is based on how and what we love, on how we live, not on someone's cruel and predestined death. Salvation comes to us just as God designed it in ancient times. We must do more than hold on to Jesus to have it.

The second flaw is Jesus never portrayed himself as the payment for our sin or as the promised Messiah. Any statement attributed to him that indicates he did either is extremely questionable. He pointed to God as the author of salvation. He believed his mission and message were directed to earthly people for earthly living so that they might enter the kingdom while they lived on earth. Any elevation of his person, message, or mission was added later by those who mistakenly declared he was something he never claimed for himself.

The third obvious and alarming thing about this belief is that it is, or easily can be, selfish. There is no place in this approach where we are encouraged or required to focus on God and neighbor. Everything seems to be about me, done for me, on my behalf and my getting to heaven. No one denies that personal salvation is very important, but by definition and the dictates of Jesus, "salvation for me" must never be the most important goal if we expect to enter God's kingdom. Concern for self is important, but salvation will likely never come to anyone who is concerned only for self or who always puts self first. Jesus did not say, "You shall love yourself with all you have and are." The two commandments proclaimed by Jesus always put God first and then put the rest of us at least second, if not tied for third. My salvation partially depends on how well I help others whom I must love as myself, not on expecting a divine Jesus to manage the process for me.

The false foundation underneath the belief that Jesus was more than human must be exposed and expunged. Jesus was always human. He was not radically different from us in mind, body, or ability. (How refreshing, or maybe frightening.) Since Jesus was like us, we cannot hide behind him until a later day or expect special favors from him, now or later. His message was for this life and this world. He was not and is not the mediator between God and us, who tries to broker some deal on our behalf that lessens our present guilt or future punishment. Our sin is between each of us and God. Jesus does not presently run interference between us and God or provide special support when we are in trouble or in prayer. He provides no special privileges based on ritual or work. No matter how hard we or others may try, he will not be responsible for our failures or successes, nor for our being either in or out of the kingdom. We stand alone, all alone, before God, just like Jesus did.

Hearing that our getting right and remaining right with God requires us to be and act like Jesus may frighten us, or it may set us free! How frightening that truth is for those who expected him to save us if we just ask or believe. How delightful that is for those to whom this provides believable hope and helpful information. Jesus showed us and told us how to live. It helps when we realize there is nothing wrong with being human because God ordained our humanness. We are not and have never been on the scrap pile of creation, regardless of who proclaimed the total depravity of humanity or that humanity's evil forced God to redesign the means by which we can avoid damnation. Jesus did not come to fix an ingrained human flaw. We have no permanent deformity caused by evil people who lived long ago. No one has or has ever had a spiritual flaw that cannot be fixed with appropriate love (no unpardonable sin). We can no longer use our humanness as an excuse for inappropriate behavior, words, or spirit. We now know we are and will continue to be human, no more and no less, but that does not disqualify us from participating in the kingdom.

The human Jesus does not let us off the hook but instead demands more of us. That is what we do not want to hear. We would rather not hear that entrance into the kingdom is strictly up to us. Having been wooed by love, we must choose to love appropriately if we expect to enter. In order to enter and participate, our love must be both a noun and a verb, patterned after the love of God and Jesus. If we choose to participate in the kingdom, we must get serious about who, what, and how we really love and how we live. There is no secret or sacred formula and no password that automatically opens the door to the kingdom. We cannot just hang on to Jesus's coattail by saying "I believe in him" and be magically transported into the kingdom of God. Jesus declared the responsibility is now squarely on us. There is no other way. If I believe Jesus, if I desire to enter the kingdom, I must purposefully do my best to always love appropriately. His message never offered a free ride to heaven, pie in the sky by and by, or a "get out of hell free" card. He taught and showed us how to daily participate in the kingdom of God, how to get out of jail from religious ignorance and false doctrines. He purposely embodied the spirit of holiness and wholeness, and so must we. Jesus was human in every way, but we almost wish he had not been.

Recognition of and emphasis on Jesus's humanness does not destroy his importance to us but actually puts his mission and message right where we live and right where it is needed. There was no magic in his person, words, or actions. They deal with life, this life, our life, not an afterlife. They are for us just as we naturally are, in our humanness, here and now, in our world. Our nature needed no patch or repurchase, but we need a real person to remind us the truth about God and us. A divine Jesus, who would not be a real person, could not do that. Jesus did not change God's ancient law, but he did tell and show us how to change our lives by following two very important directives.

The human Jesus demonstrated how we can live with our humanness without fear of it. He offered a few instructions on how to do that, based on appropriate love for God, neighbor, and self. He divided that requirement into smaller pieces with pithy sayings and probing parables that dealt with common human experiences and conditions. His entire ministry focused strictly on appropriate love, expressed in simple teachings and examples. We can no longer use our humanness as an excuse for our inability and failure to pattern our life after Jesus. For him, times were tough and neighbors were naughty, but he had no assistance beyond what is also available to us. Our humanness is permanent. We have no choice other than to live with it. We need not fear it, if we believe Jesus and act like it.

Jesus disturbed us by declaring and demonstrating there is no major difference between the sacred and the secular because all of life is sacred and every action reflects the object of one's love. Jesus's ethical and religious teachings dovetail into doable guides for daily living. He makes no distinctions between the requirements for us during lively Saturday night frivolity and the somber Sunday morning church service. Our behavior in either place reflects our god, and we have difficult hiding what it is. That truth was expressed by a simple statement in the farming community of my youth. It said, "You can tell a man's religion by the way he treats his mule." (We all plowed with mules.) This simple saying illustrates the unavoidable connection of the secular and the sacred. You cannot be religious for just one hour on Sunday or only in one area of your daily life.

The adamant pronouncement that Jesus was divine (along with all that it encompasses) may be the primary reason various people no longer attend church. Without doubt, it is one major factor for why many unchurched people never participate or join. The lack of attendance does not necessarily mean people have grown less religious. The truth is that, because of our nature, people are hungry for religious truth. Intellect and insight are rightfully washing over and eroding the erroneous foundation upon which Christianity was built. Too frequently, nothing valid is offered in its place. The argument for inerrancy of scripture, a divine Jesus, disregard for facts, accepting the symbolic as the actual, suggesting natural laws can be easily suspended, thinking Jesus and God are equal, and more no longer elicit a positive response from many people, especially the younger and educated generation. Too frequently, the Christian community offers the same erroneous message as previously offered and has no clue why their congregation grows smaller.

Recognition of Jesus's humanity is a key to enhance the church's present growth and mission. Make no mistake—people long to hear what Jesus really said and how it relates to them where they are. They want to hear something believable about God and how to respond appropriately. If we want Christianity to be relevant, if we want people to get right and stay right with God, congregations must make the two commandments of the human Jesus their primary point of emphasis and action. Those who profess to be religious or spiritual but do not believe in the divinity of Jesus or attend church services may not be as far from the kingdom as they or others think. They may even be closer than some who pronounce them far away. The message and ministry of the human Jesus is as relevant today as he was during his lifetime.

# CHAPTER 11

# MIRACLES

Since Jesus was fully human, we must give further thought to the miracles he reportedly performed. They obviously received considerable emphasis in the Gospels. Other presuppositions determine our interpretation of miracles. Controversy quickly comes among professing Christians when someone questions the authenticity of any miracle reported in the Bible. Those who believe in literal interpretation and inerrancy will always accept them as described and without question. Those who interpret the Bible differently will have serious questions about the reported miracles.

When speaking of Jesus's miracles, our first major task is deciding what can be correctly called a miracle by him. Are we referring to Jesus breaking and suspending a divine law, or are we speaking of something that was just extremely unusual, very different, and never done before? Are we speaking of unexpected and unusual things or magical acts?

The label "miracle" is often attached to whatever was very unusual, totally unexpected, never seen before, or beyond the ordinary, without necessarily assuming any divine intervention. We may have called something miraculous, but we really did not mean God did it or that he was involved in any extraordinary way. We definitely did not mean a divine law was broken. We only meant we did not understand it and it was spectacular, unusual, unexpected, or beyond our present understanding. We also understand why the less intellectual acumen available, the greater the likelihood to label some unfamiliar or unexpected event a miracle. Likewise, those more religiously inclined would be more likely to affirm divine intervention. Only with this broad definition of "miracle" can Jesus be correctly called a miracle worker.

The true miracles of the human Jesus are not identified as such in the scriptures. In the broader sense of the word, the greater miracles of Jesus are in the shadows of what the Gospels report. Jesus was a miracle, because of his unorthodox, unexpected, and peasant-centered ministry. His expressed care and compassion, teachings, and inclusiveness for the marginalized led to changes that can only be described as miraculous (unexpected, most unusual, magnificent, and life-changing), especially by those who experienced them. These were miracles created by love that provided specifically for those in need. Those acts of kindness and mercy were not officially considered miracles by Gospel writers or by most present-day professing Christians. Given the true meaning of miracle, they definitely qualify.

There are people who firmly believe Jesus actually broke or suspended universal laws. They reason that if he was divine, he could do anything he wished without harm to anyone or anything. We have no assurance that the things called miracles during Jesus's ministry were identical to the things given that label in the Gospels. Therefore, we must ponder why someone recorded these events and called them miracles long after they reportedly happened. Also, words in the Gospels reflect a different understanding of the world. If you believe God controls everything, as many of them proclaimed, then everything you do not understand is naturally explained as an act of God or a miracle. If God controlled everything, why did they not affirm the same for the things they understood? Given that belief and the conditions around Jesus, many misunderstood occurrences and events were naturally called miracles. When contemplating the reported miracles in the Bible, we must remember they are words from human writers from vastly different times and places.

We will never resolve all the different opinions about miracles held by professing Christians, but a careful consideration of at least seven major points should be helpful for those willing to think. First, during the time of Jesus, much that happened, especially if not understood, was called a miracle and automatically attributed to divine initiative. Therefore, since many believed God controlled everything, numerous common events and occurrences were automatically given that explanation, even though no divine rule had been altered in any way. The magnitude of the event or deed was not necessarily a factor. Great or small, if it was unusual, unexpected, not understood, favorably affected someone or something, and had never been seen before, it was often considered a miracle, especially by the very religious, marginalized, and uninformed. We can easily fail to fully understand the tremendous impact Jesus had among those who had so little, knew so little, and could do so little about their conditions. Conditions for many of the marginalized were likely far worse than modern ghettoes, slums, and areas where the homeless now gather. For any poor, despondent, and downtrodden person in those conditions or places, any unusual and unexpected act of kindness and compassion provided by anyone, and especially for a total stranger, was nothing short of a miracle. Given who the recipients were and where they were, they had never expected anyone to act like Jesus, and they certainly had never seen anyone act as he did. To them, Jesus's presence, compassion, and generosity were miracles. Even though they firmly believed they had witnessed a miracle, Jesus broke no natural law by demonstrating love.

Second, since Jesus was a Jew, he had been taught that any capable person should provide help and healing when possible. In Jewish families, everyone was expected to assist others who were sick or in need by using simple techniques, learned during early family and religious training. In addition to a healthy soul, a healthy body was considered very important. Family members were trained to use readily available items, such as herbs, tree bark, leaves, roots, clay, spit, financial resources, personal attention, and any other available item to assist the restoration process. (Recall my definition of love.) Jesus was certainly no stranger to the art and practice of healing minor ills and injuries. As far as I know, no one has ever mentioned the possibility that during Jesus's years of unknown adult activity, he may have received special training in the art of healing and helping the sick. Family tradition, further training, and radical love help explain the unexpected actions of Jesus.

It appears Jesus defied the norm and spent considerable time with the peasant population, including those sick in body and mind. One of the most important miracles of Jesus was his deliberate declaration and demonstration that sick people were fully acceptable in society, rather than believing they were untouchables because God had imposed an affliction on them because of some sin. Jesus excluded no one from his circle of love and help. Given the probable locations and situations confronting Jesus, healing aids would have been very scarce, which necessitated using simple things to which he had access. We do not know everything Jesus used in his healing ministry, but some of them were mind-boggling to receivers. It is highly possible that the compassionate Jesus secured meager supplies in advance and carried them to places of special need. A vast majority of those he assisted probably had little or no knowledge about, no experiences with, and no access to folk remedies and simple healing aids. Those confined to the slums had absolutely no other place or persons from which to seek help and healing, so they flocked to him when they had a chance. Jesus's genuine concern for those in need, including women, was normal for him but a miracle to them. People declared he performed miracles, but that does not mean a divine law was broken. Seeing a miracles may depend on who and where you are.

Given Jesus's spirit and behavior, we can easily understand why, in the opinion of his patients and peers, he became widely known as a healer or a miracle man. He apparently had the knowledge, ability, eagerness, and willingness to facilitate healing in people with various maladies, but it is doubtful he healed everyone in need. There is no record of another person who genuinely cared for the downtrodden as he did or who had a similar reputation. The practice of including everyone in his community of caring and sharing may be the key to his prominence in life and death. He simply made good things, totally unexpected things, happen by using what he considered ordinary things to accomplish very important results, without breaking a natural law. His healing deeds, like other events, were eventually embellished.

Third, we are unsure when the stories of miracles developed. Because of lack of understanding and the changes Jesus wrought, many of them developed during his ministry to the marginalized. I doubt any miracle story came from members of the Jesus movement because they understood his ministry. It appears some miracle stories were mislabeled, embellished, or created by Gospel writers. Other reports were probably created in the post-crucifixion community to support the resurrection theory and to prove the declared divinity of Jesus. We do not know which ones, if any, were developed by the post-crucifixion community or the Gospel writers. Regardless of their sources, Gospel writers primarily used them to promote a point and not necessarily to tell the truth. Perhaps they and their sources told miracle stories as parables or allegories to symbolically proclaim what Jesus could do for those of faith. Many miracle stories, when interpreted, pointed to the power of faith in Jesus. When examined, some miracles stories that indicate Jesus defied natural laws were intended as encouragement to faithfully follow Jesus. Little concern was given to whether they were factual or not.

Fourth, the New Testament miracle stories were often told to convey the authors' initial predetermined presupposition that Jesus was the Messiah sent from God. Unusual stories, created or actual, always got attention. They deliberately used allegorical miracles or signs by Jesus as proof of God's power working in and through him and as proof of who he was. The authors were adept at manufacturing, adjusting, and using their stories when and where they were best suited to prove their presupposition. Our awareness of their manipulation diminishes the claim made by the miracle stories and casts doubt on their authenticity.

Fifth, reported miracles were not new to Jesus's peers or the Gospel writers. Secular stories of miracles performed by kings, gods, goddesses, and others were quite common. Most hearers knew the stories were not factual and were designed to signify that someone possessed attributes above the ordinary. Caesar was said to be divine, and Octavian was called "son of god," but people knew those titles were only accolades. Secular literature, by Homer and others, told about the miracles of the gods and goddesses in hero stories. The elevated attributes simply bestowed honor upon a person, nothing more. We cannot overemphasize the fact that Jesus was an extraordinary individual, the likes of whom his associates had never seen. For them, ordinary words failed to describe such a person or his actions. Therefore, in keeping with the custom of their time, it was natural that the highest known attributes and accolades were employed to describe Jesus and his accomplishments. Over time, those ascribed attributes were easily elevated, and Jesus was later labeled as divine or having divine qualities. In the minds of many, Jesus had to be "the miracle man" who was similar to but above secular heroes.

Sixth, miracles attributed to Jesus may have had an application or implication to some secondary point beyond the storyline. There were often two points of a story. Some authors embedded a significant point in a story that was more important than the actual storyline, as in a parable. Matthew provides several significant parables and in 13:34 reports, "Without a parable, he told them nothing." Readers and hearers discovered the secondary point only after pondering the story and looking for the meaning. Original hearers were perhaps much smarter than we might imagine in recognizing what was fact and what was intended to conceal or reveal a point. They knew the difference between the possible and the preposterous. Upon hearing the latter, they immediately knew it was time to look for the hidden meaning.

Seventh, many of the reported miracles suspended, broke, or defied the dependable laws of God as we know them. However, God has never changed the natural order or rules that govern all his creation. Whatever the miracles of Jesus were, they did not and could not defy the fixed laws of the universe. Jesus no doubt did unexpected and unusual things that may be properly called miracles, but not the kind that disregard divine decrees.

The seven above points reflect serious evaluations of the miracle stories connected to Jesus. They suggest possibilities for how the miracle stories developed and from where they came. They may be the combined product of professions from the marginalized, the post-crucifixion community, Gospel writers, and others. The seven points do not suggest God's actions are always understood by us, but they offer reasons Jesus did not break God's established laws. If he had done that, he would have created chaos. Jesus was no magician. He may have done things witnesses had never seen before or that they considered impossible, but that does not mean he broke God's natural laws. It meant people either did not understand it or expect it or were deeply impressed by it. If Jesus was considered the miracle worker, the label tells more about the ones who labeled him than it tells about him. Anyone, then or now, who proclaims Jesus performed miracles that altered or suspended God's laws has failed to understand God's nature, the ministry of Jesus, the broader meaning of *miracle,* the people to whom Jesus ministered, and the pathetic conditions confronting him.

# CHAPTER 12

# RANSOM

An in-depth study of the "ransom theory" is beyond my intention. However, I am well aware that numerous professing Christians fervently believe in order for humanity to be saved, a ransom had to be paid to someone to compensate for humanity's flawed nature and consequent misdeeds. Exactly what must be paid, why, how much, and to whom is never clearly or consistently stated. Inability to provide those specifics makes the pronouncement more problematic. The theory is anchored in Judaism and not Jesus. It resulted from Paul's attempt to connect his beloved Judaism to Jesus and maintain his connection to both.

Like other proclamations, some believers base the necessity for a ransom on a literal interpretation of certain passages from the Bible. They believe it was absolutely necessary for someone to be paid something by someone so that humanity might be released from something! They never question just why a ransom is required and how it works. From their perspective and presuppositions, that is the reason God sent Jesus, why Jesus had to be other than human and had to be crucified. They eagerly quote and embellish Paul: "For you were bought with a price" (1 Corinthians 6:20).

The announced need for ransom raises several issues that deserve serious thought. It is interesting that some people who promote the necessity for a ransom often renounce the validity of the Old Testament but base the necessity for ransom on passages in it and on Jewish beliefs proclaimed by Paul. I seriously doubt Jesus ever used the term and definitely never in reference to himself.

To whom must a ransom be paid, for what, and what must it be? The answers to those questions have not been fully identified or clarified. Any emphasis on the necessity for humanity to be ransomed sounds as if people believe there is another divine and powerful being in serious competition with God, who is either equal to God or possibly able to overpower him and us unless some ransom gets paid. Humanity is not and never was in danger of being repossessed. There is no devil or other divine being in competition with God for ultimate control. That idea must be firmly denied if there is only one God who created and controls the universe. A God who lost control or can lose control of his creation does not sound like a God worthy of trust and worship. Likewise, if a ransom must be paid to God, did God eventually pay it to himself?

Some people believe our nature, at some point, was or became permanently flawed and humanity could do nothing to correct it. There was a cost or a price for restoration. For that reason, they believe we must have divine help to restore it. For them, that was the necessity for a one-of-a-kind ransom payment, the reason God sent Jesus, why Jesus had to be different from us, and why he had to be crucified—but based on what and by whom? If Jesus was divine, then it seems God killed a portion of himself through a predestined crucifixion. The argument for a predestined death to pay a ransom comes close to making God a cruel murderer, or did he just play games with us? There are other convoluted beliefs designed to cover God's cruelty, but they never really succeed. A dozen deaths of devout people can ransom no one and do not necessarily change anyone else. Our salvation depends on obedience to the logical, practical, and doable directions of Jesus, not on his preordained and cruel crucifixion that paid our debt to someone.

The ransom theory may have developed as an explanation for why Jesus died. Given the situations and conditions surrounding

Jesus, it is very likely serious-minded people repeatedly raised that question. The significance of that question and the answer given does not guarantee a correct answer, even though it apparently satisfied many people, then and now. The theory appears to have been greatly affected by Jewish beliefs and Pauline doctrines.

The ransom theory basically disregards, if not nullifies, the significance of the life and teachings of the earthly Jesus, including those based on the core of ancient Hebrew religion. The theory leans heavily toward legalism in Judaism and disregards appropriate love emphasized by Jesus. The simplicity and profundity of Jesus's primary directions for appropriate love of God, neighbor, and self gets lost in the convoluted ransom theory. Jesus never spoke of corrupt human nature that needed or could use anything other than appropriate love. When asked how to get right and stay right with God, Jesus said nothing about a required ransom, and he never considered he was one. Are we going to believe Jesus or another?

Since Jesus had no use for blood sacrifices and never mentioned a ransom for himself or anyone, apparently ransom was unnecessary and also impossible. However, long before, during, and after the time when Jesus lived, Jews apparently considered a blood sacrifice was somewhat of a ransom, a price paid for deliverance from and forgiveness of their sin. In Judaism, if the sacrificed animal blood offered by a person paid for their sin, and if, for Paul, the divine blood of Jesus, the anointed one, was offered by God for humanity's sin, the total debt was paid, and nothing else was needed. Once again, this indicates how dependent Paul was on Jewish beliefs that determine his new religion. Even though Paul's inherited beliefs may have advocated the practice of sacrificing live animals, Jesus must have been against all blood sacrifices, because he never mentions their efficacy or necessity and, as far as we know, he never participates in them during his ministry. It seems Jesus did not accept any part of the ransom theory, but it was tremendously important for Paul.

We have no idea when Jesus renounced the necessity for a ransom or blood sacrifices. Even though his parents reportedly made a required sacrifice following his birth, we have no record of what Jesus did in regard to sacrifices during his hidden years. Since the parents made that sacrifice, and since they apparently were devout Jews, it seems they would have continued to make them. Surely Jesus participated with the family during his youth, if not beyond. Was there something about life and religion in his poor family that led Jesus to question and later renounce blood sacrifices, if not all sacrifices? Were those hidden years a time of serious contemplation and eventual denial of some Jewish presupposition he had been taught? Assuming he had been originally taught basic Jewish doctrines, it becomes far more significant that blood sacrifices and ransoms were totally foreign to everything he later did and said. That may be a clue to why Paul disliked the earthly Jesus. Did Jesus wrestle for days or years in search of truth about and proper responses to beliefs within the Judaism of his day? Was his time of serious searching best described as his "time in the wilderness" or his "dark days of doubt and discovery"? Were there several "wilderness experiences" before and during his ministry? I suspect that describes the process Jesus went through in order to resolve several issues, especially when he made the radical declaration that the sacrifice of living animals was null and void as a means of salvation. The Gospel writers did not tell the story that way, but that makes more sense, especially since he was human.

It seems none of the original members of the "the Way" believed Jesus was a ransom, and they did not create the theory. The practical, profound, doable, and ancient directives of Jesus had no need or room for such a belief. There is no way to deduce a ransom theory from what Jesus said and did. In order to promote that theory, you have to begin elsewhere. Someone did, perhaps shortly after Jesus's death. We do not know all the particulars, but we do know there was one dominant voice, perhaps the loudest religious voice heard in the gap of time between Jesus's death and the formation of the Gospels. That voice and person was none other than Paul, the one who discovered through a vision the final part of what he needed to perfect his Judaism. He proclaimed to his hearers, "You were ransomed with a price" (1 Corinthians 6:21).

Did Paul develop this idea, or did he have help from others who knew or knew about Jesus? In 1 Corinthians 15:3–4, he indicates others informed him that "Christ died for our sins in accordance with the scriptures." Is that a possible contradiction to saying no one assisted him with his beliefs about Jesus? Paul had help in promoting the ransom theory. We do not know the effect of that idea during the early days or months after Jesus's death. We do know that some form of the ransom theory has traveled for two thousand years down the highway of human history. It presently lives among us. A large percentage of professing Christians fully affirm their belief that humanity needed a ransom, and Jesus was it.

The lack of thinking, learning, and logic are extremely obvious in the ransom theory. It supports the Judaism that Jesus firmly rejected. It offers nothing about the goodness of God and his forgiveness. It provides no recognition of the message and ministry of Jesus. It points specifically to Pauline theology. I firmly believe living by the two great commandments from Jesus leaves no room and no need for a ransom. Anything presently used to support that theory is not from Jesus.

# CHAPTER 13

# CRUCIFIXION

We know extremely little about the crucifixion of Jesus. Was he conveniently crucified during a seasonal celebration, or did someone manufacture this story for various reasons and from various tidbits of tradition and information? Given the magnitude of this event, it is extremely strange that we do not know its date, exact location, or specific circumstances. That alone should be a caution for us. Lack of information, coupled with misinformation and vivid imagination, rob us of simple truths about it. Because of the late compositions of the Gospels, along with their specific purpose and inadequate information, we have extremely little or no data from which to draw any firm conclusions, other than Jesus met a cruel and unnecessary death at an unknown time and place and for unknown reasons. However, because of belief in the ransom theory, some would vehemently argue against the unnecessary death.

We do not know what specific cause or excuse precipitated Jesus's apprehension and the punishment administered. We have no records of him having been officially warned by anyone to "cease and desist or else!" There were a few reported conflicts but no formal or final warning. There may have been times of serious conflicts about which we have not heard. There had to be a driving force behind the utter dislike expressed against Jesus and his ministry, perhaps by both the civil and religious authorities. I suspect the crucifixion was not the expression of a sudden and unexpected dislike for Jesus, but rather he had been a continuous *burr under their saddle* by what he did and said. He may not have been as humble or docile as the Gospels suggest.

The Gospels indicate greater danger arose late in Jesus's ministry and in Jerusalem. I doubt the crucifixion slipped up on Jesus and the disciples; nor did they believe it was predestined. If he was sternly warned more than once, each additional warning was accompanied by fear of an arrest and possible crucifixion. That was how things were, and Jesus knew it. Even if forcefully warned, Jesus did not alter his lifestyle or teachings. Based on hints offered, Jesus may have been arrested more than once and may have been well known to the authorities as a recurring troublemaker. If that is true, we can better understand the reason for his final arrest and subsequent crucifixion and for the response of the disciples following Jesus's apprehension. Perhaps, based on their conversations with Jesus about what they should do if Jesus was suddenly apprehended, the disciples made a wise choice immediately following his arrest. They knew there would definitely be no request for a character witness at his trial, and there was no need to join Jesus in a crucifixion. They all knew they could not help him and rightfully feared for themselves. They hid, but it is unreasonable to think they all hid in one place.

The stories of Jesus's trials and crucifixion appear contrived and improbable. Our transcript of the trial provides no real justification for a crucifixion, but apparently little was needed. Given the conditions surrounding the trial, no supporters of Jesus were present, and if they were and if identified, they would have also been in danger. Because of the severe cruelty of a regular Roman crucifixion, it is very doubtful any family members witnessed the trial or crucifixion. No concerned person or close associate could safely follow close behind the prisoner (the reason for Peter's denial). Therefore, no correct information on the specific treatment of the prisoner would be available. Likewise, family and friends were not allowed to observe from a distance when a person was physically hung on a cross. No family member or friend likely knew exactly where or when the killing occurred, where the corpse actually was, or who was near him. Persons who showed special attention to the event or who asked for favors regarding a candidate for execution were often also arrested and crucified along with them. Likewise, the corpse was not given to anyone, even if a disciple or family member requested it through someone in authority. No wonder the disciples disappeared.

The existing reports about the crucifixion have facts, fiction, and faith entwined to the degree that it is impossible for us to separate them. Since Jesus's crucifixion was likely little different from a host of others that regularly occurred under Roman rule, it seems safe to draw some specific conclusions. All evidence indicates Jesus was subjected to a horrible death, the likes of which is hard for us to imagine. Given the Roman soldiers' delight in cruelty, everyone apprehended probably received the worst they could give. To be more specific about their treatment of Jesus is unwise because there were no reputable witnesses. We must remember that Gospel writers often used Old Testament words and phrases as if they were original for events they described, and the crucifixion story is no exception. If anyone had witnessed any portion of another crucifixion, they knew the gory details. Given these facts about a crucifixion, any specific information provided in the Gospels is questionable.

The trial, crucifixion, and their aftermath were undoubtedly a gigantic disruption to those who had expected the continuation of Jesus's earthly ministry. They knew of no predetermined time, place, or purpose for Jesus to die. There is no doubt his followers, whose number and identity remain unknown, were devastated by his sudden death but perhaps not totally surprised. If Jesus disrupted the status quo to a significant degree, they knew the price for such behavior. They did not live in a vacuum.

Strange, different, and unusual stories about the crucifixion probably arose at different times and places and for different reasons, primarily because no one other than a few of the cruel Roman soldiers witnessed the slaughter. Those who crucified Jesus probably had no idea he was any different from all the others they crucified during a normal day's work. Likewise, they and others were not informed of the exact time of his death by a heavenly disruption. It is very doubtful soldiers gave any reports about Jesus's crucifixion or death. Stories, true or imagined, pertaining to Jesus's crucifixion events likely developed in an effort to answer questions asked much later. Certain crucifixion stories probably developed after the resurrection stories and were designed to make the reported resurrection stories more believable (very important). The reported resurrection became the primary framework upon which the major beliefs about Jesus were later built. Since the resurrection became the primary emphasis, stories pertaining to the crucifixion were emphasized, altered, and invented to support it.

If we are confused, in what state of mind do you think the disciples were during and after the mock trial and cruel crucifixion, especially if they did not actually witness either? Were they able to sneak a peek from time to time, as Peter attempted? What gruesome reports did they hear? We have no front-page pictorials from a special edition of the *Jerusalem Gazette* that inform us of the event. If there had been such a possible source, it probably would not have even mentioned what was considered a routine crucifixion or its effect on the victim's close followers. This crucifixion was just an ordinary event on an ordinary day for most people, since that was the common treatment for criminals. However, it was far different for the disciples.

Did Jesus instruct his disciples on how to respond if he were killed? Some of those recorded questions in the Gospels from Jesus to the disciples, or the disciples to Jesus, may be hints of such discussions on many other unrecorded occasions and subjects. Jesus's question to the disciples in Mark 8:29, "But who do you say I am?" could easily be a prelude to and part of that type of discussion. John 6:60–68 and the entire content of chapters 14 through 17 sound as if they were discussions for the disciples' benefit, but they were most likely concocted by John. Were the disciples as dense as a doorknob and just didn't get it? Were the disciples' stated responses the product of someone's imagination and creation? The answers are unknown, but given the social level of some disciples and the diversity of those who followed Jesus, some of them probably misunderstood what

Jesus meant—but certainly not all of them every time he spoke. The Gospels' reported announcements Jesus made to the disciples about his impending and predetermined death and resurrection are certainly later creations, either by the authors or by someone in agreement with them.

The crucifixion was not predestined. It was not necessary. It occurred not from the design of God but from the desires of some evil people. Any argument that it was predestined for a specific purpose, to occur at a specific time and place and according to a designed format is based on assumptions far removed from the nature of God, the teachings of Jesus, valid presuppositions, and common sense. A predetermined crucifixion is only a part of a larger collection of erroneous presuppositions. Any argument for its necessity arises out of Jewish doctrines and overlooks God's original salvation process proclaimed in the teachings of Jesus. The argument that a crucifixion was necessary is one more effort to disregard, diminish, or deny Jesus's stated sufficiency for getting right and staying right with God.

# CHAPTER 14

# RESURRECTION

Numerous professing Christians believe Jesus's physical body was resurrected. Since they have heard it proclaimed for many years, they have no reason to believe otherwise and consider it sinful if others disagree with them. Many eagerly anticipate the same for themselves, while forcefully and frequently proclaiming that inherited presupposition which was implanted long ago in their box. Many of them, even entire denominations, make the belief in Jesus's bodily resurrection the litmus test for being called a Christian. However, some of us who also call ourselves Christian believe otherwise. We believe there was no resurrection of Jesus's physical body, and there will be no bodily resurrection of our own.

We do not know if the subject of resurrection ever became an important concern for Jesus or his immediate followers before, during, or after his death. Neither the idea nor the term, whatever it meant at that time, was created by them. Long before Jesus and Judaism, ordinary people had undoubtedly discussed, "What happens to us after this life?" Numerous answers were offered by concerned people ever since the first search for the indescribable something. Specific ideas about different forms of resurrection offered today will probably identify the major religious group to which one belongs. The Judeo-Christian concept about a possible future life is only one idea among many. Most, if not all religions of the world are predicated on the presence of an indescribable something being "out there," on how we relate to it in this life and its effect on us beyond death. Regardless of the multitude of answers, many people expect personal continuation of life in some form, including reincarnation, resurrection, the continuation of an undying spirit, and others.

Biblical records remind us that the subject of resurrection was definitely not a new concern after Jesus's death. It is normal for a person to ponder the possibilities beyond this life, and they have done so for many, many years. They had questions concerning divine rewards for good behavior and punishment for the opposite. Long before the time of Jesus, there was great concern about justice for those who had no justice while they lived, including the peasants, the marginalized and all who suffered the misfortune of ruthless rule over them. If a person believed God controlled everything and always righted the wrongs, he naturally asked how, when, where, and for whom does this apply? Given the conditions under which they lived, resurrection in some manner was the only answer that made sense for many of them and gave them hope. If most everyone who knew or followed Jesus believed God controlled everything, and if they believed Jesus was seriously wronged in this life, it is easy to understand why they thought one possibility for him was resurrection in some form.

Desperate people who seriously need some acceptable answers for unanswerable questions are more inclined to reach or accept conclusions that partially satisfy. If an answer makes someone feel good, or just less bad, he or she is less likely to question it. Words from Josephus, the great historian, address this point. He wrote, "When humans suffer, they are readily persuaded; but when the con artist depicts release from potential affliction, those suffering give themselves up entirely to hope" (*Jewish Wars*, 6.285–87). Some people will always think any proposed belief that provides a bit of relief is better than no relief, better than saying "I don't know," and much easier than personal research.

We do not know what the disciples and other close followers of Jesus believed about resurrection in general and for Jesus in particular. There are strong clues the disciples believed Jesus's spirit continued to exist among them without a bodily resurrection. The Jesus movement in the scattered communities likely agreed with the disciples that Jesus's body died but his spirit remained among them. Some people speak of a spiritual resurrection instead of a physical one. Technically speaking, that was no spiritual resurrection for Jesus, since his spirit did not die.

Inquiring minds must ask probing questions about the development of the resurrection stories proclaimed in the Gospels and by Paul. Recall the vital issues about dates, authenticity, preconceived purpose, and others, especially within the Gospels and Acts. From where did belief in the bodily resurrection of Jesus come? When? Why? If there was a bodily resurrection of Jesus, it would have been dramatic news, so why did it not radically reverberate throughout the local area and the entire region when it happened? Did specific stories about Jesus's resurrection exist prior to Paul's vision? If most Pharisees believed in resurrection, Paul probably held that basic belief prior to his vision. Paul obviously believed in the significance of Jesus's death and resurrection, but did he believe only in a spiritual resurrection, as some scholars now believe? I find that difficult to accept because, within the context of a long passage about resurrection, Paul plainly states, "If there is no resurrection of the dead, then Christ has not been raised; and if Christ has not been raised, then our proclamation has been in vain and your faith has been in vain" (1 Corinthians 15:13–14). That seems to say he believes correct theology depends exclusively on a bodily resurrection. Unless I am very mistaken, Paul repeatedly affirms that belief to different people and in different places.

Since all Gospel reports about the resurrection came long after the events, how dependable are they? On what date did this most unusual event happen? Matthew's record of events at the tomb borders on ridiculous. The very dissimilar stories and limited number of those who reportedly saw the resurrected Jesus cast further doubt on the validity of the reported events. Reports indicate only a small number of people initially knew about Jesus's resurrection. The women who went to anoint Jesus's body, whomever they were, are the ones who first became aware of a resurrection, having been first informed by an angel. Did they tell "no one" (Mark 16:8), two disciples (John 20:2), "the disciples" (Matthew 28:8), or "the eleven and all the rest" (Luke 24:9)? Other than Mary Magdalene, no one saw the resurrected Jesus at the tomb and only in John's Gospel, the last one written. Two other people reportedly saw Jesus shortly after they left the tomb, while on their way to tell the disciples. A few others saw an empty tomb, and angels told them what happened to Jesus. Later in the day, two people, not from the eleven disciples, were some distance away from the tomb and reported contact with the resurrected Jesus.

According to the Gospels, no disciple saw Jesus until after others had seen him. How strange. Few people initially saw a resurrected Jesus, and few others immediately received that information. The source of information (angels), the limited number who saw Jesus, and the small number informed about his physical resurrection raise serious concerns about these reports. If Jesus's bodily resurrection was extremely significant, why was his immediate appearance so secretive? Why was he first seen, with one exception, by only a few close unnamed associates, none of whom was from the inner circle of disciples? Reports of angels on guard prove nothing and are difficult to believe. At what level of followers was the cutoff point for those allowed to immediately see the resurrected Jesus? Why were not all of the close followers allowed to see him immediately? If they were previously and repeatedly informed that a resurrection would occur, why were they totally surprised, and why were they not all gathered for its occurrence? Why was his mother shocked? This is a strange story.

As proof of resurrection, it would have been most appropriate for Jesus to appear at a religious gathering and to the authorities. Likewise, if a walking corpse of a well-known person from an empty tomb appeared and was recognized, that would have been the talk of the town. Regardless to whom he appeared, they could not keep a secret or limit it to those who had a need to know.

There is also the matter of an empty tomb, supposedly caused by a resurrection. No person witnessed the reported resurrection event? It is indeed strange that at the tomb, several inquirers were told what had happened by an angel. According to the story, after all that had transpired, no one other than two disciples and a few women got excited about the empty tomb of Jesus, which was reportedly occupied for only two nights and one day. A recently occupied but now empty tomb of a known hero with a large stone rolled away from its entrance would have received special attention and created numerous questions. However, no follower of Jesus remained there to explain to inquirers what happened. I guess they assumed the angels remained on duty. The Gospels, for whatever reason, provide no record of any questions from outsiders about an empty tomb or a resurrection. It is extremely strange that the empty tomb story received little emphasis at any point beyond its immediate telling and is not used beyond the initial stories as proof of resurrection. Why?

It is strange that Paul, the earliest New Testament writer, placed absolutely no importance on the empty tomb. Paul's vision of Jesus was the primary point from which he began, and prior events related to Jesus were of minor concern. He provided no physical particulars about the resurrected Jesus who confronted him in his vision, because he heard words but saw no physical body, which means Paul had no need for and made no mention of an empty tomb. It is highly possible that stories of the empty tomb and a physical resurrection of Jesus were nonexistent at the time of Paul's vision. If at some point Paul believed in a spiritual resurrection, did he add it to his belief in a physical resurrection or vice versa?

Even though Paul lived relatively close in time to the event of Jesus's proclaimed resurrection, he provided no particulars about it. The Gospels were separated from the event by forty to eighty years and offer minute details. What are we missing? If the disciples did not believe in the physical resurrection of Jesus, where did the Gospel writers get that idea? We do not know, but we do know it was extremely important to them. Since their chosen purpose was to prove Jesus was the Messiah, perhaps they created, borrowed, or rearranged beliefs about a physical resurrection and applied them to Jesus as further proof of who he was.

During his earthly life, Jesus was a man like no other man his followers had ever known. That impressed others during his life and troubled them after his death. In the Gospels, Jesus seldom if ever spoke about resurrection, and any indication that he did was likely ascribed to him by the author. Since we have no idea about the religious background of his followers, we have no way of surmising who among them might have believed or even been aware of the possible resurrection proclaimed by some of the Jews. Generally speaking, the Pharisees believed in it but the Sadducees did not. Some followers of Jesus may have come from the group who believed in resurrection. Did they, at his death or later, purposely draw ideas from those Jewish beliefs in an effort to make some sense out of Jesus's cruel crucifixion? If they did, to what degree? If they believed resurrection was a possibility, and if God rights the wrongs and rewards those who deserve it, that opened the door for them to develop a belief in Jesus's resurrection.

Given the diversity of both religious and secular beliefs surrounding the initial followers of Jesus, they could have been affected by other religions and cultures. For hundreds of years, people had believed in different forms of resurrection and life after death. It was expressed in pagan religions and folk tales. The Egyptian pyramids reminded others of belief in the afterlife of a pharaoh. Certain cultures believed that the dead had power to sustain the living. Some believed those who accomplished great things would be rewarded with or in another life. Some members of the Jesus movement may have been influenced by outsiders who believed in resurrection. Having heard those stories, perhaps some followers of Jesus were determined to surpass all pagan stories about resurrections with symbolic stories of their own.

The resurrection stories that came to us could have been affected by symbolic words and exaggerations, because people of that day often spoke of impossibilities as if they were possible. Jesus's life and ministry surpassed all they had ever known. They interpreted reported events in light of presuppositions and faith that made sense to them but perhaps not to us. Some of the verbiage with which they reported events may have been purposely more parabolic, symbolic, and mythical than intended fact. They could hear and accept the symbolic message without accepting its content as factual. The initial beliefs and stories about Jesus's resurrection were formulated within that culture and context. If only a spiritual resurrection was originally proclaimed, it was only a short period of time before it was transposed into a physical one. In addition, the initial stories repeatedly received adjustments, various interpretations, and authoritative declarations prior to reaching their present written form. For the sake of absolute honesty, it is extremely doubtful we have actual reports from the scene and time of the reported resurrection.

Where were members of the Jesus movement during the formation and proclamation of stories about a resurrected Jesus? If there was a physical resurrection of Jesus, they would have publicly proclaimed that unusual story long before Paul came upon the scene, and Paul would have been on the "second team." The story apparently developed out of Paul's ideas, not theirs.

The New Testament writers affirm Jesus had a physical life and a cruel crucifixion. For an unknown period of time, he ministered to diverse types of people. Beyond that certainty, we must move with caution. We do not know the spot of his crucifixion, the year it happened, what happened there, the nature of Jesus's suffering, or the disposition of his body. Those facts raise the question just how important was the resurrection at that time? That is the material from which diverse stories could be easily imagined and developed. We ponder how widely Jesus was known and how many people were immediately affected by stories of his death or resurrection, whenever they appeared. We are certain that crucifixions were common, everyday public events, and his crucifixion was not unusual to the public passerby. The crucifixion of Jesus was likely little different from the norm.

We are certain the Gospel writers were not present at the crucifixion or immediately after the reported resurrection. We are also certain the resurrection events differ greatly in the Gospels. We are certain no authentic words of Jesus tell of any intended resurrection for him, even if the Gospels report otherwise. We are uncertain why the crucifixion and reported resurrection events were not discussed or described by Paul. The absence of his attention to them casts further doubt on their authenticity.

We are certain no known secular information validated the bodily resurrection of Jesus. There are almost no secular references to his physical existence. All reports were an inside job. That raises the serious issue of his importance and the significance of the Gospel stories told about his life, death, and resurrection. Did Paul and the Gospels make Jesus more famous than he actually was? Did they manufacture the resurrection stories to make Jesus more important, or did they borrow hero stories others had concocted? Did someone borrow folktales from another culture and substitute Jesus as the main character? In spite of all these possibilities, no reputable scholar doubts Jesus lived, that he loved appropriately while calling others to do the same, or that he died a horrible death. The resurrection is another story.

We also know that after his death, the Jesus movement emphatically proclaimed the physical life and actual death of Jesus. That emphasis was designed to specifically counteract the Gnostic heresy that proclaimed a radically different Jesus. The Gnostics believed Jesus brought to earth special knowledge. They said he also had a secondary spirit that remained dormant in his body until near the time of his crucifixion, at which time his primary spirit escaped the body and was not in him during his time of cruelty and crucifixion. They said the real Jesus did not die, only the body and his secondary spirit. The Gnostic belief had additional concepts that created serious problems within the early Christian movement and among the church fathers.

The disciples acted decisively soon after the crucifixion. The exact time delay is uncertain, but something dramatic happened to them, without the appearance of a resuscitated or resurrected Jesus. Whatever happened to the disciples had more to do with events during Jesus's life than with any specific event related to him after his death. After his death, they were transformed from fearful men in hiding into bold and faithful men with a firm proclamation. Given our concern about the truthfulness of the Gospels, it is not exactly clear why or if the disciples said "He is risen" or "He is alive." If said, the words were not meant to be accepted literally. If they used that phrase, or something similar, they were not referring to a bodily resurrection or a resuscitation. If at some point they thought the human body was restored to its former earthly state, that would be a resuscitation, not a resurrection. The story is not about resuscitation. A resurrection would necessitate a different, nonhuman lifeform about which they would have absolutely no insight or understanding and likely would not have recognized. The Gospel stories seemingly depict Jesus rotating between two lifeforms. That new lifeform is not necessarily impossible just because we have never experienced it. To believe that it is possible or has happened is rather problematic, since we have only questionable sources that report such a lifeform in all of Judeo-Christian history. The reports of what happened and what was said at the time of and soon after Jesus's death were not provided at that time of or soon after his death, not by the disciples and not by eyewitnesses. That should alert us to problems with the Gospels' reports on Jesus and the resurrection stories. We simply do not know what to believe about the immediate response to Jesus's death by his close followers. The best we can do is offer educated guesses and proceed with caution.

I believe the disciples said "He is alive" or something similar. Their words had no reference to a physical resurrection or resuscitation of Jesus's body, and they would probably be shocked to learn anyone thought they did. My guess is they proclaimed "He is alive" because they concluded nothing could kill the essence of what he was, the spirit by which he lived, and the truth of what he taught. Did they understand, as we have not, that he was and we are primarily spirit? There had to be a valid, reasonable, and compelling explanation for their radically changed behavior and new fearless commitment. Something compelled a small group of scared and hidden men to suddenly blow their cover and charge forth with a firm public message, totally disregarding any impending danger. They were not empowered by a sighting of the resurrected or resuscitated Jesus. Their transforming experiences were not because of divine intervention or superhuman action. They were changed, like us, by a personal experience that came from a historical event. The disciples' exuberant response and verbal proclamation were caused by an indescribable, unverifiable, transforming, and very personal experience that came to them after the crucifixion. There was no outside verifiable proof of their inner experiences, other than the change in their spoken words and obvious behavior. They left no doubt a change had occurred in them. They had a new presupposition. Through faith, meditation, memory, reason, experience, and revelation, they discovered, like so many of us, that truth, goodness, and actions of God are revealed in earthly situations and human experiences.

The disciples of Jesus, or some of them, believed what Jesus had said, and they finally understood what he meant. They suddenly got it. They were converted. Their faith in the absolute truth of what Jesus taught was resurrected, not Jesus. Their hope, commitment, courage, and confidence were resurrected, not the body of Jesus! The cruel crucifixion had severely wounded, if not almost destroyed, their faith in the Jesus movement, but their personal experience resurrected their faith in, hope for, and commitment to it.

No one knows exactly what led to or happened during the disciples' transforming experiences. It seems reasonable to assume something like the following occurred. The fearful, confused, and disappointed disciples had secretly gathered soon after Jesus's horrible death. They had previously discussed with Jesus and each other the impending danger or death for him and them. His death was not, and could not have been, a complete surprise. The Gospels indicate too many confrontations between Jesus and his adversaries to believe otherwise. Soon after his death, some of the disciples, if not all of them, secretly gathered together, perhaps more than once. Their earlier discussions did not destroy their present dilemma. Pondering his cruel death, they repeatedly asked, "Where to from here?" With heavy hearts, they slowly began to speak in hushed tones about Jesus. They recalled and recited favorite stories about his life of compassion and love. They told of what he meant personally to them. They reiterated how good it made them feel to be near him and join him in ministry to the marginalized. They recalled the transformation in those whom he treated as his equal and those whose bodies and souls were restored and refreshed. They remembered love in action.

They vividly remembered and quietly recited what he said, exactly how he said it, along with what he did and the spirit in which he did it, especially his demonstrative love and compassion that created a community of unusual and diverse followers. They spoke about the life of a fellow human being who lived on a moral, religious, and ethical plane they had not dreamed possible, and they were witnesses. They realized Jesus told them things they never expected to hear, and he demonstrated Godlike love to a degree they had never known before. He pointed them to God and embodied the spirit of holiness and wholeness. He proclaimed a doable and meaningful lifestyle far different from the Judaism of their day. They concluded the life and ministry of Jesus demonstrated the presence of God's kingdom among them and, of all things, he had invited them, even them, into it.

At one of their meetings, like cream slowly rising in a bowl of milk, the ramifications of his message and ministry slowly surfaced. Almost simultaneously, or at least within a short span of time, the majority of those assembled had a genuine conversion experience. Their memory of Jesus was so vivid, it was almost as if Jesus was present among them. (There is a theory that memory can be so vivid it is as if it were real.) It dawned on them that even though his body died, there was no way to destroy the essence of who and what Jesus was. Death had not killed the eternal truth and Godlike love he embodied and proclaimed. They did not for a moment deny his physical death and decimated body, but they could no longer keep silent about his spirit that was alive. They sprang through the door of their hiding place like a high school football team through a paper spirit banner. They shouted, "He really is alive! He is alive, not because he came back from the dead, but because you cannot kill the essence of God's truth and love, nor can you seal it in a tomb." The stone of disbelief was rolled away for them. They were resurrected from disbelief and fear, and they acted like it.

Sunday schools and sermons have repeatedly stated that the disciples had faith because of the physical resurrection of Jesus, but that is really not true. The disciples were empowered, not because of the resurrection of Jesus's body but by restoration of their faith. They did not have or need a resurrected body. It would have prevented the discovery of truth, for them and us.

In the final analysis, a close examination of the resurrection stories in the Gospels tell us nothing believable about what happened to Jesus's body following his death. Were these stories concocted to cover the bitter truth about the end results of Jesus's crucified body? Who wanted to hear the truth that he, like numerous other victims, had his unidentified bodily remains devoured by predators whose mission was to destroy the obvious and visible evidence of cruel crucifixions? Did it seemed more soothing to say his remains were buried as a special person rather than to truthfully admit that meager remains were scattered at an unknown spot on that gruesome hilltop? The stories about Jesus's body being placed in a tomb by a secular authority seems contrived, but it conveniently sets the stage for a salvaged body and the resurrection stories. Who would have ever believed he was the promised Messiah if the story ended with his disintegrated body on an unidentified cross at an unknown location in an inaccessible killing field?

We have no factual data on what happened immediately after all, or just some, of the disciples were transformed. There are hints they were not all on the same page. Given the exuberance and assurance of at least some of them, I believe they fervently continued to act like Jesus because they embodied his spirit. I do not believe Paul's arrival with his new beliefs caused them to alter theirs, but we have few records of their immediate or continued activities. The Jesus movement appears to have been widespread but loosely connected. What and when did Jesus's scattered followers hear about his death, and did they ever hear about a resurrection or need to? If there were large pockets of support for Jesus in distant areas, how slowly did the exuberance and understanding of the disciples spread, or did it need to? Perhaps it was already elsewhere because Jesus had been there! Perhaps we have overlooked the dynamic effect Jesus had wherever he went and the degree to which his spirit and teachings lingered long after his departure. Perhaps those scattered followers of Jesus, like the disciples, needed no resurrection.

It is extremely significant that Paul's proclamation about a resurrected Messiah did nothing to change the Judaism of his day. Jewish authorities totally rejected his argument that Jesus was the expected Messiah. If there had been widely publicized sightings of a resurrected body, it is difficult to believe it had no effect on or comments from the existing Jewish authorities. Apparently, the idea of a physical resurrection had no support from Judaism or the Jesus movement.

For many reasons, I do not believe there was a bodily resurrection of Jesus. First, it was totally unnecessary for our salvation. Based on Jesus's authentic words taken from the ancient Hebrew leaders, Jesus knew the process for salvation had been correctly identified by the Hebrews soon after they recognized their one God. It was the original and only process ever needed or possible, a fact Jesus recognized but Judaism and Paul denied. Therefore, belief in a bodily resurrection of Jesus has absolutely nothing to do with getting right and staying right with God. A physical resurrection of Jesus would not help us love God above all else and our neighbor as ourselves.

Second, the reports of a bodily resurrection lack credible content. There are too few believable records for the magnitude of the story. Too few people knew or told believable stories about it. The few stories are very different, seeming to lack information that is believable, practical, truthful, and simple, unless we disregard all we know about God's rules for life and the universe. There is no extended story about the disciples' actual response to the crucifixion events. After all, they were Jesus's chosen disciples. Later stories about the appearance of the resurrected Jesus to many others have too many unanswered questions to be taken seriously. Likewise, Paul's vision tells more about Paul than about Jesus.

Third, the secular community would have publicized an unexpected and immediately empty tomb because of a resurrected or resuscitated body, if it had happened. Small communities are inquisitive and observant. Unexplained empty tombs would have been the talk of the town and front-page news. The absence of any stories about Jesus's resurrection in secular history should cause us to pause and ponder the stories we have. All stories came from the inside and reflect faith instead of facts. Since the resurrected Jesus was reportedly seen only by particular people, the mystery grows and becomes harder to believe. An event of such magnitude could not have been known only by those on the inside. This lack of outside factual data lends support to the disciples' proclamation that he is alive in spirit but not physically resurrected.

Fourth, a unique event of this magnitude surely deserved a date by someone who told the story. The absence of a known date diminishes its impact and raises other significant issues. Either we are missing important factual information or that information never existed. I accept the latter.

Fifth, the bodily resurrection of Jesus was impossible because of the unchangeable laws of God. No one can return to life days after death, instantly change forms, go through walls, suddenly reappear as a recognizable person, and then totally disappear into thin air. God's unchangeable laws of the universe totally forbid such things. The argument that Jesus did those things because he was divine does not compute, especially since he was not divine. God does not suspend any law for any reason, even with Jesus, or the universe would implode. There could not be a bodily resurrection.

Sixth, since Jesus was just as human as we are, the resurrection stories were created to enhance the acceptance of him as the Messiah. The dividing line between actual and symbolic Jesus is too blurred to follow. If we remove the concept of a divine Jesus, there would be no need or justification for his resurrection as reported.

Seventh, it is difficult to understand just what Paul believed about resurrection. Given the English translation of his forceful words in numerous places, it seems he believed in a physical resurrection of Jesus. However, it seems his attachment to Judaism may have molded his beliefs more than anything he gathered from Jesus or Jesus's disciples. Apparently, Paul originally knew nothing about a resurrection of Jesus, or he did not believe it until after his vision. That adds further problems with a physical resurrection.

I have wrestled for years with the proclamation that Jesus's physical body was resurrected. For me, his physical resurrection joins the ranks of erroneous beliefs that were intended to answer serious questions. However, that proclamation has been harmful for many professing Christians and without their knowledge. I remain steadfast in affirming there was no physical resurrection of Jesus, but his spirit did not die. The resurrection story appeared after Jesus's cruel death, told by people of faith, but they were not factual. The belief in a bodily resurrection for Jesus is beyond acceptance, irrational, and perhaps un-Christian.

# CHAPTER 15

# WHY WAS JESUS'S DEATH IMPORTANT?

Professing Christians continue to debate why Jesus's death was important. Most of them support one of two basic reasons, but those reasons are distinctively different. One group emphasizes what they personally gained from it, but the other focus on what we lost and learned. The first group believes it was important in order for us to have salvation. The second group mourns the loss of such an important man in human history, but we also look for what his death taught us, especially about appropriate and inappropriate love.

The first group encompasses those who accept the ransom and bodily resurrection theories and all beliefs connected to them. They have no problem declaring a specific, simple, and straightforward answer that is always absolutely fixed, regardless of the variable verbiage they use to state it. For them, humanity went terribly astray, and Jesus was the predetermined fix. He was a ransom whose shed blood paid for humanity's sin, especially theirs. God sent us Jesus, who was predestined to die so that we might have salvation. Jesus had no choice in how he lived and in how or when he died. Without a predetermined death, a ransom, and a resurrection, there would be no readily available means of salvation. This group affirms Jesus died so that salvation would easily be available to us.

The second group radically differs from the first. We also believe Jesus's cruel death was very important. However, it was totally unnecessary for our salvation because there was no need or possibility for God to change the original rules, which Jesus recalled and reiterated in his two directives. Any importance attributed to his death must be measured and valued primarily from what we learned and what was lost. His death was important because we lost the life and ministry of a unique spokesperson for God. His death left a huge hole in human history. We know not when or if the truth Jesus taught would have been recognized had he not proclaimed it. His admonition to love God above all else and our neighbor as ourselves was explained and exemplified in ways that have never been equaled. We all lost a man whose life, teachings, ministry, and spirit offered genuine help and hope for all who believed him and acted like it. He offered "light to the world," but that light was snuffed out, perhaps largely by religious people, and that was no insignificant thing.

For many of us, Jesus's death was more tragedy than triumph, devastating but not demanded, humanly directed and not divinely ordained, and an unnecessary loss from which came reminders of great truths. We are saddened because evil scored a goal by usurping the life of a unique man who was motivated only by appropriate love. His demise robbed his followers of a living example and a loving leader but made them responsible for the continuation of the ministry he began. The trying circumstances that led to his death demonstrated his unwavering commitment to a holy cause for which he would not compromise and for which he was willing to die. His examples call us to make similar commitments to similar causes, even when unpopular and possibly dangerous. The untimely and tragic death of anyone who gave himself for the betterment of others is always an irreversible loss. The death of anyone who revolutionized life and religion by loving others is irreplaceable. Anytime religious and secular authorities joined forces to destroy a proclaimer of truth, that was and always will be a grave injustice affecting all of us and should deeply disturb us. The death of Jesus, like the death of anyone, was important, especially to his family, friends, close followers, and the entire Jesus movement. Make no mistake, Jesus's death was extremely important, even for those of us who do not accept the ransom theory, the resurrection, and other beliefs connected to them.

The death of Jesus is tremendously important because it reminds us the extent to which some religious and secular authorities will go to maintain their control. Prominent religious authorities are not always controlled by Godlike love in what they believe and do. Even though they claim to be divinely led and acting for the good of others, their beliefs and actions can adversely affect us. Their god can be an idol, and we must carefully decide whom to follow. If the Gospel records can be trusted, Jesus had committed no crime against a law that was punishable by anything other than verbal rebuke. He just made some rich and powerful people angry by doing so much good for so many poor and abused people. Given the character of the authorities, they were afraid of good people doing too many good things. They were afraid of truth and love that, by their standards, had gone wild and might further expose them for what they were. Since religious and secular authorities were apparently "scratching each other's backs," neither could tolerate a man who repeatedly made both of them look bad. They simply could not allow such a man in their midst. Jesus's popularity with the poor posed problems, but the authorities could certainly prevent their continuation by erasing their leader. Therefore, either the secular or religious authorities, if not jointly, calculated a backdoor scheme to destroy Jesus. They simply murdered him of their own volition. Those circumstances that led to Jesus's death serve as reminders of how destructive selfishness can be in personal, religious, and governmental decrees. We must be aware and alert because little has changed in our day. Jesus showed us not only how to live appropriately but also how and for what to die. Living the truth does not guarantee a long life, but living a lie has no lasting value for which to live or die.

I do not believe Jesus had to die as he did. However, because of his death, good things developed. Tragedy sometimes opens our eyes to truth we previously overlooked. Like the fictitious and ancient phoenix, new life can come from the ashes of serious disappointment and tragedy. In fact, new life may be encouraged or necessitated by the death of someone or something. After every human tragedy, some people accept responsibility for who and what they are, as well as for what they seek to become. They look to the future, try to pick up the present pieces, rationally rejoin them as best they can, seek to follow truth, and accept responsibility for their actions. However, there are others who look back for someone on whom they heavily depend to take them into the future.

Why was Jesus's death important? The answer depends on the one who answers. I do not believe Jesus had to die for our salvation, but the way we respond to his death may determine whether or not we have salvation.

# CHAPTER 16

## CONCLUSIONS ABOUT JESUS

We know very little factual data about Jesus, but I believe we can correctly conjecture certain things about him. He was the son of a poor and humble Palestinian Jewish couple who lived and worked in or near the small town of Nazareth, where Jesus was born at home. Because of the conditions and customs of that time, his mother was a young virgin who, according to social customs, was betrothed and possibly married at a young age. Most young ladies were betrothed at an early age for protection from undesirable suitors and sexual predators, because unclaimed and unattached women were prime targets for both. Marriage may or may not have immediately followed a betrothal. Therefore, we do not know Mary's age when Jesus was born. Jesus was conceived in the normal way, by two nondescript Jewish parents and without divine intervention or instruction. His birth was very similar to all other human births, with no heavenly response and no foreign or heavenly visitors to celebrate it. There was no journey to Jerusalem for his birth, no unusual fanfare or extraordinary miracles associated with him immediately after his arrival and no required escape to Egypt shortly thereafter.

Jesus was a member of an ordinary Jewish family, but references to his family relationships and activities are extremely scarce. Even though our records indicate there were several opportunities to do so, at no point did family members recognize or affirm he was more than human or that his birth was different from theirs. Luke's story of the missing lad who was finally found three days later in the temple discussing religious matters with authorities made no impressions on his parents (Luke 2:41–49). One biblical story (Mark 3:31–35) indicates his birth family's unfavorable opinion of him because he was meeting with a crowd and forsaking the family. His mother and siblings attempted to get him away from those crowded around him and take him home. His answer to them is somewhat of a rebuke. Obviously, they did not know of any unusual birth or purpose, not even his mother!

One biblical record casually reported Jesus had four named brothers, and more than one unnamed sister but gave no indication he was different in any way from them. God needed nothing different or spectacular for Jesus's conception and birth, since the natural process is always best described as miraculous. If the spectacular events related in Matthew or Luke had occurred at his birth, the whole known world would have soon heard about it, talked about it, and remembered it. Those events obviously did not occur. There is clear indication his parents were poor, because at their purification and the dedication of their firstborn to the Lord, they sacrificed only two pigeons and two doves, which was the sacrifice of less-affluent parents. The exact date of his birth is unknown but can be placed within a specific timeframe, most likely prior to or during 4 BCE. His prominence, if he had any, came not from his special birth or death but from what he did for the poor, where he did it, how he did it, and what he taught. He may have received some notoriety late in his ministry but primarily well after his death. That fact alone is revelatory. It tells us little about who Jesus was but rather who and what people later decided and said about him.

We know almost nothing about his formative years. Some people have said Jesus probably could not read or write, because most peasants were uneducated. There is nothing to indicate he was a poor peasant. If he was, that does not mean his parents had always been peasants, that he remained one, or that he automatically lacked those skills.

His inability to read is doubtful, because of his brilliant religious insights, profound words, and unusual actions. There is at least one biblical reference about him reading scripture in the temple, but that report may not be factual. Assuredly, he was raised in a devout Jewish home where Sabbath worship and a Jewish lifestyle were faithfully followed. To some degree, he would have been homeschooled, as in any Jewish family. Jesus was originally a devout Jew but undoubtedly became a dissatisfied and disappointed Jew. Current Jewish practices and beliefs were extremely familiar to him. His familiarity with the message and lifestyle of Old Testament prophets most likely added to his dissatisfaction with Jewish practices around him and helped shape his own teachings and lifestyle. From family, synagogue, personal perceptions, and the Old Testament came a profound understanding of God as a loving Father who freely offered and wanted the best for everyone, regardless of class, creed, or origin. That became his model for life.

We can only guess the level of society into which Jesus was born and in which he lived at any given time. It seems he was or became a member of a higher class in society in order to offer help to the marginalized. Regardless of his social class, his association with and ministry to the outcast were strictly voluntary.

According to the custom in every Jewish household, Jesus's father likely taught him the family trade. There are indications it was carpentry and possibly masonry, but he could have learned another. The Greek word that designates Jesus's trade is best translated "a worker with wood," which includes construction of buildings and making other practical items such as doors, boxes, crates, and other wooden items. In modern terms, he was a construction worker and a handyman. Nothing indicates he had only one trade. Opportunities for carpentry and masonry work were readily available because Nazareth was located only four miles from Sepphoris, the site for one of Herod's gigantic building projects. If desired, gainful employment was readily available for him, his family, and all who were able to work at the nearby building projects. Jesus may have been gainfully employed as a teenager and young adult, before devoting full time to ministry, if he ever did. He may have been gainfully employed and also engaged in his ministry, like a modern part-time pastor. The opportunity to be gainfully employed may have enabled him and his family to attain a social class above, perhaps well above, the very bottom. Likewise, if gainful employment was readily available for all who were able and willing to work, that provides valuable insight into the deplorable physical and mental condition of the unemployed, ill, and marginalized with whom Jesus spent some of his time.

We do not know exactly what Jesus did or where he lived during what some people believe to have been approximately thirty years prior to his public ministry. There are numerous possibilities, some of which may have greatly affected his later activities. Since Jesus must have been a rather ordinary person during those years, normal activities and gainful employment would have been appropriate. If he were a builder or carpenter, that tells us he had a common skill and knew what it meant to work for a living, like many of his peers. Men his age were normally married and had a family. There is some indication he had a special relationship with a woman but no indication of marriage or children. We do not know when or where he began his public ministry, if it can be correctly called that. It is reasonable to believe he had been practicing ministry by his lifestyle long before he became widely recognized, if that time ever came. There is no creditable information about any trip to Jerusalem prior to his public ministry, even though he may have gone often or even periodically lived there. Conjecture again suggests he spent extended time in the temple in Jerusalem, because it appears he was very familiar with it and knew exactly what transpired therein. Devout Jews wanted to visit the temple, and Jesus probably visited it on several occasions during those unknown years.

There is an interesting possibility worth considering. If Jesus's parents dedicated their firstborn to the Lord or temple, as some devout Jews did and Luke may suggest, Jesus may have spent extended time during his very young life living apart from his biological family and within the confines of the temple, where he lived, learned, and labored under the watchful eye of a seasoned rabbi. The dedication of a firstborn to the temple was not new. The firm possibility that Jesus was a temple child would explain why, at age twelve, he could have an intelligent conversation with learned men in the temple, why he was well informed about temple activities and religious teachings and practices within Judaism, why he had a different understanding on how we get right with God, and why he gladly associated with anyone from any social class. These possibilities might provide one answer to why people in his hometown were later astonished and wondered where he got such wisdom, because he was just one of them (Matthew 13:54–56).

There are other plausible possibilities, but no proof, for what Jesus did as a teenager or a young adult. Given his ability to help the sick and lame, he could have studied the art of healing, which helps explain his knowledge and ability to assist the sick. Being a devout Jew, he may have also studied under the tutelage of a rabbi, either full time or part time. He could have lived and worked in or near Nazareth, Jerusalem, or anywhere and actively participated in or even officially served as a rabbi in a local synagogue. If he was gainfully employed, that would have provided financial resources he needed to minister to the marginalized, who likely migrated to places of employment, gathered along the way to and nearby it, where helpful handouts were more readily available. Those too sick, too lame, and too far away to gather at such places were even more desperate and needy. Jesus's occupation may have offered him opportunities to travel from town to town to construct or repair buildings. Everyplace he went and worked provided another place to assist those in need, both along the way and at his destination. The reported changes in his locations may have been more for employment than for intended ministry. Any earned income beyond what he needed for his basic needs may have been used to secure specific supplies to share with others, many of whom he seemingly sought and not just for those who sought him.

The specific time or age at which Jesus entered public ministry is unknown. Likewise, the length of that ministry remains a mystery. His generosity and concern for the marginalized may have been quietly practiced in nonpopular places long before his public ministry and may be the behavior that originally gave him notoriety. Careful calculations from events and dates in our existing records provide no valid answers to when or where his ministry began. Known and dated secular documents outside the New Testament canon provide little specific information about Jesus. Whatever else that tells us, they affirm he was not popular outside very limited areas, or there are no records of it if he was. Secular records vaguely affirm his ministry but make no comment about an unusual birth or unusual attributes in life or after death. There are a few known documents, also called gospels, but they are not included in the New Testament. They are also from the early Christian communities and contain snippets of information about him and sayings attributed to him. Some of those sayings appear to be authentic and were most likely written before the canonical Gospels. A few of those sayings appear almost word for word in Matthew, Mark, and Luke. The noted secular historian, Josephus (37–100 CE), does little more than mention Jesus's existence. If the spectacular events told by the Gospels actually happened, why were they not widely known throughout the country and prominently mentioned in popular secular writings? Josephus and his fellow historians who loved Jewish history would have certainly known and written about those events at great length. The lack of further religious and secular verification for an extraordinary man who reportedly participated in extraordinary activities raises other questions that deserve careful consideration.

Jesus undoubtedly had a private life, even though we know almost nothing about it. The unknown date of his birth, the secret years of his youth and young adult life, the unknown date for entering and ending his public ministry, exactly what he did and where leave gigantic empty spaces in our desired knowledge. We know Constantine was converted to Christianity on October 28, 312 CE, but we do not know when Jesus was born or when he died. That strongly suggests no fanfare at either event, or someone would remember the exact dates. From every indication, his ministry was offered to any who would receive it, but the greatest impact was with the marginalized, outcast, poor, women, and any who were downtrodden, left out, unimportant, sick, or lonely. Some prior training or study as a medic and rabbi would have greatly facilitated his ministry and increased his effectiveness. He conversed with those in need, ate with them, ministered to them, included them among his friends, and enabled them to feel included and important. His inclusive gatherings with such groups, during which he shared bread and wine, are probably the origin of our Communion services, rather than some formal gathering in an upper room. During his conversation at meals, or "table talks," he proclaimed a new and possible way for them to participate in genuine worship apart from the Jewish requirements. His doable directives on how to get right and stay right with God were music to their ears and relief to their spirits. His new information and his demonstrative love, expressed in words and deeds, made him truly a savior to them in more ways than one. He literally saved them from many things. His extended and successful association with a large following from every level of society likely got him in serious trouble that led to an excuse for his death.

We also have a few unusual and interesting comments about his personal life found in several of those noncanonical gospels. Some comments are believable and others are not. Those gospels have no problem relating how human Jesus was and often spoke of him as "the human one." One indicates Jesus may have been married or at least had a special woman in his life, but there is no reference to any children. Mary, otherwise unidentified, was a very special person to him. Someone reported that one gospel speaks of him "kissing Mary on the lips," but I can find no exact reference. The Gospel of Mary has Peter say, "Sister, we know that the Savior loves you more than all other women" (6:1). In one reference, the disciples are disgruntled because Jesus had not given them information he had earlier given to his special friend, a woman (Gospel of Mary 10:3–4). Even though the original manuscript is damaged, verse 10 of the same chapter has been translated: "For he knew her completely and loved her steadfastly." Perhaps it was not by accident that "Mary" was the first woman, or among the first, to reportedly visit the tomb following the Sabbath. That would be the natural thing for a wife to do.

Marriage was a common practice for Jewish men during that time, so it should not surprise or disappoint us if Jesus was married. If it does surprise or disappoint us, it is probably because of a presupposition about his lack of humanness. If he were married, it should change nothing about his teachings or actions, and it makes him more like us. That would greatly diminish the possibility of his divine nature. At least one or two reported events in the synoptic Gospels would make more sense if the presence of his significant other was recognized and properly named. The synoptic Gospel writers were not personally acquainted with Jesus and apparently began with the assumption that he possessed, at some point, a divine nature. Because of that assumption and certain presuppositions about sex, they may have purposely denied or disregarded reports on a natural birth, the humanness of Jesus, and especially any close association with or an emotional attachment to a woman.

Most scholars believe Jesus seldom if ever gave long discourses, but John's Gospel reports lengthy discourses attributed to Jesus. For many obvious reasons, that was for John's own purposes and not quotes from Jesus. Some lengthy passages attributed to Jesus may encompass subject matter briefly mentioned by Jesus. Lengthy discourses attributed to Jesus do not fit his known pattern and must be questioned as his words unless composed by joining together several of his sayings. Information traveled primary by word of mouth, especially among the poorer people. Jesus usually framed his intended message about God and proper human response in short, pithy statements, parables, or stories. Each usually focused on one subject or point so that it could be easily understood, remembered, and correctly recited. Most parables in the canonical Gospels are rather short, easily remembered, and about well-known things or events. Likewise, most if not all noncanonical material thought to be the possible sayings of Jesus are that type. If elongated, they related a short story easily remembered and recited. Scholars have discovered at least one brief document believed to be a collection of some actual sayings from Jesus. The document is entitled *"The Gospel of Thomas,"* which has 114 brief statements or short stories attributed to Jesus. Several statements in the New Testament Gospels reported as the words of Jesus are identical to or closely resemble those found in Thomas. These few pithy and pointed statement attributed to Jesus may be as close as we will ever get to what he said and who he really was.

The width and depth of Jesus's popularity are completely unknown at every point during his life and after his death. The Gospels' reports on attendance at his gatherings may not always be mathematically correct. The extent to which his pithy statements were shared is unknown and depended on the popularity of Jesus during his earthly ministry or the proclamations of his words by his followers after his death. One or more limited and unidentified collections of words attributed to Jesus may have been the nucleus from which Mark was motivated to formulate his individual Gospel. Other collections of sayings attributed to Jesus may have motivated Matthew and Luke to either add to or correct Mark's Gospel.

The synoptic Gospels indicate the human Jesus was an extraordinary man whose humble life and behavior drew the attention of others. This man with a godly spirit reportedly changed individual lives and entire communities. He embodied a spirit of loving concern like no one had ever witnessed. His gathering with and assistance to the marginalized were no doubt far more extensive than reported and made him famous, at least among them. His purposeful, casual, and conscious association with the outcast, poor, sick, needy, and well-to-do was not a common practice for other people around him. His behavior was most unusual. We can only speculate on what his ministry among them extracted from him in terms of time, effort, energy, and material possessions. He demonstrated that love for others will always cost us something. Jesus's genuine interest in and assistance to marginalized individuals enabled changes in them that can be properly described as healing for both their bodies and minds. If those results were totally unexpected, previously unknown, or very unusual, for the lack of a more correct term, it could have been called a miracle, which simply meant out of the ordinary, most unusual, and totally unexpected. They could have correctly called him Messiah because, to them, he was sent from God to provide healing, justice, and peace. They properly called him Savior because he saved them from extensive misery and improper religious beliefs. However, those terms were most likely applied without any assumption that Jesus was divine.

I suspect people were more at ease and felt better if Jesus was present in the community. Some of us witnessed a somewhat similar situation during the years shortly after the Depression. My small hometown got very excited and grateful when Dr. Henry moved his medical practice into it. He came to live among us and help heal us. His presence and potential to meet our needs, even if we were not sick, made us feel better. That may have been true in some places where Jesus visited and lived.

Let us not forget Jesus also gathered with those who were not physically sick, hurt, or marginalized. There were many others to whom he pronounced his message of God's requirements to love appropriately and act accordingly. His confrontation with the Pharisees may have been more prominent and problematic than we have been told and an excuse for his death.

It is probably safe to say no one had ever spoken or acted like Jesus. No person had ever demonstrated love for the marginalized and all others as he did. No one within his current religious community had explained and simplified the doable requirements for godly living as he did. There is no wonder why religious authorities considered him a heretic or why other people thought he was a hero. No one had seen any designated religious leader humbly practice or personally embody a message of love. He repeatedly reminded everybody that they lived in God's world and should act like they appreciated the privilege. He never called attention to himself but always pointed to God, whom he called Father and with whom he never dared claimed equality. His basic insights into life and righteous living were so revolutionary and refreshing, yet so simple and applicable, that the people were totally amazed. Astonished by what they heard and saw, they wanted to know who he was.

If Jesus was a temple child, his teachers most likely forced him to study Hebrew scriptures. He would have been forced to study them even if he were raised in the home of a devout Jewish family. His teachers, whomever they were, did not convince him to accept their interpretations and follow current Jewish beliefs and practices. Even if Jesus was no temple child, he became well informed about religion and many other things. At some point, he consciously made a complete commitment to love and serve God above all else and to love others as he loved himself. That probably came from his study of ancient Hebrew religion. If Jesus was ever a member of the marginalized, his personal experiences would have affected his future choices for beliefs and behaviors. If he was not one of them, his behavior toward them indicates his religious knowledge and loving nature. We have no indication why, where, or when Jesus purposely chose from all ancient Hebrew teachings two primary directives as guides for his life. He chose them because no others are sufficient. He knew these were all anyone needed. That choice was likely made before he began his public ministry and may have been the foundation for it. We have no indication he struggled over that choice, but I suspect he did, since it was so radically different from the religious teachings and practices he inherited and confronted. That struggle, and perhaps others, is likely symbolized by the story of his wilderness temptations. His declaration of those two directives is definitely believed to be authentic, based on statements specifically attributed to him in three Gospels (Matthew 22, Mark 12, and Luke 10). The first directive is the ancient "Shema" (Deuteronomy 6:4–5) which was and is daily repeated by devout Jews as a reminder to love God above everything else. His second guiding principle was taken from Leviticus 19:18, which says "love your neighbor as yourself." Someone asked Jesus how to get right and remain right with God. Jesus answered the inquirer by telling him those two commandments are the sum and substance, the totality of what God requires of us, that and no more, but also no less. Jesus knew these were rules we did not make and cannot break, if we wish to get right and stay right with God.

Everything else Jesus taught and did was intended as commentary on and implementation of those two commandments. In essence, he said anything contrary to or disconnected from those two directives must be disbelieved and discarded, even if found in the Hebrew scriptures, Jewish practices, the Jesus movement, modern beliefs, or elsewhere. Being translated and applied, Jesus spoke to us. Any part of the Bible or modern religious beliefs and practices contrary to living by those two directives is unnecessary and must be rejected, including much of Paul's doctrine. Ponder the gigantic fights within Christendom, from its very beginning to this day, over issues that had nothing to do with facilitating those two directives of Jesus. Extensive arguments over the nature of Jesus, the need for a new salvation process, the requirement for a blood sacrifice, a bodily resurrection, and all that goes with them have denied and diverted the very heart of what Jesus was and taught. I think it is not too far afield when I declare that disregard for those two directives has been the primary cause for every false doctrine and major religious conflict within Christendom from its beginning to this day. Didn't someone say something about guaranteed problems for a house built on an unstable foundation?

It would be interesting to know how many people asked Jesus how they could get right with God and enter God's kingdom. I suspect most of them did not have to ask, because he gladly informed them, even before they asked. His "table talks" and "fireside chats" covered that and more. If someone did ask, I imagine Jesus answered something like this: "You can enter now because the kingdom of God is among you. It is here where you are and available to you now. You have no need to do anything other than make the necessary changes that will enable you to graciously follow what God has designed, which is live by and embody the two great commandments to love appropriately. They are the foundation and summation of all God will ever require of anyone who wishes to participate in his kingdom. God is love and only loves. Learn what it means to love as God loves and then act accordingly. You need no animal or human sacrifice to pay an unidentified somebody for your sin. A priest, pastor, sibling, your mother, my mother, or any person, even I, cannot usher you into or kick you out of the kingdom, but you alone can do either. Offering the blood or body of a bull, ram, bird, firstborn child, or anything actually offends God. There is no requirement or way for you to earn or pay your way into the kingdom. You participate in God's kingdom here on earth by choosing to appropriately love God and neighbor in every part of your life. Participation in the kingdom of God on earth is its own reward and not preparation for a greater one that will come by and by in the sky. Dear friends, believe nothing you have heard, or will hear, that is contrary to this."

How extremely radical was that, compared to what they had previously heard and what we usually hear? Jesus never claimed to be anything other than a human child of God, like everyone else. Jesus had absolute faith in God's sovereignty and believed God's spirit was always present. He purposely sought and firmly sensed God's sprit around and within him and therefore loved intently while asking his followers to participate in the spirit of love and truth. The extent of God's spirit within him was and is available to any and all. His spirit was akin to God's spirit. At no point in time did he say or suggest he was the expected Jewish Messiah, a special creation of God, equal to God, the scapegoat for everyone's sins, or that God had decreed he must be crucified as a blood sacrifice. He never claimed any accolades, positions, or privileges as if he were due them because of an unusual birth or being. He asked for and expected nothing that was not rightfully because of those with whom he lived and to whom he ministered. He most likely sacrificed physical things such as money, food, time, and effort so that others might have more. Even though he was first of all a man, he was an unusual man, deeply devoted to demonstrating his love for God and others. Since that lifestyle was so radically different from the norm, it easily separated him from the crowd. That lifestyle was not easy or automatic but it was possible for him and is possible for everyone with similar devotion and determination.

Even though our information about Jesus is unclear and incomplete, there are several points of which we are quite sure. Jesus ministered to people from different levels of society, from the bottom to the top. He definitely cared for the marginalized and gave much of his time and possessions in ministry to them, the extent of which is unknown. It was undoubtedly they who first heaped accolades upon him. Given his two basic guides for life, how could he be unconcerned for those in need of physical or religious help? Faithfully loving God and neighbor necessitated a personal relationship with all others, including but not limited to the poor, oppressed, and sick. He provided godly love through personal care because love was also a verb to him. His devotion to God and determination to help others provided the framework for his ministry and the excuse for his crucifixion. The strength to endure the opposition against him came from his unwavering faith in God and commitment to truth. He believed the only thing for which to live was following his two guiding commandments. If necessary, that was also the only thing for which to die.

Jesus was a most unusual man. He joined the few previous and remarkable spokespersons who understood the primary presupposition pertaining to God's nature and what he requires of us. His unwavering commitment to appropriate love and a lifestyle through which he practiced it may have caused him to be misunderstood, mislabeled, and murdered. We must emphasize Jesus inherited the true requirements for entrance into God's kingdom, first specified by Moses and repeated by the Hebrew prophets. He reiterated, not created, God's requirements for all who wish to be saved from their sin of inappropriate love. (That is the definition of sin.) Jesus is often called "our Savior." We must be extremely cautious about using that term, or we will say what we do not intend. If we say "Only Jesus can save," we have disregarded and denied God's saving process, not only for now but also for all who lived before Jesus and all who are not professing Christians. Technically, Jesus cannot be the savior, because only God can be that, and Jesus never became God. Jesus instructed us about God's salvation process and showed us how to participate in it, but beyond that, our salvation is between us and God. Jesus pointed us to God, warned us about erroneous beliefs, identified misdirected behavior, and showed us a life directed by appropriate love. Others have done and can do the same. Jesus was and is a conduit to God, but there have been and presently there are other conduits. Trouble abounds when "Jesus saves" means more than "we get on the right track by believing Jesus and acting like it."

Given that fact, Jesus can be our savior only because he lived, not because he was crucified and resurrected. Jesus did not save us by his life or his death. We move toward salvation by choosing to believe Jesus and acting like we want it. Our salvation does not depend on what Jesus did but rather on our proper relationship with God, just as Jesus said. Jesus's death did not change God's original requirements on how to get right and stay right with God; nor did it remove the requirement for us to live by appropriate love, if we want to be right with God. Jesus never insinuated he was other than fully human, and he always emphasized the primacy of God in all things. Jesus embodied the spirit of holiness as few others have done, but that did not make him God or indicate he had capabilities superior to ours.

Jesus was one of history's most remarkable men. I doubt he could have solved calculus problems, but he thoroughly understood the crucial matter of how we get right and stay right with God. Some of us have no need to solve calculus problems, but all of us need the proper information Jesus provided about the salvation process. Salvation is available to us, not because Jesus died but because it is and always has been God's free gift to us. We move toward it when we believe Jesus and act like it.

# PART THREE

# FOLLOWERS OF JESUS

# CHAPTER 17

# EARLY FOLLOWERS

The New Testament Gospels spent extensive effort trying to prove what and who Jesus became, but they provided little information about his earthly life or his initial followers. However, perhaps unintentionally, they reveal far more than many of us realize. Matthew, Mark, Luke, and John focused on the "Christ of faith," which means the authors were obviously unconcerned with or did not have much factual information about the human Jesus or his followers. Because of when they wrote, their statements about the human Jesus and his followers may be largely conjecture at best. Several noncanonical Gospels offer some additional information on Jesus and his followers.

Paul provides almost no useful information on the earthly Jesus or Jesus's immediate followers. Paul had no concern for the human Jesus, believed Jesus's followers were mistaken, refused to gather information from Jesus's disciples, and apparently shunned any who believed as Jesus did. Because of Paul's prior and adamant persecution of the early followers of Jesus, he certainly knew specific information about them and Jesus, or else why did he persecute them? He refused to share why he did it or what he knew about Jesus and them. If Paul learned anything about Jesus and his followers during his short stay with Ananias, he never admitted or mentioned it. It appears he sought to avoid further contact with the early followers of Jesus. Recorded meetings with Jesus's disciples were sparse and perhaps not very pleasant. His rejection of them is affirmed in Galatians 1:16–17 by saying he received no instructions from any human beings, including the apostles, but "went away at once to Arabia."

The book of Acts, written by the author of Luke, is largely a possible travelogue and diary for Paul, with little factual information on early followers of Jesus. Because it was written after the Gospel of Luke (after 85 CE) and by the same author, the initial followers of Jesus and Paul were likely deceased. Much of Paul's ministry and life were not recent history for the author of Acts, and it sometimes conflicts with Paul's personal reports. We read and wonder.

Other New Testament writers tell about activities and teachings within the Christian churches and communities, with few references to the original followers of Jesus. Secular literature written in the first century does little more than mention Jesus or his followers. Therefore, we are left with little factual data about those who knew Jesus best. With careful analysis of the information we have, logical thought, and reasonable conjecture, we may open windows through which we can look.

Various types of people associated with Jesus, beginning with his diverse disciples. We must remember there is a distinct difference between those who followed only to hear or see Jesus and those who seriously followed him in belief and behavior. We have no guest list for his large or small gatherings, no tally sheet containing their headcount, and no list of those who signed up for service. Those thousands who reportedly gathered may have been someone's purposeful overestimate of the crowds to prove a point. We can only guess who or how many gathered around Jesus at any given place or time. (How many people does it take to make a crowd?) We must remember Jesus did not always wait for people to come to him, but it seems he went to individuals and small groups.

Some people surely came to hear Jesus out of curiosity, but many came for very personal reasons. Some followed because of his compassion, ability, and willingness to facilitate the healing of body and soul. Other were attracted by his revolutionary insight that enabled everyone to truly worship without making an expensive blood sacrifice. Because of several hints, we surmise that many of his followers were less than affluent, but he freely associated with people from all social classes, including the sick and women. Even though large groups may have occasionally gathered around him, individuals and small groups likely consumed most of his time. He probably had his greatest influence in small groups by sharing meals, visiting, worshipping, casual conversations, and making everyone feel significant and included.

There is a story about a man who said to his friend, "Your wife sure lights up the room when she enters." The husband replied, "Why not? Everything she has on is charged." Gospel writers indicated Jesus lit up the town and charged up the community wherever he went. However, those reports may be inaccurate, at least in some places and to some degree. Villages were small and separated. We have no valid information on how far people traveled to hear him, how far they physically followed when he left an area, or if he made a lasting difference when he was no longer there. Did he visit small villages or only the larger towns or both? Given the conditions of that day and the people, extensive crowds who traveled great distances to hear or be with Jesus were the exception, if not almost impossible. If huge crowds repeatedly gathered to hear him, there is more to the story than we have been told, specifically about food, water, sanitation, places to sleep, and other necessities.

Contrary to what Gospel writers insinuate, it is reasonable to assume Jesus was not liked by everyone he met during his traveling ministry, not popular every place he went, not always greeted by friends, and did not necessarily gather a huge crowd at everywhere he went. For Jesus to be whom the Gospel writers declared, he had to be popular everywhere he went and had to draw large crowds on whom he always had unusual and positive effect. Reports that large crowds desperately clamored to be near Jesus was another possible way that authors attempted to prove his prominence. The authors proclaimed,

"See, everybody in town knows who he is, and they follow him," while many did not, and some people even despised him.

At some unknown times and places, the crowds became significant enough for the Roman and religious authorities to get concerned. There may have been no problems with authorities in small villages and the open-air meetings, but things were different when Jesus came to the big cities. The pronouncements of any popular man and the size of the crowd following him were both carefully monitored in certain places under Roman rule. The size of a crowd may not have been as important as its exuberance, frequent gatherings, and assumed purpose. "Little but loud" groups probably gained immediate attention from the secular and religious authorities (Triumphant Entry). If Jesus was designated by the authorities or local people as a miracle worker or healer or popular or different or a troublemaker, he and his immediate followers may have been under early and close scrutiny, especially in cities like Jerusalem. Apparently, there were some specific conflicts with the Pharisees that may have contributed to his eventual demise. We have no indication when or where Jesus and his followers were put under observation or if he or they were ever warned to cease and desist whatever they were doing.

Who provided Jesus and his followers with food and lodging, both daily and during his travels? Did Jesus have a home, wife, family, and job prior to and during his ministry? If so, how were they affected? Did he primarily provide for himself wherever he lived and wherever he went? With whom did he stay over extended stretches of time while away from home, if he had a home? Did faithful followers accompany him with adequate supplies? Did he or they furnish funds to purchase what was needed? Were there predetermined places along the way that provided for his or their physical needs? Were there public accommodations for travelers? Did Jesus travel alone and, like the Cynics and other roving preachers of his day, depend on the generosity of those he met? The lifestyle of a Cynic is strongly indicated for the traveling Jesus and his disciples. The Gospels indicate that he carefully instructed his disciples on more than one occasion, prior to sending them on a preaching mission, to carry almost nothing and depend on the generosity of those they met for their physical needs. That instruction caused no alarm for the disciples, because that was apparently how disciples and peasant preachers normally lived and traveled. Jesus's specific instruction to his disciples causes us to suspect he normally traveled in that manner, but there were probably periodic and extended exceptions.

Jesus's strongest support probably came from ordinary people who supported him as best they could with the best they had. It is difficult to believe otherwise. I experienced that kind of hospitality when my family and I lived on the Greek island of Crete. We were traveling in the countryside, and total strangers rushed out to the road, stopped us, and insisted we join their party, because they knew we were away from home. If we were visiting a small village near nightfall, it was quite common for a total stranger to ask if we needed food and lodging. If, perchance, you visited anyone's home, you absolutely must eat or drink something! Refusal to do so was a serious insult. Be assured, whatever they gave you was the best they had, regardless of its taste or texture. On our visit with an elderly, emaciated Greek Orthodox priest, he provided fresh almonds. At his insistence, he shelled them one by one and handed them individually to each of us. That was the best, if not all, he had, to give us. I believe the peasant people treated Jesus in a similar manner, whether they knew him or not.

Was there a specific group of followers who always accompanied Jesus everywhere he went? The specific number and names of disciples may have been a partial creation by the Gospel writers for their own purpose. If there was ever a select group designated as special disciples, it is highly possible their number was more or less than twelve at any given time or location. Thirteen people traveling in a group during the entire travels of Jesus is far beyond reasonable, because of many practical issues. It is doubtful that twelve disciples, or a specific one or two, always accompanied Jesus, especially if they or he had a family or a job. It is possible that one or more may have accompanied Jesus and acted as a scout, helper, companion, and confidant. If so, was one of them his wife, who added a special feminine touch to his caring and healing ministry?

There is no indication of the order in which Jesus addressed the needs of those who sought his help. Conjecture tells us Jesus did what he could for as many as he could. An often-overlooked and extremely significant fact is that no record tells us if Jesus tried to meet the physical hunger he confronted. Given the environment in which we believe he did his ministry, there was undoubtedly much hunger, both physical and religious. There are no indications Jesus sought to alleviate physical hunger but surely he did. If Jesus had been divine, he would have also addressed and fulfilled that vast need. His apparent inability to meet that need indicates the type and degree of healing he could perform, likely limited to certain physical, social and religious disorders. His ability to help in any one of those areas was enough to command a large following. Since he was only human, he primarily gave from himself because that was basically what he had to give. Those who received new life and new hope through what he gave were so affected they correctly called him *savior*.

For obvious reasons, many of the marginalized had no perfect attendance award from the distant temple or a local synagogue, but it seems many of them longed for meaningful worship. Jesus demonstrated and taught reasonable religious beliefs and doable worship practices for any who needed or wanted them. By willingly administering to certain physical needs of the poor, Jesus thereby demonstrated a radically new religious response of love and concern for others, previously unknown by the marginalized and unpracticed by the affluent religious leaders. Since Jesus was obviously at odds with some Jewish practices, did he and some of his followers, at some point, no longer worship in the temple and synagogues but worship primarily outdoors and in nontraditional places? By that action, Jesus gave a new meaning to worship. Given the composition of the those who followed him, certain ones may have been forbidden to worship in the temple or synagogues. Likewise, Jesus's confrontations with religious authorities were most often at places other than the temple.

We do not know if Jesus abandoned temple worship, but most of his known ministry seems to have been in places far away from and far different from a temple gathering. If there were synagogues in various places he visited, we lack information on how he was received by them.

Jesus gave worship a new meaning. He purposely modeled worship for his followers through sharing and caring sessions, prayer, quiet meditation, and ministry to others. The shared meals may have been special bonding times of inclusive fellowship and meaningful worship for the diverse attendees. Shared meals and small groups appear to have offered numerous learning opportunities. They were the most meaningful and enduring "worship services" because they bound diverse participants together and emphasized equality for all members of society, including women and the sick. The odds are that Jesus was often the host who provided the meal at his expense, and it may have consisted of only bread and wine, a regular meal for many. Those shared meals were unforgettable experiences for participants who later used similar ones as a reminder of who Jesus was and who they were. Those meals proclaimed inclusiveness in God's kingdom on earth. They were visual aids for genuine worship. Those gatherings encompassed various types of participants to whom Jesus proclaimed their oneness with him and each other in God's kingdom, regardless of class, health, condition, or gender. The proclamations in and by those worship services were about as opposite of Jewish worship and practices as Jesus and his followers could get.

Were followers of Jesus strongly discouraged from participation in regular Jewish worship? There are no indications of any vociferous opposition to Jewish worship by Jesus, but there are indications he tried to reform it and enlighten others. He participated in a different religious life and lifestyle from the Judaism around him. Jewish worship centered around offering live animal sacrifices, but Jesus focused on worship of and service to God wherever he was and by whatever he did. More than once, he reportedly told them something different from what they had been taught. To what degree he did that, in what spirit he said it, or if he said more or did more, we do not know. Accusations brought against him during his trial, if there was a trial, may indicate teachings that bordered on deliberate opposition to Judaism and his encouragement to shun it. The charges brought may not have been anything close to what he actually said or the real reason to destroy him. The number of his followers who had renounced formal Judaism was never mentioned, but their rejection may have been a major reason for the Jewish authorities' dislike of Jesus and his subsequent crucifixion. Did Jesus's open opposition to formal Judaism make him popular among the poor and public enemy number one for religious authorities? The crowds who occasionally followed him may have been more of a threat to the religious authorities than to Rome. Jesus advocated the sufficiency for salvation according to the messages of Moses, Amos, and Micah. That was in direct opposition to the local legalistic religious teachings and the lucrative business associated with required sacrifices in Jewish worship. Why would his followers need or want to attend the temple or synagogues?

Followers likely heard Jesus, a devout Jew, recite the Shema (Deuteronomy 6:5–6) every day. He may have quoted it often and openly during his daily worship or private meditation or even as the text for his Friday night homily. Having informed them of this requirement to worship God above all else and having explained its meaning, he no doubt added and emphasized another requirement that said, "You shall love your neighbor as yourself" (Leviticus 19:18b). The marginalized were likely stunned to learn these two directives from Moses summarized the entire commandments from God and the Torah. They were further amazed when Jesus told them they should and could follow those two ancient directives and thereby enter the kingdom of God, without meeting the sacrificial requirements imposed upon Jewish worshipers. That brought welcome relief to any who struggled with Jewish worship that required expensive animal sacrifices and legalistic living.

Sacrifices required for temple worship were major impediments to the poor followers of Jesus. They undoubtedly discussed with him their predicament, of which he was already keenly aware. He probably reminded them of the ancient Hebrew prophet, Micah. (Again, Jesus selected answers from ancient Hebrew teachings. Nothing new was needed.) Long ago, Micah knew expensive sacrificial offerings were major impediments to worship for the poor. Jesus may have told them Micah's story, how he had seriously contemplated the required sacrifices and repeatedly pondered, "With what shall I come before the Lord?" (Micah 6:6). Micah contemplated several possible answers, including burnt offerings of one-year-old calves, thousands of rams, ten thousand rivers of oil, or even the sacrifice of his firstborn son. He eventually concluded not one of those, all of them combined, or anything else was required because sacrifices of that nature were totally unnecessary. Then Jesus told them Micah's powerful conclusion was "He has told you, O mortal, what is good; and what does the Lord require of you but to do justice, and to love kindness and to walk humbly with your God" (Micah 6:6–8). Then Jesus said to his followers, "Believe Micah and believe Moses. Each of you can meet their directives with what you have and where you are." Having heard, heavy burdens were slowly and surely lifted, and the words of Moses and Micah became another doorway for the poor to join the Jesus movement.

After the hearers recovered from the shock of what Jesus had just said, the diehards probably protested. Perhaps Jesus added, "If the words of the Shema and Micah are insufficient to explain how each of you can enter the kingdom of God, there is at least one other profound prophet who made a similar point." He then shared how Amos, speaking on behalf of God, declared God despises raucous religious festivals and solemn assemblies; no grain or large burnt offerings are acceptable, and the worshippers' disgusting music could no longer be tolerated. Instead of that nonsense, Amos declares, "But let justice roll down like waters, and righteousness like an ever-flowing stream" (Amos 5:24). That simple message about justice was definitely understood by many because injustice had been a part of their life. They knew what it was like to be poor and suffer injustice. Since the marginalized were often too poor to participate in organized worship and the incapacitated were very unwelcome at Jewish worship services, Jesus's message was music to their ears, because they already had everything needed to worship God. Jesus gave worship a new meaning from what they had previously thought. The hearers were absolutely amazed and said one to another, "We now know the reasons for his behavior."

Having said all this, we must confess we do not know from what section of society the majority of Jesus's followers came or to what degree his teachings were accepted, believed, and practiced. Gospel writers were probably correct when they indicated his followers were primarily the marginalized and poor, but I firmly believe his followers were from all classes.

We have been led to believe Paul swooped in, herded all the followers of Jesus into Paul's theological sheep fold, declared himself the chief shepherd, and named the newly formed flock "Christian." However, we must not identify the early followers of Jesus as Christians or assume after Jesus's death they immediately became followers of Paul. Both conclusions are incorrect if we can believe brief comments from Paul. He said that very soon after his vision, he purposely separated himself from the Jesus movement by purposely going to Arabia. For several years, he focused specifically on the Gentiles, but the followers of Jesus focused on the Jews (Galatians 1:13–2:9). If those comments are correct, the Jesus movement and Paul's followers remained somewhat separate and continued their ministry in two different locations for years. However, for several reasons, I doubt the dividing line for ministry was that precise, especially for the Jesus movement. The Jesus movement was and perhaps remained anchored in ancient Hebrew doctrines but different from the Judaism Jesus confronted and the Judaism that launched Paul. Just because Paul sought Gentile audiences does not mean members of the Jesus movement avoided them. The name *Christian* was not established until year later and was probably given to the followers of Paul, because of one of his specific beliefs.

The early followers of Jesus continued to promote the portions of ancient Judaism that Jesus emphasized. The Jesus movement was reformed Judaism but a form of Judaism nonetheless. Paul, also a

Jew, introduces a third Jewish movement that was radically different from the ancient Hebrew religion Jesus taught and different from the Judaism of Paul's day. The exact process by which the name *Christian* came into use is unknown and debatable, but it seems followers of Paul became known by that name, not because of what Jesus had taught or done but rather because of Paul's presupposition that the crucified and resurrected Jesus became "the Christ" or the English translation of the Greek word *Christos*. At some unknown point, those who believed with Paul that Jesus was the Christ became known as Christians, a word that perhaps was originally used in derision. We have no separate name for those who remain members of the Jesus movement and believed Jesus.

Did Jesus and his followers intend to start a new religion? There is no valid argument they did and strong evidence they did not. Jesus made deliberate efforts to restore Jewish worship to its Hebrew core, not replace it. Jesus openly opposed the fallacies of Judaism, but by no means did he renounce the very core of Hebrew beliefs. He said or did nothing contrary to that core, which the current Judaism ignored. Jesus was a devout Jew, remained a Jew, and his followers knew that. From Jesus's perspective, the Judaism of his day was the new religion, far removed from its core. In modern sports terminology, Jesus blew the whistle and called the fouls, but he did not cancel the game, abolish the sport, initiate a new game with new rules, or let the air out of the ball. He and his followers intended to play the game vigorously by the original rules and encouraged others to join them for everyone's good. These facts should be shouted from every pulpit in the land, because Jesus and his followers were Jewish reformers who sought only to restore Judaism to its proper foundation of appropriate love. Nothing else was needed or intended.

We are puzzled because we have no record of any immediate follower of Jesus joining with him to deliberately challenge the status quo within Judaism. Likewise, we know of no one among the followers of Jesus who resisted Paul. Were any followers of Jesus capable of such action, or were they largely a motley band from the lower social classes in society who could do little more than believe, witness, march, and shout? If Jesus was as prominent as our records indicate and if his message was as contrary to the religious and secular teachings of his day as we have been led to believe, surely some of his followers joined him in open opposition to existing religious and social conditions and would have later confronted Paul. The absence of recorded opposition may not be because it did not happen but because it was unknown, considered unimportant, or objectionable.

It should now be clear that within a brief period of time, the early Christian community was seriously affected by three distinct and very serious disruptions or breaks. The first irreversible break came between the Jesus movement and the existing Jewish community, because of Jesus's unsuccessful attempt to restore Judaism. The second break soon followed, between the early followers of Jesus and Paul because Paul disassociated himself from the followers of Jesus, totally disregarded the teachings and practices of Jesus, and focused primarily on the significance of Jesus's death and resurrection. The third major break came between Paul and the Judaism of his day because Paul declared Jesus was the Messiah, which altered the prevailing Jewish beliefs and practices he had previously and recently proclaimed. Each one of these three major breaks had its own history, emphasized its own presuppositions, and had its definite influence on Christendom.

Paul created a new religion that had a most interesting twist. He claimed to have one foot in the Jesus movement and one in current Judaism, but he actuality had a foot in neither. He was affected by and claimed to be a follower of Jesus, but he did not follow Jesus's two doable directives or care for the marginalized. Paul believed the current Jewish emphasis on an expected Messiah and said Jesus was the "anointed one," but the Jewish authorities totally disagreed. Paul denounced Jesus's declaration that appropriate love was sufficient for salvation, declared the necessity for Jesus's death and resurrection, and radically altered current Jewish beliefs. Paul's new presuppositions were far removed from current Judaism and from Jesus's teachings and ministry, which means he also started a new religion.

We do not know what effect Paul's new presuppositions had on the original Jesus movement. According to Paul, he did not purposely attempt to demolish it. However, it is as if the immediate followers and teachings of Jesus fell off the pages of history shortly after the crucifixion. If Jesus traveled as much and as far as indicated, his followers were widely scattered. If terribly scattered, that may explain the lack of a firm leader, the loss of collective strength, and few reports. Those conditions and the social status for the majority of Jesus's followers inevitably contributed to their being outflanked and disregarded. Even if Paul had not told us the followers of Jesus continued their ministry, reason reminds us that there was no way they were demolished overnight and disappeared without a fight. Paul may have shunned them, but that did not destroy them. They did not sit around and wait for Jesus's return and the end of time. They were committed to the lifestyle and ministry of Jesus and did not surrender, even without a resurrection. Bits of information beyond the Gospels indicate some of them continued their ministry. Threads of their beliefs appear in New Testament writings and the discussions by church fathers.

Persecution of the Christians is another big book with many blank pages. The who, why, where, and when remain unknown. There is ample evidence that it repeatedly occurred, perhaps beginning with Paul (Saul). The practice and presence of further persecution apparently provided the backdrop for several New Testament passages. We can only wonder if persecution was primarily against the Jesus movement, the Pauline believers, or both. Paul reported considerable opposition and persecution for himself, but that provides no information on the extent of persecution for members of the Jesus movement. Widespread persecution proves that some form of the Christian movement was somewhat successful. Willingness to suffer and die for "the cause" may have been rooted in the example set by Jesus.

To what degree were the immediate followers of Jesus affected by the disciples' affirmation "He is alive"? Without doubt, at least some of them continued to care for the marginalized as best they could, break and share bread as they met together, recall and emphasize what Jesus said, share with others their experiences with him, worship

God as Jesus directed, and invite others to join them in building a community of appropriate love, all without witnessing a resurrection of Jesus. That was their life and lifestyle. But what about those who were beyond the circle of close disciples? Did the disciples become traveling evangelists, or was that necessary? Perhaps Jesus's previous presence and ministry in distant places left behind a few outspoken witnesses who already knew Jesus's spirit could not be destroyed. They already knew what the disciples later proclaimed after Jesus's death. They believed Jesus's spirit was alive, and they acted like it. They continued to minister without need for or having heard of a resurrection, which emphasized the impact Jesus had on those who heard and believed him.

The early followers of Jesus were diverse and determined witnesses. It would be very informative if we had accurate information from those who personally knew Jesus and continued his teachings, ministry, and lifestyle following his cruel death. We must settle for the little we are able to deduce from the skimpy records and from what we can surmise. If we had those records, I believe they would reflect the Jesus movement remained very much alive and its members continued to believe Jesus and act like him.

# CHAPTER 18

# PRESENT-DAY FOLLOWERS OF JESUS

What have professing Christians done with, to, for, and because of Jesus? Would his initial followers recognize the person, gospel, and God proclaimed by us? We can only guess how comfortable or uncomfortable they would be if they walked into a multilevel ornate sanctuary with a gigantic pipe organ or a huge megachurch with loud and lively music or a church where very pious clergypersons were wearing their brightly colored uniform of the day. Would they be more at home in a small, informal country church with no air conditioning that did have hand-held wooden-handled cardboard fans with an advertisement for a funeral home on one side and a picture of Jesus knocking on a closed door on the other? Perhaps they would be more comfortable at the cowboy church without walls, with guitar music, among the horses and seated on the fence, a bale of hay, or a saddle. Maybe they would prefer a worship service for the homeless under a bridge or in the makeshift chapel in the corner of the dining room at an assisted-living facility. How would they feel in a church that spoke in tongues or exuberantly proclaimed, "You must be washed in the blood of the lamb to be saved"? How would they feel if Jesus were the primary focus of worship and God was seldom mentioned? How would they respond to those whose worship is based on "What's in it for me?" We tend to think they would be delighted to worship where we regularly attend, and we believe they ought to have some question about the integrity and effectiveness of at least some of the other places.

Regardless of what Jesus's initial followers would think, professing Christians must pause and ponder if we intend to follow the dictates of Jesus. Many among us presently endeavor to worship God as Jesus directed. Even though we are doing the best we know, we may need new insight and adjustment. It is wise for us to reconsider where and how we intend to worship God and live by appropriate love. Since "Every tree is known by its fruits" (Matthew 12:33 and Luke 6:44), I fear the fruits of many professing Christians are different from Jesus's directives to love God above all else and to also love our neighbor as we love ourselves. I am afraid the intended purpose for church buildings and the intent of those who worship in them are not always for the glory of God and the betterment of everyone.

## A.  Bothersome Presuppositions

Previously, I discussed some beliefs about God that seriously disturb me. Professing Christians also proclaim certain presuppositions about Jesus that give me great concern. Beliefs are serious matters with vast consequences. I am amazed at the number of people who want to ride into heaven on the coattail of Jesus but disregard his emphasis on the necessity for appropriate love for God, neighbor, and self. Jesus is extremely important to and for us, but getting right and remaining right with God demands far more than saying, "I believe in the crucified and resurrected Jesus." Those bothersome beliefs are expressed in various ways and with different words. A few examples follow.

### 1.   Jesus Is Enough

Professing Christians naturally have concern about the procedure for getting right and remaining right with God, commonly called *salvation*. For many, one prominent presupposition affirms that believing in or on Jesus is the only key for anyone to acquire it. "That is enough," they say. They have the Jesus-only syndrome. For them, getting right with God focuses almost exclusively on Jesus, and God takes a back seat! Their expressed requirement decrees one must believe specific things about Jesus, not God, and do certain things related to Jesus before they can have salvation. Jesus is the one necessary connecting link between God and our salvation. That presupposition often arises out of other assumptions related to a belief in the fall of man, human depravity, a required ransom, and a resurrection. They assume humanity's condition is such that there is no hope without divine assistance, and only Jesus can change our fallen nature and pay our debt by his crucifixion and resurrection. They exclaim, with little explanation, "All we need is Jesus!"

Earlier, we discussed two particular Old Testament directives that give specific requirements and opportunities for getting right and staying right with God but they were not "believe in Jesus" or "believe on Jesus." Jesus identified and proclaimed both ancient directives, but neither focused on him. The necessity for a particular kind of love and the recipients of it are prominent in each directive. The primary focus is on love for God, never on Jesus as the Messiah, never on a ransom, never on a resurrection, and never on "What's in it for me?" We must also appropriately love self and others, but not first. From all the possibilities contained in the ancient Hebrew and Jewish religious traditions and all the available rules in the current Jewish religion (613), Jesus quoted those two ancient commandments. Nothing more was required, but also nothing less. I do not believe that is the usual meaning of "Jesus is enough."

If we only believe in or on Jesus, that fails to fulfill either of Jesus's two directives, which require designated beliefs and specific actions. Failure to fulfill one directive is an unavoidable failure to fulfill the other. In a previous book, *A Pain in the Gut,* I indicated how we always love God, neighbor, and self either appropriately or inappropriately and simultaneously. There can be no exception because they cannot be separated. They move in tandem. Loving God appropriately necessitates appropriate love for neighbor and self. Inappropriate love of neighbor or self makes it impossible to appropriately love God. That is exactly why Jesus gave his answer. That is why focusing only on Jesus and believing in or on him is not enough. However, Jesus is extremely important because he demonstrated how to fulfill the requirements, not because the requirements for our salvation were fulfilled by what happened to him.

## 2.   Getting to Heaven

Getting to heaven is a major concern for many professing Christians. Some of them do not enjoy their earthly life because they are overly anxious about the next one, where they anticipate spending time with Jesus and their loved ones. They are preoccupied with keeping all the prescribed and precise requirements for their entrance into heaven, as dictated by some religious authority. That is their primary guide and goal for life. Continuously haunted by the fear they will fail to keep all necessary requirements, they wonder if there might be one more rule about which they have not heard. They often eagerly seek one more leaderless Bible study where they join with like-minded people to do little more than pool their ignorance (but the fellowship can be positive). Contrast this fear and effort with the words from Jesus. In statements believed to be authentic, Jesus seldom if ever mentioned the afterlife but instead spoke of the kingdom being present among us as we live by appropriate love, not fear. Instead of attending additional Bible studies, some people may need to attend just one with an informed leader, resulting in more time to love and care for the needy, lonely, and sick who live in their neighborhood. Perhaps it would help if they included the homeless in their Bible study and then took them out to lunch. Perhaps they need to believe Jesus and trust in God's grace as they purposely practice appropriate love and forgiveness. The next life never concerned Jesus, but he said selfishness in this one will make us miss the available kingdom. Likewise, he clearly stated entrance into the kingdom of God is here among us, not at some other place. It is now, not later. The Gospel of Thomas, a pre-New Testament document, speaks of the realm of God as a possibility for ordinary people on earth where everyone loves appropriately. The quality and opportunities for this life, not the next, deeply concerned and consumed Jesus. Any biblical words attributed to him that emphasize the next life are most likely not his words.

Diligently trying to get to heaven initially sounds good, but exerting extensive effort just to get there can be very selfish, totally irrelevant, wasted effort, and unchristian. Those whose primary purpose in life is getting to heaven will likely be unsuccessful, but those who live by appropriate love will have a taste of it here on earth. Willingness to serve God at any cost is primary for a follower of Jesus, not the consuming effort to get something for self. Participating with God's spirit in this life produces in this life what they expect in the next. Some of the most frustrated, unhappy, and anxious people I have known were those who had no doubt they were heaven bound and believed they could not be stopped. Something is terribly wrong when love of God and others appears to be in short supply among those who are absolutely sure they have already been saved by the blood of Jesus. Contrast one's consuming efforts to get to heaven with the question, "Who is willing to be damned for the glory of God?" Consider the words of Dietrich Bonhoeffer, a Christian martyr at the close of the second World War. The first line of the preface to his book, *The Cost of Discipleship,* reports him having said, "When Christ calls a man, he bids him come and die." Let all professing Christians ponder these matters. Getting to heaven must not be our primary concern if we love God above all else.

### 3. *"Jesus Has Saved Me"*

Some professing Christians firmly hold on to a presupposition that actually piggybacks on the previous one. In order to get to heaven, they declare a person must personally believe in or on Jesus and then publicly declare not only that Jesus saves but also declare, "He has saved me." Note that it has already personally happened. They affirm that all who fail to publicly speak these specific words prior to their death will be sent to eternal punishment. There are at least six serious problems with this belief. First, Jesus does not save. He points us to God, who saves after we do our part. Second, that is far different from what Jesus declared as the keys to entering the kingdom. Third, it emphasizes particular words as if they contain magic. There are no magical words in attaining salvation, and there are other appropriate words that can reflect a person's confidence in his or her relationship with God. Fourth, apparently, some people do not know that words can be spoken without believing them, to save embarrassment, from fear of not saying them, to get someone off our backs, and just because others are saying them. Fifth, it indicates words, not a loving spirit, put us in the proper relationship with God. For Jesus, loving actions must follow our words. Sixth, no person has the authority or responsibility to proclaim final rewards or punishments for another.

### 4.  Once Saved

Having publicly said those special words and believing salvation is absolutely secure, some professing Christians add another dimension by affirming, "Once saved, always saved." It sounds as if it is one and done, with no need to ever be concerned again about salvation or behavior, because there is no possible way to break their right relationship with Jesus. Notice their relationship is with Jesus, not with God. Also, once you say the proper words and join hands with Jesus, you become a member of the heavenly union from which you will not and cannot leave; nor can you be kicked out under any conditions or for any reason. Any New Testament words in support of this belief certainly did not come from Jesus. The two commandments offered by him are not one and done, not just public proclamation of specific words, but rather they require a constant commitment to truth and love in our being and behavior wherever we are and as long as we live. Believing in or on Jesus does not make us a member of a union that has unconditional and unending membership. Our membership in the kingdom requires continuous and purposeful participation in appropriate love or the relationship will be broken.

## 5. *Saved by the Blood of Jesus*

Numerous professing Christians speak of being saved by the blood of Jesus and washed in the blood of the Lamb. Those words reflect a host of proclamations, most of which are directly connected to Paul, who would not renounce the Judaism of his day. Earlier, I told how he infused Jesus into his Judaism; the present proclamation, "saved by the blood of Jesus," reflects Pauline theology. According to Jewish doctrines, in order to attain salvation, an unblemished and live animal must shed its blood, its life-giving substance, in a sacrificial offering to expiate the sin of the one who offered it. The animal's blood is a sacrifice and a substitute for the one who offers it. Paul accepted that Jewish concept and believed, through the sacrificial death of Jesus, the Anointed One, God had recently provided humanity a substitute of such magnitude it negated any need for another. A blood sacrifice was still required for salvation, but that requirement was already met if one believes Jesus was it.

Those who accept Paul's presuppositions refer to the salvation process as being saved by the blood of Jesus. I suspect many who boldly declare this statement have no idea of its origin or meaning. I am deeply bothered by this belief because it is based more on legalistic Judaism than on the words of Jesus. Likewise, there is no emphasis on our responsibility to abide by appropriate love as Jesus insisted. It denies our responsibility to love appropriately.

## 6. *Anything Goes*

Modern presuppositions sometimes affirm almost anything goes, so long as we just profess a belief in God—but do not ask anyone who believes that to explain what it means. Once again, we confront a stated belief system without directions and required behaviors. It is as if the universe has no core values or rules and each of us is free to declare our own. Unless I have missed something, that is the recipe for chaos and destruction in every area of our lives. If we desire to live by appropriate love, that is not a lifestyle for which we make the primary rules, choose the place of application, determine the number of hours per week we work, set the conditions under which we agree to serve, and dictate our pay scale. We must know about Jesus's two directives and also make a conscious commitment to always abide by them. By design, accident, luck, grace, love, and personal effort, we can and must do both. It is necessary to have times and places to properly worship, study, pray, examine, search, confess, forgive, meditate, fellowship, discuss, and serve. As an individual or group, we must refurbish, refine, and renew our commitment to love appropriately, or we may unexpectedly slip away from love and truth and carelessly, perhaps even purposely, clasp an unhealthy hand. (No "once saved, always saved" here.) Since we are only human, we must establish and maintain some proper beliefs, boundaries, guides, and supports, or we can carelessly surrender our commitment by thoughtlessly accepting easy, pleasing, selfish, and less-demanding presuppositions. Those who live by appropriate love cannot subscribe to "anything goes as long as we profess a belief in God." Appropriate love must be consciously chosen and purposely practiced but also be so prevalent within us that it is most often unconsciously applied wherever we are.

Since beliefs largely determine our behaviors, those beliefs named above as bothersome are only a few among many that should concern us. They bother me because they seem to be less than truthful, and anything less than truth inevitably robs and destroys.

## B. Christian Worship

Present followers of Jesus need to be aware of what we really worship and how it affects our daily lives. Because of our nature, worship is unavoidable (chapter 2). Given that belief, I am concerned that too few professing Christians recognize or understand it. I previously identified worship as our response to whatever we value most, which means it is continuous. It is reflected in what we are as well as what we do. Our public and private worship may differ in format and location, but the purpose remains the same. We too frequently depend on others to direct our activities in formal worship services for one or two hours per week, but that may or may not be a part of genuine worship for us. Prescribed formal worship services that demand and dictate specific rituals, rites, robes, recitations, etc. are a long way from what Jesus practiced and prescribed. On the other hand, it seems Jesus never forbade anything that aided appropriate love of God, neighbor, and self, even if it radically differs from what pleases me.

Worship of God is not observing acts performed by someone specifically trained and attired, nor is it simply participating according to a designated format facilitated and encouraged by a leader or a printed program. Worship is a personal response that rises from the core of our being in reference to whatever we value most, whether in public or private. From the Judeo-Christian perspective, our worship reflects that either God or an idol is our highest value, and we demonstrate what that is by how we live. When guided by appropriate love, our formal worship is not a preordained series of designated hoops through which we weekly have to jump on one leg, with eyes closed, fingers crossed, reason renounced, and waiting to be yelled at if we yield to temptation by peeping with one eye during the "come to Jesus" altar call. Rather, our participation in organized, private, and appropriate worship of God has no specified time, format, or place. However, there may be particular practices, people, and places that enhance our worship. Regardless of place, time, or method, we are free to make a meaningful, joyful, and grateful response to God, while seeking enlightenment and empowerment to always love appropriately and act accordingly while at church, work, or play. Public and private worship demand effort and thought from us. The basic desire to appropriately worship God never changes, but the format, time, and place are unlimited.

My second concern associated with present followers of Jesus relates to the physical structure, if there is one, in which our worship occurs. What would Jesus think about the cost of our various places designated for worship? I suspect he would apply the same standard of judgment against their size, cost, and location that he would apply to any other thing we do; namely, does it reflect the love of God above all else and love of your neighbor as yourself? Whether an ornate edifice, a one-room wooden building with a tin roof, an open-air arena, or any other possible place of worship, the same judgment always applies. Our efforts to justify the ornate and gigantic buildings with their melodious and majestic pipe organs might not always receive an A+ if graded by the standards of Jesus. The size, purpose, and effectiveness of a white clapboard country church might not necessarily score well either. Overkill in size, aesthetics, and comfort, either accidentally or purposely, may seriously detract from helping the needy and unchurched for whom Jesus had great concern. Make no mistake, I love beautiful churches with pews comfortable enough to take a nap, with pipe organ music that soothes the mind and softens the heart, churches that have cardboard fans with wooden handles, or open-air locations with their accompanying animal odors and sounds, but I really wonder where we should draw the line on the expenditure for places we say are for the worship and glory of God. Is seems appropriate to ask, "What does the structure boldly say about what we worship, the priority of resources, and the god of those who worship there?"

A third concern is to or for whose glory these places of worship were established, even when reportedly erected for the glory of God. Members of many individual churches have recognized their purpose and have excelled in promoting love of God and neighbor, even with a few or several nonessentials. We are deeply grateful for those whose members show us what it means to appropriately love and worship God, regardless of the size, cost, and location of the building or the composition of the congregation. However, because of erroneous and unexamined presuppositions, buildings are too frequently monuments to Jesus or an edifice that identifies an affluent member and donor whose name appears first on its marquee ("Person's Name Memorial Church"). Perhaps this identifies a problem in

Christendom when monuments to Jesus and people were established instead of places whose intended and specific purpose was to worship God. If we disregard Jesus's two directives, the size, cost, location, and purpose for any place identified for worship may easily illustrate selfish desires, the misdirection of its mission, and worship of an idol. Though size and elegance may be intended to show commitment to love and truth, opulence may actually illustrate selfishness and idol worship. Magnificent or small churches with huge budgets spent primarily on salaries, upkeep, and internal programs too often seek personal comfort for their participants and forget the homeless near their door and the hungry of the world. Members of self-centered city cathedrals and the segregated country churches have not yet learned the identity of their god or the actions appropriate love would elicit from them. Everyone who proclaims their church was designed, dedicated, and is operated for the glory of God needs to back away from it and take a long, critical look.

A fourth concern is where and when we worship God. Other people inescapably affected our early understanding of worship and shaped our practice of it. They filled our box with presuppositions long before we knew what they were doing. Eventually, each of us became responsible for what, who, how, and where we worship, even if we never purposely made those choices. If we do not know what Christian worship is or how and where we participate in it, we may spend extended time in worship services without participating in the worship of God. Likewise, we may spend extensive effort to obey specific directives and wonder if we have done enough. If we are going to truly worship God, we must begin with the recognition of who God is and our proper response to him. That does not automatically come through osmosis but through learning and experience. Jesus provided some vital clues on the worship of God that are worthy of our consideration. He knew who his God was, and it was not himself. He was consciously concerned with loving God above all else and then acting like it by sharing Godlike love with others at all times and in all places. His life was worship. Worship was expressed in and by his relationship with God and other people.

215

He spent far more time outdoors or in buildings not specifically designed for worship. His loud and clear message states there is no recess period during worship. There can be no separation of behavior between weekday activities and Sabbath-day worship, because each is anchored in what we value most. It can be very helpful to spend an hour or two at a designated and special place, during which we sometimes think and talk about God or Jesus (or take a nap), but that does not free us from loving and living as Jesus directed for the remainder of that day and every other day of the week. What we do beyond the church building will always be connected to who, what, why, and how we worship inside it, and vice versa.

If an early follower of Jesus evaluated our church and our worship, what would he or she say? I suspect they would joyfully affirm those who worship and live by appropriate love. Our format and process for worship would be different but of little concern, as long as it facilitated genuine worship of God and not Jesus. They might warn us of the serious dangers if we forget who and why we worship and the ease with which that can occur when we erect our buildings, design our programs, and go about our daily lives. Perhaps they would remind us that just as Jesus reached back to Moses to get his directives for living, we must reach back to what Jesus taught and how he lived. Our world may be very different from theirs, but the rules for appropriate love and genuine worship of God remain the same.

## C. Love for Others

Present followers of Jesus speak of love and usually admit love for others is necessary. Having said that, they frequently qualify that love and identify those whom they love. Many find it difficult to appropriately love those who do not believe like them, look like them, and are not of their race, church, country, sexual orientation, etc. Their love (or is it just *like,* if it even goes that far) frequently gets iffy when they say, by word and action, they will love *if* this or *if* that. Jesus issued no "if certificates" on behalf of God and no exceptions for loving everyone as yourself. How shocking for some to learn they must appropriately love even those who are very different, those they dislike, and even those they detest.

The requirement to love your neighbor as yourself is problematic for many, perhaps because they do not understand the meaning of this kind of required love. It does not mean you have to be their best friend, invite them to dinner every Sunday, repeatedly stay overnight in their home, or sleep with them. My previous definition of love is very helpful. "Love is wanting for someone or something to have what they need for their health, happiness, and wholeness and wanting it to the extent that I am willing to freely give up something I have in order for them to have what they need." That does not allow us to decide whom we will love, but it does give guidance on what it means to love everyone, including self. It does not state what we give, but it will be something they needed and something we have. It further states that when we love, we will help others when we can, including our enemies. That kind of love changes enemies into friends and helps both giver and receiver.

How to decide what another needs is and will always be debatable. However, it is not as difficult as we sometimes pretend, because we are to love them as we love ourselves and to treat them as we wish to be treated (the Golden Rule). It may help if we ask, "If I were in their condition and position, what would I need and want?" If we do that and respond accordingly, we will most often demonstrate appropriate love. Like it or not, all of us are important, and each of us has some responsibility to help others, which always requires a rational response to the situation. Loving them is not just for their good. It is also necessary in order for us to *be good.* If we take seriously the teachings and ministry of Jesus, no one, not even our vicious enemy, can be left outside our circle of love. Godlike love includes everyone.

Regardless of who they are and what they worship, we must admit the religious DNA found deep within every person reflects a kinship with us because the core spirit of everyone is connected to God. Anything other than appropriate love divides, robs, and destroys, including those unwilling to love as well as the unloved. Do we want everyone to have "the fruits of love," as directed by Jesus, or just the ones we choose? Any attempt to limit the ones we love is inappropriate love, a sure way to prove we disbelieve the directives of Jesus, and it is the forerunner of serious difficulty. The alarming truth is those people who love appropriately but are declared misfits and cast aside by some professing Christians may be closer to the kingdom of God than those professing Christians who cast them aside.

## D. We Want to "Be Good" (Love Appropriately)

Most modern followers of Jesus say they want to be and try to be good people. Most declare they have been basically free from major mistakes and have lived peacefully with their neighbors (most of the time). Many attend, at least occasionally, the church of their choice and express firm belief in the doctrines of their denomination, even if they have no idea what they are or mean. Most of them believe that is enough to qualify as Christian. The majority believe they were taught correctly and are following those teachings to the best of their ability and the best they know. "The best they know" is often less than and different from the inclusive directions of Jesus, but they pride themselves on being good Christians.

Given our nature, I believe that in the core of our being, we long to be good, to get right with God, and that we will be uncomfortable, dissatisfied, ill at ease, etc. until we do. Our innate spirit longs to be closely associated with God's spirit (our search for the indescribable something). Nothing else will satisfy our inner self, and nothing else will enable us to be at peace. Like a washing machine in the spin cycle with an unbalanced load, we spin and bump against the constraints until we get right with God through appropriate love, or we remain unbalanced in many ways. In his *Confessions*, St. Augustine reminded us our hearts are restless until they rest (get right) with God. This is certainly true for professing Christians and possibly for everyone everywhere.

Those who practice badness are seldom happy, and very few of them believe they are good people. Their unwise search for goodness may even generate further badness as they mistakenly search for appropriate love in all the wrong places and ways. The badness they perform may even be an attempt to do something good or to feel good. None of us is always able to get it right, but I suspect there is a correlation between getting it right and having the right spirit within us. There is also a correlation between having the right spirit within us and the environment in which we were born and lived.

I have spoken with faithful, kind, loving, generous, caring, and well-educated worshippers who expressed their desire to be good but feared they were not good enough. However, they are good in so many ways through purposeful living, kindness, and generosity. There are few obvious flaws in their beliefs and behaviors. Few others would suspect they have that fear. It appears that most of them firmly hold on to old and erroneous religious presuppositions, implanted earlier by religious authorities, that insist on perfection, and they are afraid to let them go. That response in not uncommon or unexpected. That is the normal outcome for people who begin to think seriously about presuppositions and firm admonitions that demand legalistic religion. Most often, they conclude they are not good enough because they or their predecessors failed to fulfill all religious requirements. Like Paul, trying to fulfill the law will always lead to doubting our goodness. Those old, inappropriate presuppositions insist they cannot be good without being perfect, but they know perfection is impossible and attempting to be perfect cannot give peace. They hurt but they want to be good. They need new insights about their humanness. They need new and positive presuppositions that affirm their humanness, their present goodness, and the fact that they can be good if they choose.

We can never be perfect, but we can attempt to love appropriately. Getting right and remaining right with God does not depend on how well we obey laws but rather on how we love. When appropriate love directs us, we will be good, and that will be good enough.

## E.  Love Hangs On to Us

Some present followers of Jesus believe we survived our erroneous proclamations and behavior only because some of us hung on to appropriate love. There may be a modicum of truth in that, but the better statement is that God and truth hung on to us. Because of God's indestructible nature, his pursuing love never gave up on us and never will. We never need to ask for his spirit to come where we are, and if we do, that is an affront to God. We cannot remove its presence or stop its pursuit. Erroneous presuppositions, inappropriate love, and human ignorance endanger what love is allowed to do for and in us. The number of those who obviously carried the flame of love and truth may have periodically waned, but the ever-present spark remained among us, even in unlikely places and through strange circumstances. That hidden spark has previously burst into flame in unexpected places, times, and people. Throughout all the years of misinformation, erroneous presuppositions, and false proclamations, love and truth remained among us, even when we did not know it. Like the symbolic picture of Jesus on the country church fan, love always knocks on our door and offers us a better way to live. That is what love and truth always do and are presently doing. Because of its essence, appropriate love always invites, or perhaps demands, us to participate with it in order to find greater purpose and inner peace. Our future will always be disrupted and in doubt if we blatantly disregard love's directives.

In spite of what we believe or do, love and truth always hang on to us and offer us a chance and a choice to hang on to them. Because of God's nature, love will always hang on to us, but in order to complete the connection, we must make some effort to claim it and hang on to it by what we love and how we live. We must consciously seek to hold on to love or suffer the consequences. Our promise lies in the sure fact that love will always hang on to us, but our quality of life and love always depend on how well we hang on to it.

## F.  Need Good Neighbors

Followers of Jesus want and need good neighbors. Everyone is a neighbor. My neighbor is anyone and everyone beyond me. The presence or absence of appropriate love automatically affects everyone's treatment of their neighbor. At our birth, we moved into a new neighborhood, which deeply affected the kind of neighbor we became. Any attempt to rearrange the rules by any insider or outsider was often rejected. We slowly learned the rules for participation in that neighborhood and then a much wider one. Our initial neighborhood largely determined whom we considered a neighbor and how they should be treated. Eventually, knowingly or unknowingly, we decided who was our neighbor.

The directive from Jesus tells us to love our neighbor appropriately. This is an undeniable part of Christian living, because it is contained in the absolute rule for getting right and remaining right with God. Appropriate love of our neighbor benefits the neighbor and us. Likewise, our neighbor will unavoidably love us in some way, but we need their appropriate love, just as they need ours. Anything less from either adversely affects both, just as appropriate love strengthens both. There are no one-way streets in a neighborhood dominated by appropriate love. Any attempt to create one destroys the neighborhood and results in a very unhappy or unhealthy lifestyle for more than one person. In an effort to be a good neighbor, we cannot isolate ourselves or our neighbor. Two imperfect sticks, even when bent and partially broken, can sometimes prop each other up but only if they are nearby neighbors who willingly support each other. "Love your neighbor as you love yourself" is not just a good suggestion. It is another absolute rule, reiterated by Jesus, which he did not make and which we cannot break.

## G.  Christians and Persecutions

Followers of Jesus have been persecuted from the time of Jesus to this day. Some people who really believe Jesus and endeavor to act like it are presently under persecution by ways we seldom realize or will admit. It can be unintentional, because of lack of understanding, but most often it is purposefully done. Purposeful and painful opposition directed toward others does not always go by that name. Persecution comes to those who garner the headlines as well as to those who get no noticeable publicity. It is somewhat ironic that those who believe Jesus and act accordingly are often severely ridiculed, publicly renounced, and sometimes physically attacked by others who boldly affirm, "I believe in Jesus." In fact, the "I believe in Jesus" crowd usually do more harm to those who believe Jesus than those who make no claim to follow Jesus at all. (That fact should disturb us.) How sad that those who adamantly profess to believe in Jesus do not know what it means to believe Jesus and act like it.

Many of those who believe Jesus and act like it have met serious, sometimes furious, opposition from places you never dreamed, in forms you never imagined, and from people you never expected. I know from experience. That is one reason I have special concern for those who believe Jesus and act like it. Just as in the day of Jesus, the opposition usually comes from both religious and secular authorities. It is well organized, adequately funded, vociferously proclaimed, and widely publicized. That was certainly true in 1963 when twenty-eight United Methodist ministers joined together to publicize their opposition to segregation. For me and others in that group, the most hateful, cruel, derogatory, untrue, demeaning, purposefully destructive words, actions, and threats came from denominational officials, fellow pastors, peers, and strong church supporters. All of them adamantly claimed to believe in Jesus. In an official gathering of ministers, one fellow pastor suggested those of us present who had recently signed a declaration supporting integration "should be lined up before a firing squad and shot." No other pastor in the group came to our defense or chided him for his comment, not even our supervisor. Shortly thereafter, my supervisor declared me unfit for further pastoral assignment, and my bishop concurred, even though the bishop had recently signed a similar statement and the law of the church said I must be given a pastoral assignment. Their intent was to publicly declare I did not know the truth, rob me of further ministry and witness in that state, deny income, and necessitate a different profession or relocation in order to financially support myself, my wife, and our two small children.

In large and small ways, similar persecutions remain among us, especially for those who proclaim an unpopular religious truth. The urgency to believe Jesus and proclaim that belief is upon us. The religious world does not appear to be moving toward unity and compassionate understanding. It may be moving farther away. Obedience to eternal truth in human history appears to imitate the up-and-down movement of a yo-yo, closer to truth at the top and then farther away. Humanity has never reached the top or bottom of the string. Presently, the yo-yo appears to be very far from the upper end. In the name of professed Christian religion, major sections of society renounce the rights, needs, and personhood of those who are different from them. Modern religious expressions tend to emphasize "What is in it for me and my group?" and not love of God and others. Present conditions emphasize the need for appropriate love to be proclaimed and lived. There is nothing else that can save us. Those who believe and act like Jesus will meet opposition from those who firmly hang on to presuppositions they have never pondered. The conditions in our world point to the urgent need for truth and appropriate love, or else we may reach the bottom of the string and destroy the world as we know it.

I contend there are many people who want to hear more about what it means to love appropriately. Some people are presently imprisoned by the content of their boxes. Their gatekeepers prohibit any change in beliefs, but they hurt. Some of them suspect why they hurt but cannot find strength to overcome their fear of what change would necessitate. Some who consider change must secretly seek information because any open search would engender persecution from their peers, parents, or even pastors. They need a good neighbor.

I cannot tell anyone exactly how to personally believe Jesus and act like it while under persecution. No one can. Having been in that situation for an extended time, I learned a few things and developed some ideas that may be helpful for any who face the same fate.

1. Stand firm in what you believe. Always be truthful to your belief, and do not water it down for any reason. There is nothing other than truth behind which to seek safe shelter because truth and love are the foundation of the universe. It helps to present the truth as kindly and gently as you can. Much earlier, I affirmed that only truth will set us as free as we can be. Your truthfulness will be under attack and often disbelieved, but unfounded lies from adversaries will be readily accepted as truth by others. Even then, calmly and patiently proclaim your beliefs as clearly as you can.

2. After a while, your presence will be your proclamation. Practice the "ministry of being" by endeavoring to embody the spirit proclaimed in the two commandments Jesus gave. Respond as best you can to all confrontations with love and truth, seeking to do and be what you proclaim. Be a good neighbor. Someone may get inquisitive and ask for your secret.

3. Be alert, observant, prepared, and waiting, never fooled or surprised at anything others say. Think carefully before speaking. People will bait you with less important issues, ask ridiculous questions, and try to trap you or to see if you are trustworthy and if they are important to you. There are many uncomfortable people seeking truth, many of whom will only secretly and safely discuss serious issues. Make sure they have that opportunity.

4. Look for humor and share it. Nothing softens opposition like humor, and it reflects your freedom to be you.

5. Having done your best to protect yourself from harm, do not be terribly afraid of what the opposition may do to you. God's spirit of love and truth will be present. Be assured, the two commandments prescribed by Jesus offer the only valid purpose and process for which to live and, if necessary, the only lifestyle for which to die. Unless we reach that level of complete commitment and are perfectly content in it, we have not given up idol worship and will have difficulty convincing others we really believe Jesus.

Religious persecution, under various names and practices, continues in far more places and by far more people than we want to admit. Unless we are very careful, we can inadvertently participate. Those who suffer from it need the care and encouragement of others who believe Jesus and try to act like it.

## H. Consequences of Loving

Our expressions of appropriate and inappropriate love have their inescapable consequences. There is no agreement on what the consequences are or will be. We already know some of them. When we get right with God, he does not negate all the damage we unwisely did to ourselves and others when we were selfish, mistaken, and misinformed. He does not clean up all the mess we made; nor does he guarantee we will always remain right with him. Divine forgiveness does not create, restore, or guarantee human perfection. It gives us a chance to remove and remodel our mess as best we can and then consciously try to do better. Like Jacob (in the Bible) our limp may remain, but we must do our best with what we have. Like him, both the ability to love appropriately and inappropriately will always be present. We decide which love will direct us. Whether based on appropriate or inappropriate love, a life of love is its own reward, here and now. Inappropriate love produces misery, disruption, and destruction, but appropriate love engenders personal joy and peace while seeking to love God above all else and our neighbor as ourselves. Most professing Christians are sure there will be a next life in which they will be rewarded with unending and indescribable joy, but all others will endure permanent punishment.

## I. The Next Life

What if there is no next life? What if the rewards and punishments for how we live in this life come to us in this life, not later and not elsewhere, just as Jesus seemingly specified when he said, "The kingdom is among you" (Luke 17:21)? Some noncanonical Gospels emphasize a present kingdom of love with no references to a next life. The lack of a next life staggers many minds and torpedoes major beliefs called Christian. It is essential to remember that any presupposition for the next life is, and has always been, the product of human minds, regardless of the credit given to God, Jesus, the Holy Spirit, or Paul. From the dawn of human history, people have wanted or needed to believe there is something reserved for us beyond this life. Efforts to appease the indescribable something were often intended to have favorable effects both in and also beyond this life.

Three questions about the next life have echoed across the corridors of time. They simply ask, "Will there be another life?" and if so, "What will it be like, and how do I prepare for it?" The answer to the first question is usually a resounding yes, but not from everyone. "How do I prepare for it?" has been repeatedly answered throughout human history with a multitude of diverse conclusions. Jews and Christians cannot agree. There is a plethora of possible answers to "What it will be like?" Those answers include nonexistence, diverse types of reincarnation in various forms or things, a personal bodily or spiritual resurrection, and others. Imagination, personal desire, misinformation, and faith are the foundation upon which a multitude of presuppositions have been offered and believed. Since these presuppositions remain unproven, no mortal knows the answers.

Do professing Christians need or just selfishly want a next life? Do we personally believe in it or do we accept what certain others have professed? Do we fear we have wrecked this life and need another one and also a special agent to remove the mess we made in this one? Are we selfish and foolish enough to believe what we have been and done deserve special rewards for our good beliefs and good behaviors? Will believing in Jesus or believing Jesus qualify us for everlasting joy and peace in our personal, private, and plush mansion, with unending room service and no chores? Do those who were evil in this life deserve eternal damnation because of what they did not know or what they knowingly or unknowingly did? Many professing Christians have their reasons for fervently believing in the next life, but from where did those presuppositions come, and how dependable are they?

There may not be a next life for us. That possibility is based on several significant points. First, I have found nothing in the authentic words of Jesus to his immediate followers that specifically addressed this subject. In authentic translations of scripture, Jesus does not speak of heaven in his model prayer. The "In my Father's house are many dwelling places" (John 14:2) sounds wonderful, but it is extremely doubtful Jesus said that. Apparently, the next life was not a hot topic for Jesus or his early followers. His entire ministry and mission were primarily concerned with meeting the needs of the marginalized around him and encouraging everyone, by words and examples, to live by appropriate love and then trust God for the results. Jesus's emphasis on appropriate love had almost nothing to do with future rewards, but it had everything to do with what controls our spirit, and thus our behavior, here and now. Paul radically changed the emphasis to a resurrected Jesus and an afterlife for Jesus and us.

Second, Jesus spoke words that indicate no next life when he declared, since the kingdom of God is among you, there is the possibility for God's spirit to rule in all who dwell on earth. If that is true, there is no need for another life, because the best God has to offer is already available in this life. That means we must accept personal responsibility for developing and maintaining the spirit Jesus demonstrated and proclaimed. No one can do that for us, no matter who claims otherwise. Given the human conditions that surround us, it is difficult for us to live by appropriate love, but we must consciously try. That possibility does exist, and if attained, we would then dwell in "the Father's house" here on earth. Perhaps living in the Father's house here on earth has to do with serious intent as well as actual accomplishment.

Third, I have serious doubts Jesus ever spoke about "treasures in heaven" as some future rewards. There are questions about the translation of that phrase and if he actually said that. His use of the phrase in Matthew 6:20 and Luke 18:22 most likely was referencing a lifestyle and spirit, not a specific location. If Jesus used "kingdom of heaven," he was not speaking about a future dwelling place but was offering encouragement for a life of appropriate love here on earth. Perhaps *heaven* was a symbolic term referencing the possibility for a life purposely guided by appropriate love here on earth.

Fourth, Jesus was concerned about life here and now. Pie in the sky by and by did not concern him, or he would have followed a drastically different lifestyle. No existing records indicate one iota of selfishness in Jesus. He was vitally concerned with appropriately loving others by providing healing and comfort for those on earth who were hungry for physical food, reasonable health, and religious truth. Proclaiming the good news about God and caring for the needy was far more important to him than a next life. Getting to heaven was not his primary topic, if he ever mentioned it. Jesus set the example for us.

Fifth, no mortal has been to the next life and returned to tell about it. Everything said or believed about it is human conjecture based on desire, imagination, assumptions, and hearsay. Even though some base the ideas on scripture, that does not change the source from which it originally came. Believing something is true because it is in the Bible does not guarantee it is.

Sixth, belief in a next life does not rest on a rational foundation. This belief hints at selfish wishes more than solid wisdom for those who believe it. Everything I know or believe about God appears to be rational, practical, and always coincides with other known systems that are interconnected with law and order. There is no rational foundation or connection for this belief to what we believe we know.

Seventh, since our individual essence is spirit, any argument for a next life must address the storage of individual spirits, both good and evil, until the day of judgment and then afterward. How and where that will or can be done is unimaginable and unnecessary.

Eighth, eternal punishment does not sound like "God is love and only acts from love." Since God is and acts only from love, he will send no one to a physical punishment of unending hellfire, even if they ask for it by the way they live.

Ninth, heavenly rewards sounds as if there are rewards for being what we should have been and for doing only what we should have done in this life. Even if that were true, none of us reaches that level.

Most of us were assured there will be a next life. Presuppositions based on personal desires, ours or our predecessors, can lead to pleasing conclusions, but that does not mean they are correct. Belief in the next life appears to depend more on human wishes than on solid wisdom, more on selfish desire than on common sense, and more on hearsay than on serious thought. Since life was given to us by God, it will reach its full potential only when we, like Jesus, become saturated with the spirit of holiness and basically lose the self in appropriate love, asking for nothing in return. When we do that, there is no need for a next life.

# CHAPTER 19

# HOW DOES IT END?

I do not know our eventual end or if there will be one. However, consistent with other expressed presuppositions, there are some possibilities that presently appeal to me. Even though we are dominated by either appropriate or inappropriate love, the possibility for the other is always present. Each thought and action may unknowingly add strength to one love and possibly diminish the other. One love gets stronger with use, even when we are unaware. I doubt there is a divine scorekeeper who records each occurrence, daily updates the checklist, and eventually, on some Judgment Day, will tally the numbers and hand out the scorecard stamped *passed* or *failed*. That is unnecessary, because each of us possesses a personal recorder that cannot be deceived for long. Having chosen our god, obedience to it will subconsciously bend our spirit in its direction. Obedience to our god rewards us with added strength to follow it. Even when unintended, we asked for it.

Our primary presupposition that inevitably became our god largely determines how we live and what we love. The source from which we inherited that god had a strong influence on what we consciously or unconsciously chose and why we worship it. The contagious spirit absorbed from the community into which we were born, the presuppositions consciously and subconsciously implanted into our boxes, plus the degree of our exposure to and acceptance of truth will follow us throughout life. However, we eventually become responsible for ourselves and can no longer blame others for what or how we love.

Even though I do not know if or how our existence will end, I am totally confident God's unchanging spirit of truth and love will respond to each of us at death just as in life. God will respond to each of us on the basis of his love and our love, regardless of what and how we loved, who we are, what we did, or what, how, and whom we worship. God is love and always acts only from love for everyone, even for those who are seriously mistaken, do not know how to love appropriately, worship differently, call their god by another name, worship idols, do not know what they worship, and do not know about Jesus. God shows no partiality to any of his creation. However, even though God loves everyone, the end result will not be identical for everyone; nor is there universal salvation. The determining factor is what kind of love possesses us and how we respond to God's love. We will receive our rewards in this life, based on our true spirit. There will be no need for God to act as judge at our death, because our spirit will enter the next phase for which we personally prepared, based on our love in this life. Death will usher our spirit into our final phase.

Getting right with God is not limited only to those who knew or know about Jesus. If that were true, all Old Testament heroes, including Abraham, Moses, the great prophets, and others, had no hope. Where would this leave Jesus? If God is what I have affirmed him to be, his love also reaches beyond the Christian, Jewish, and Islamic faith groups to every group and person, even if they do not recognize it. We do not know what label appropriate love may wear in other religions and cultures, but the basic design of human nature declares its possible presence in everyone. Even in the numerous places where the indescribable something does not have a Judeo-Christian name or assumed nature, and in places where Jesus is unknown or unimportant, there are three specific reasons it seems logical that the laws of appropriate love are always operative in some manner. First, God is spirit and is everywhere. Second, God created everyone with the ability and necessity to love something and to love either appropriately or inappropriately. Third, Godlike love, God's spirit by whatever name, is the foundation for personal peace and growth, but its opposite always disrupts and destroys, regardless of name, place, or time.

Because of human nature, I suspect people in all cultures have an innate desire to find and follow an indescribable something. Their response gives meaning to their lives, even if professing Christians call those who differ with them "idol worshippers." However, those not called Christian may follow God and care for self, neighbor, and the universe far better than many professing Christians. If we believe the Jews' and Christians' God controls the universe, that his nature is love, and that he acts only from love, then he deals with everyone in life and at their death according to his nature and their love. Based on the unavoidable application and profound significance of the two ancient directives proclaimed by Jesus, I believe those directives extend across all time and cultures. They are the inescapable laws for everyone's life. Based on human nature, there is no place or people totally devoid of the possibility for appropriate and inappropriate love, called by whatever name. Just because others interpret God differently than we do, that does not mean they are necessarily and totally incorrect, even if they have never heard about Jesus or the Judeo-Christian God. I believe it can be no other way because "God does what he is and he is what he does," wherever he is, in everything he does, to and for everyone. Appropriate love comes in flavors other than Hebrew, Christian, and English. Professing Christians do not own or completely understand the indescribable something, nor do our narrow interpretations necessarily limit his or her nature and actions. This broad application of God's love and laws further discounts the absolute necessity to believe in Jesus for salvation, and it further affirms salvation comes only through appropriate love as reiterated by Jesus.

Those who profess to be a Christian may not act like one. Those who have never heard of Jesus may be motivated by appropriate love.

Likewise, those kind souls among us who profess erroneous beliefs may sometimes unknowingly renounce them and be guided by a deeper presupposition to love appropriately, as best they can. Those expressed erroneous beliefs may not actually guide their life. The key to our quality of this life, regardless of who or where we are, is the expression of appropriate love.

Contrary to what many believe, salvation refers to the spirit of appropriate love operating within us and it does not mean we have already reached a final and fixed condition or position. It is having the right relationship with God that presently directs what we are and do. No person or group owns the copyright. Salvation is somewhat like a boat ride on a lake. There are ever-present potential dangers during the travel. As long as we remain in the boat, keep the boat upright and on course, we are *safe,* but we will be *saved* from the dangers of the journey only after we go ashore. Likewise, all who maintain the right relationship with God while in this life are safe, but they are not saved until death, because we can possibly break the required relationship as long as we are alive. All humanity has the potential for a safe boat ride, but they must do their part to safely reach the shore. There is danger if we rock the boat.

God's inclusive love does not mean everything will one day be peaches and cream for everyone, living or dead. Even though God is love, there will be no universal salvation, because of human choices and divine decrees. Universal salvation would mean everybody eventually receives the same rewards, regardless of what they believed or how they lived. That would negate any reason for appropriate love and our efforts to be good would be only a joke. Our nature as cocreator and protector of the universe requires accountability for behavior. Either we love appropriately in this life or suffer the consequences in this life. Everyone is responsible for and will be affected by what we love most. There can be no other way, based on the proclamations of Jesus and Moses, as well as human experience, logic, reason, and practicality. Everyone, to some degree and in some manner, will be affected by what we did with the opportunities we had to live by appropriate love, by how well our spirit and actions were aligned with God's spirit and actions.

I do not believe there will be a Second Coming of Jesus with a cataclysmic announcement of the end of time and a final judgment. For several and various reasons, some of which I have already stated, I do not expect Jesus to come again in any form. That is another impossible presupposition based on someone's imagination or desire, not on what Jesus said or on reasonable conjecture. Erroneous presuppositions caused New Testament writers to assume Jesus would return and end humanity's time on earth. Since it is stated in the Bible, many people still expect it. Rational insights point us in a different direction. The universe includes far more people than Christians, so it is illogical that only their ideas will come to fruition. I believe people will continually inhabit this world and reap returns based on beliefs and behaviors, unless they destroy it by abuse and neglect. The universe embodies the essence of appropriate love because it offers self-giving love to us and asks only the same from us. As long as it is protected, it will provide for its inhabitants. There may be a cataclysmic destruction of earth's human inhabitants, but that will not announce the return of Jesus. It will clearly announce human failure. That would only end humanity's time, not necessarily all time and the universe. Please notice, I have drawn a definite distinction between *the end of time* and *the end of human inhabitants on earth*. It is essential to maintain that distinction. The assumption that humanity's demise will coincide with the end of the universe is presumptuous and claims information we do not have and importance we do not possess.

Based on what I have said, I anticipate no final Judgment Day. A final Judgment Day also assumes there must be an end of time as we know it. By God's grace and our nature, coupled with opportunities and abilities, we chose, within limits, our path and destiny. Therefore, God does not need to be a judge, because our final destiny depends primarily on our prior choices and not on his summation and judgment of them. If judgment were to come only at the end of time, the storage space for previously deceased people awaiting a decision raises other unanswerable issues. The logistics of a Judgment Day seem impossible and unnecessary, even for God! How can all the people who have ever lived be separated into designated groups, based on exactly what and how they loved? There would be approximately as many groups as people, since we each believe and act somewhat differently. The minute differences would make proper judgment of each individual highly improbable, if not impossible. How could there be an equitable dividing line, given all the variables? None of this makes sense, and God is always sensible. There has to be another way. God lovingly chose another process and gave us the responsibility and privilege to decide our destiny while we live.

Based on prior presuppositions, I propose the following possibilities. Since the essence of God is Spirit, it can never be destroyed. Our nature, the core of who we are, is also spirit and, in that sense, our nature is closely aligned with God's nature. God has made us somewhat like himself. The spirit implanted in us at our beginning must grow and love something in some way. We, like God, must unavoidably love something, but we must choose what and how to love, largely affected by the community into which we were born. The spirit that gave us life at birth develops during life and departs from us at death, but because of its essence, it is not immediately dissolved. If that spirit given us at birth developed into love as God loves, our spirit cannot be destroyed (eternal life). Inappropriate love destroys itself. Since we had no knowledge of our existence while in the womb, perhaps the same is true after our death. I believe the spirit of love in us at death will merge with or infuse into its like spirit and may in some way supplement and support it, without our awareness and without maintaining our identity. Our love, appropriate or inappropriate, will affect others and the future of our planet. By its very nature, our spirit will linger after death, be alive, supportive, and remembered for a while among those who knew our name and the nature of our spirit. (Remember the disciples realized Jesus's spirit was yet among them.) After death, the Godlike spirit in us eventually rejoins the Spirit from which it came. Since inappropriate love is always destructive, it will eventually destroy itself, but its effect (spirit) also lingers, at least for a while in and among others. The degree and length that our spirit continues among others may be in direct proportion to the degree that spirit was demonstrated by us while in this life. Eventually, the remembrance of our individual spirit will fade from those who knew us, and we will become a name on a page. Not many of us will be as effective and remembered as Moses, Jesus, Mother Teresa, and others, but the door of possibility is open to us. Regardless of who we are, rewards or punishments will come during life, not after death, unless being remembered and influential can be called a reward. Based on this, there will be no need or possibility for a physical resurrection at some future date to renew our lives in some form.

Obviously, my presuppositions eliminate heaven and hell as physical places. Logically, there is no need or place for them. Neither of them has anything to do with how we get right and remain right with God. Neither facilitates a daily life of appropriate love for God, neighbor, and self. Both emphasize unending and after-death experiences about which we know nothing. No one has ever returned from the other side of death and told us what is over there. Neither can be a logical storage or resting place for something that will have no later use or existence. Heaven and hell are imaginary places that exist only in the presupposition declared by misinformed people, even if they were people of faith. Logic, love, laws, and common sense destroy them as future and physical places.

If—perhaps I should say *since*—my above major presuppositions and conclusions are somewhat correct, major adjustments are necessary for the beliefs and behavior within Christendom. Change will be adamantly opposed because presuppositions identified as religious are always the most difficult to adjust. I have previously identified many necessary changes, and others are quite obvious, but the full ramifications of the necessary adjustments are too numerous to discuss here. However, numerous changes would naturally follow if a few fundamental presuppositions were removed or adjusted. It would be most helpful if God and Jesus were restored to their proper places, if we believed Jesus instead of Paul, and if the Jesus-only salvation theory, with all its accompanying baggage, was squashed and replaced with Jesus's emphasis on appropriate love. Unless there are changes, many congregations will continue to sing their favorite old hymns that often reflect erroneous doctrines, certain teachers will frequently espouse theology that disregards or misinterprets the teachings of Jesus, and unwise pastors will boldly proclaim to their flock that Jesus became what he never was and was never intended to be and tell them "all they need is Jesus." Worship services and church programs designed to make congregants feel good will do little to challenge the status quo and will actually reflect idol worship. Given the extent to which erroneous beliefs and behavior are entrenched within the present religious environment, the future of what we commonly call the Christian community appears in grave danger. The destructive power of inappropriate love continues to impinge upon us. National unrest, poverty, persecution, nuclear proliferation, disregard for truth and honesty, climate change, racial disharmony, divisions over sexual orientation, lack of rational thinking, persecution of other church members, the splintering of major denominations, and the decline in mainline church attendance are some vivid illustrations of present and possible dangers.

There is hope for us, the church, and the world, because God and the Jesus movement are not dead. I trust what I have said confirms that. I have offered selected and sensible presuppositions that countermand the undue emphasis on a divine Jesus, getting to heaven, hellfire, punishment, rewards, resurrection, ransom, the Second Coming, being saved by the blood of Jesus, and others. I strongly advocate appropriate love that will set us free from these and other erroneous beliefs. When we become confident the God of the universe loves us and when we fully accept Jesus's two primary directives, we are free to pay less attention to ourselves and freed for more joyful participation in the kingdom among us by loving and helping others. This freedom gives us inner peace and directions for which we innately long. I am fully confident appropriate love must be the ever-present gatekeeper to our beliefs and the policeman on the street where we live. God's spirit of love and truth hangs on to us and invites us to hang on to it so that we may consequently love each other appropriately and thereby make the world a better place for everyone. Through appropriate love, a major portion of our human problems can be resolved, and the remaining difficulties can be greatly reduced in number and effect. If we want to get right and stay right with God, we must demonstrate, by our spirit, words, and actions, that we *believe Jesus!*